IN
OTHER
WORDS

IN
OTHER
WORDS

ORAL HISTORIES OF THE
COLORADO FRONTIER

MARIA M. ROGERS

FULCRUM PUBLISHING
GOLDEN, COLORADO
1995

In Other Words

*Dedicated to those who conducted the
oral history interviews.*

Library of Congress Cataloging-in-Publication Data
In other words : oral histories of the Colorado frontier / [compiled by] Maria M. Rogers
      p.   cm.
      Compiled from tape recordings in the oral history collection of the Carnegie Branch Library for Local History in Boulder.
      Includes bibliographical references (p.   ) and index.
      ISBN 1-55591-218-4
      1. Boulder County (Colo.)—Social life and customs. 2. Frontier and pioneer life—Colorado—Boulder County. 3. Oral history.
      I. Rogers, Maria M.
      F782.B6I5   1995
      978.89'63—dc20   95-599
                                                                         CIP

ISBN 1-55591-218-4

Printed in the United States of America

0 9 8 7 6 5 4 3 2 1

Fulcrum Publishing
350 Indiana Street, Suite 350
Golden, CO 80401-5093

CONTENTS

PREFACE

In Other Words is a story about life in the old West from the Pioneer era to Prohibition, as told by those who experienced it. For ten years I have been listening to well over six hundred oral history tapes that focus on Boulder County, Colorado, an area that evolved much like many other counties in the West. Narrations by cattlemen, farmers, housewives, politicians, business owners, miners, and teachers describe everyday occurrences, and in so doing, portray a somewhat different picture of a period in American history than is typically depicted in popular Western movies and novels. From the collection I have chosen anecdotes, single sentences, and long descriptions from 182 recordings to present this kaleidoscope of impressions and memories, which are fitted together like pieces of a puzzle to tell a story that is uniquely American.

Hearing a tape of reminiscences is similar to listening to a good friend talking at the kitchen table. One comes away with a splendid feeling of camaraderie and a lasting impression of the time or the place about which the friend was speaking. But as with a friend's account, one must be aware that the facts presented in oral histories may not always be strictly accurate. How many people can remember offhand the exact year of a flood or what a store was originally called? What is accurate, however, is how the person felt about an incident, how he or she lived through it and what images came to mind. These are not edited versions that have been double-checked with history books, but rather are recollections of personal experiences. As Cecelia "Sallee" Gorce said, "You had to be there—to live through it—to know what it was."

Except for the paragraphs at the beginning of each chapter that set the stage for the subsequent narrations, every word in the text is a direct quotation from one of the recordings in the collection at the Carnegie Branch Library for Local History in Boulder. Quotation marks are used only around quotes within quotes. The name of the narrator is in brackets at the end of his or her statement, not necessarily at the end of the paragraph.

Finally, brief instructions are included in the Appendix for anyone interested in taping the recollections of his or her relatives and friends. The task is not difficult; the only stumbling block seems to be the time that it takes to set up the interview and actually carry it out. Since an audio- or videotape of a person's memories of life fifty years ago is a unique treasure, the hours it takes to make the tape become time well spent.

ACKNOWLEDGMENTS

My sincere thanks go to the primary contributors to this book: the 182 people who were kind enough to record their life stories for our oral history collection and the fifty-seven volunteer interviewers. The historical information amassed by these and many more citizens of Boulder County will be safely housed in the years to come at the Carnegie Branch Library for Local History. There are also a few individuals I would like to thank who have been of particular help in putting this book together and in supporting the Carnegie Oral History Project since its beginning: long-time friend and historian Anne Dyni who submitted thirty-six of the tapes referred to in this book; Ann Bramhall and Jewel Wolcott who have been loyal members of the Project for the past eleven years; former Carnegie Library archivist and manager, Lois Anderton, who willingly attended to all library-related oral history matters; and assistant archivist Jody Corruccini who facilitated the assembling of photographs for this publication in every way she could. Finally, I would like to thank my husband, Andrei, for his encouragement and his computer, both of which were vital in putting this book together.

DANCING, WORKING, TALKING, AND LANDING IN BOULDER COUNTY

Patricia Nelson Limerick
University of Colorado, Boulder

I can live on a dance floor, seems like.
> –Ralph Yates (p. 104)

Well, I always thought you was a crackerjack dancer. I always liked to dance with you.
> –Beth Dodd (p. 106)

Our predecessors in Boulder County danced as hard as they worked. "We used to go to dances, you know, every week," Charles Perkins put it. "We'd have dances four, six, seven miles away, you know. ... Dance all night" (p. 103). At the dances, "[t]here was a bench 'long by the piano," Sanford Wagner remembered, "and there would be one, two, three, there'd be a dozen little kids sound asleep there, you know, layin' out in the blanket or basket or crib or somethin' else. Yeah, you never picked your coat up without tryin' to shake it a little first to see if there was somethin' (or someone!) in it" (p. 104).

"[Y]ou get started in that darn square dancin'," Harold Eddy recalled the process, "and they keep bringin' in new calls. Every week you gotta learn a new dance." But novelty came from sources beyond the commands of the square dance callers. There was the time, for instance, when the idea of dressing up for a dance took a special culinary turn. "We were dressed like eggs or potatoes," Eddy said. "And all you could see was our feet, and the body would be the whole tater, and we just had eyes" (p. 105).

It is important to realize that the people we call "pioneers" were fully human, with characters and customs too varied and too unpredictable to fit any stereotype. There are few better ways to reach this realization than to spend a moment contemplating the image of a room enlivened by a vigorous square dance, with eggs swinging potatoes and potatoes do-si-do-ing eggs.

In Other Words

While they danced hard and worked hard, Boulder County residents talked with even greater vigor. Selecting memorable passages like this one and grouping them thematically, Maria Rogers has scouted through tapes of interviews with 182 women and men who lived in Colorado in the late nineteenth century and the early twentieth century. Sometimes they had emigrated into the area; often they were the children of early settlers. Late in life, they told their stories to interviewers, and the results were deposited in the Carnegie Branch Library for Local History. As different as their experiences had been, life had trained all these people in one shared skill. They knew how to talk. Repeatedly, the quoted words in this book demonstrate the punch of oral language, the power of deeply felt speech to capture and convey the lived reality of the past.

What was it like to undergo an invasion of grasshoppers? C. Clarence Waneka's grandmother "saw this black cloud, and it was the grasshoppers coming just in swarms. She rushed in the house and got some rugs to throw over her tomato plants. ... They may not have any crops, but at least she was gonna save her tomato plants. After the horde of hoppers passed by, she went out and the rugs had been consumed" (p. 28).

How snug were houses in mining camps? How much did they protect residents from the elements? Russell Flarty gives us an indication: "Durin' the evening we didn't have much to do so one of the fellas built a little windmill. ... We fastened it to the corner of the table, and that windmill never stopped turnin' for six months just from the wind that blew through the keyhole" (p. 156).

What was life like before trains, automobiles, and buses speeded up the process of transportation? Della Friedman tells us: "We just walked. We just walked. We just plain walked" (p. 61).

How did women respond to the unsettling move from a familiar home to a new and unknown place? "[G]randmother," Gertrude Tower said, "wouldn't leave her flowers behind. ... We still have some dwarf iris that she hid in her dresser drawers, because she just couldn't leave *everything* behind" (p. 6).

What was it like to live in a town dominated by a "great big mill"? "You could hardly hear yourself think in the vicinity," Anabel Barr remembered, "but it's a funny thing, in the middle of the night if the machinery would break down and stop, everybody in the village would be wide awake because the noise was all gone" (p. 56).

What was it like to take one's first automobile ride in an open car with the wind rushing through? "I do remember the first car I ever rode in," Elizabeth Wiest Farrow said. "It was my Uncle Joe's. It was a touring car with a top that could go down or up. Most of the time the top was down. ... Uncle Joe chewed tobacco, and if you sat directly behind him—that memory is very keen" (p. 73).

INTRODUCTION

With descriptions like this one, delivered by such skilled talkers, you feel for a moment as if you had been there, riding along in Uncle Joe's car. And then, in the next minute, and also as a tribute to the talkers' talents, you are glad you were born far too late to ride with Uncle Joe. Even when experienced vicariously, some memories remain "very keen."

Talking about their lives repeatedly brought many of these reminiscers to the topic of work and to the contrasts between work then and work now. "It was hard work all the time all the way through," Birdie Mather said, "because we had so much to do and nothing to do [it] with, ... hardly" (p. 86). For farmers as much as miners, for housewives as much as cowboys, daily life was a very demanding round of physical activity. Anyone who thinks that gender roles protected women from real exertion need only contemplate the process of doing laundry: making soap, heating wash water, removing heavy wet clothing from wash pots, hanging up clothes, starching, and ironing. "I can remember when I learned to iron," Elizabeth Wiest Farrow said. "I hated men's shirts and hate them to this day." Ironing those shirts, with an iron repeatedly heated on a stove, was "a thankless job if ever there was one" (p. 81). "As we girls grew older," Pearle Yocom remembered, "we were taught to dust and wash dishes. ... There were a lot of dishes. Sometimes I used to wish the table would fall over, and they would all break" (p. 79).

"Our family, there was twelve of them and times was tough," Louis Varra said. "We all had to work. ... That's all they knew was work" (p. 22). Work was constant, and yet attitudes toward memories of work could vary tremendously. "I'm retired and I'm glad of it because there was a very dangerous and a very hard work in that coal mine," Rick Martinez appraised his work experience (p. 41). But compare this to John Jackson's judgment: "If I could start to mine tomorrow, I would go—at seventy-six years old. ... It's different every day. You learn something new every day. It's hard work" (p. 51). Martinez's coal mining and Jackson's precious metal (or hard-rock) mining were clearly different experiences, but there were also good reasons to appraise work, on some occasions, as a valuable means of developing character and, on other occasions, to appraise it as a draining and debilitating burden. Seemingly contradictory, both judgments could make equal sense.

After working in the hayfields for twelve hours a day, Jacob Schlagel remembered, "I tell you one thing, you got pretty hungry when you come in. You didn't need a diet or anything" (p. 24). Appetite was not the only beneficiary of exertion: "I'll tell you what," said Schlagel, "you slept! You didn't need sleeping pills" (p. 25). Or, as Joseph Malcolm remarked, "You didn't have athletic clubs around the mining camps. Those fellas had plenty of exercise" (p. 112)!

These references to diets, sleeping pills, and athletic clubs draw a clear contrast between then and now, a contrast that makes our own times seem distinctly silly. Then, calories were essential fuel for powering the day's labor; now, calories are a bane that we plot to avoid. Then, people slept because they were tired; now, we trick ourselves into the sleep that our addled bodies do not know we need. Then, people used their muscles for a *purpose*; now, we schedule—and pay for—special time in athletic clubs to see that our muscles get used at all. Drawing her own version of this contrast between past and present, Delores C. "Dee" Bailey turned to the telling example of the postal service. "If you wanted [the mailman] to bring up somethin'," Bailey remembered, "he'd bring in hay to feed the cows or the chickens." She then pointed out the change probably already in many readers' minds: "Different from now days, [when] you're just lucky if you get a stamp" (p. 63)!

If one directs one's attention selectively and strategically, the past *can* look considerably more attractive than the the present. There is real substance in the opinion of Charles Perkins: "We had hardships and everything, but we enjoyed our life more than we do today. ... Then we enjoyed everything. We had time to do it. Now we don't have time" (p. 103). And yet one's yearning for a more enjoyable and enjoyed past flags a bit when one imagines actually *doing* all the work described by these speakers. Nostalgia comes to a complete halt when one reads the descriptions of the devastation of the 1918 influenza epidemic: "Luckily I only had a touch of flu for one day," Grovenor Ketterman said. "But, oh my, people were dying just right and left. ... I remember our milkman was a great, big, husky, well-built man that you'd think would never get sick. Well, he took that flu and died in just a day or two" (p. 145).

The yearning for a happier past runs into an equally rough time when it confronts descriptions of race relations. The displacement of Indian people and discrimination against Mexican and African Americans were also part of the social landscape. "There was prejudice here against the Mexicans," Jack Rowley said. "Those people were pretty much supposed to stay to their own" (p. 59). When Henry Amicarella remembered that his "brother and I and some of the Mexican kids that were friends of ours and Filipinos ... had to get away from the schoolhouse and go to the side of the creek to eat our lunch, because we didn't want to be embarrassed" (p. 59), he offered an important reminder that Western American society has long been riddled by faultlines of ethnic hostility and misunderstanding. Similarly, Joseph Malcolm gave the abstractions of prejudice a down-to-earth meaning with the story of a swimming pool:

The town decided they needed a swimming pool so they
built one. Now, of course, many people in town were of

Mexican descent, and they helped with the work. ... Well, then
there were some people in town who looked in [at the pool].
There's Mexican children swimmin' with their children, and
they thought, "Good lord, this cannot be; this is not right!"
They had a big argument about it, and they filled [the pool] up
[with dirt]. Believe it or not they filled the swimming pool up.
Isn't that ridiculous (p. 59)?

Malcolm's unambiguous disapproval of this response deserves as much of
our consideration as does the response itself. And yet, even with the recognition
that individuals like Malcolm kept their distance from these prejudices, the image
of a filled-in swimming pool that *no one* could swim in strikes a well-deserved blow
against the idea of a lost golden age of community harmony.

Positive and negative experiences were not poles set at opposite ends
of a continuum. In the past as well as the present, positive and negative have
been the warp and weft that wove life together. When African American children were excluded from after-school activities with white children, the children showed their enterprise and self-reliance by turning to nature. "[Y]ou
stay out of our way," Ruth Flowers remembered the patterns of exclusion,
"and we'll see that you don't have any contact with us." But "we had to do
something—the young people did—so we formed ourselves in a little group,
and we roamed the mountains. I know practically every canyon and every
mountain in Boulder because for four years that's what we did" (p. 97). Racial
exclusion was a practice designed to demean and reduce the soul; the children's
turn to the canyons and mountains restored and strengthened the soul. Here,
as in many of these stories, positive experiences and negative experiences were
braided, inseparably joined with each other.

Many memorable stories in this collection demonstrate the complexity of
human nature and of human experience. Our predecessors were not, these stories
remind us, "our heroic and superhuman pioneer forebears"; they were people among
whom consistent nobility and sainthood were as rare as they are among us. There
was, for instance, Ernie Ross, who appreciated the local enthusiasm for holding
dances, but who was not himself a dancer. "I couldn't dance," he said, with admi-
rable frankness, "but I could drink." On one occasion, he borrowed a friend's horse
from its pasture and rode to a dance. At the end of a festive evening, he began his
ride home. After that, things became vague: "I don't know where I did pass out.
But when I woke up the next morning the gate was open, and the horse was in the
pasture, and I was on him, and a little bit cold; it was in the winter. I never fell off
that horse, but I sure slept on him the rest of that night" (p. 105).

Again, the contrast between past and present seems very clear; the ability to stay on a horse without benefit of consciousness is a skill much in decline in recent times. Compared to the unhappy consequences of modern drunk driving, old-fashioned drunken horseback riding seems a pleasant and unthreatening sport. In the same spirit, one reads Martin Parsons' tribute to Charlie Temple with more in the way of admiration than of regret over Temple's missed educational opportunities. Temple was a man who "just could write his name, and that was about all." But "when it come to knowin' a cow," as Parsons put it, "by god, he knew 'em from the foot to the horns" (p. 20). It is perfectly appropriate to spend a moment wondering what topic or subject, in the very complicated world of 1995, one stands a chance of knowing as well as Charlie Temple knew cows. In a world of astonishing technological complexity and general information overload, is there any topic left that a human can know from "the foot to the horns"?

Envy is a perfectly logical response to many of these stories. And yet, despite the temptation to place these stories in that vague historical era known as the good old days, many of the honest and forthright storytellers quoted in this book cut short any retreat to a fuzzy-minded nostalgia. "They talk about the good old days ...," Maude Washburn Wagner challenged nostalgia directly. "It was hard work; it was awfully hard work" (p. 78). But if it was work, it was also dancing. If the times were troubled by epidemics of disease and by high rates of child mortality, the times were also enlivened by picnics, neighborly visits, and halloween pranks demonstrating considerable youthful vitality, with cows led up to the second floor of schoolhouses and wagons placed on church roofs. If the streets of towns were, alternately, awash in mud or clogged with wind-borne dust, those streets were also filled with commerce, conversation, and community. Good and bad, positive and negative, festivity and illness, conversation and mud, neighborliness and discrimination, dancing and work came in one, very complex package.

In Boulder, Ruby Roney and her friends made the most of the possibilities of winter by sledding down Nineteenth Street. While sledding offered the charms of exhilaration and adventure, like any vigorous way of passing through time and space, it also presented the problem of momentum: where to stop, and even more important, how to stop? For Roney and her friends, there was a happy answer. "My grandfather always took a piece of the fence down," she said, and "put straw in his backyard so that we would come down the hill and land in the straw" (p. 109). That feeling, earned by people who have taken a rough ride and yet made a safe landing, radiates from this book. From Ruby Roney landing safely in her grandfather's straw pile, to Ernie awakening in a familiar pasture after a mysterious ride home, that feeling of "landedness" and arrival carries tremendous appeal.

IN
OTHER
WORDS

Cabin—West University Hills area near base of Flagstaff, Boulder, ca. 1880. Carnegie Branch Library for Local History, Boulder Historical Society Collection.

CHAPTER ONE

ROLLING WEST

People move because of dreams: dreams of a happier life, of an easier life. These dreams were the force that induced inhabitants of many countries to leave their homes for a land across the sea, and once in the United States, to move westward. The dream of wealth and prosperity could be realized with a little luck and a lot of hard work. It had happened for others; perhaps it could happen to anyone.

In the 1800s many people were disillusioned with their homelands and were searching for a better life. Over a million men, women and children migrated to the United States from Ireland between 1815 and 1845; Irish farmers who survived the potato famine of the 1840s were driven out because their land was being converted to pasture land. Swedish and Norwegian farmers left their country because of a depression in the 1880s. Political and economic upheaval of the Slavic states forced emigration. A sharp increase in the growth of the German and Italian populations along with crop failures pushed people out of those countries and into the open space on the other side of the Atlantic. In England, an increase in the size of the population, along with the development of factories, which put many craftsmen out of jobs, fostered emigration and caused skilled workers to seek higher salaries in the United States. Migrants who sailed across the Pacific from Asia worked on railroads and farms at low wages, undercutting the salaries offered to United States workers. Remittances were then sent back home so that other family members could come to this place of promise, a practice that was common with most immigrants.

There was prosperity in the United States. It was the land of second chance, just as the immigrants said in their letters to their loved ones who stayed behind, and just as the shipping companies advertised in order to profit from passengers. But life was by no means easy. There was also turmoil on this side of the Atlantic. The panic of 1837 resulted in widespread unemployment. In 1857, the United

States experienced another panic that deprived farmers of the funds needed to produce goods and forced able-bodied men into unemployment. The devastation of the Civil War (1861–1865) stimulated the need for farmed goods, causing many to move West—to open, uncultivated, fertile lands. But these problems did not dissuade people from coming, and an independent, fighting spirit drove them on from one day to the next.

Communication services eased the stress of migrating to the open range. The first stagecoaches to the western territories began their routes in 1858. The Pony Express started mail deliveries in 1860, which helped friends and family to keep in touch. By 1883 the railroad system had become so complex it was necessary to divide the country into four time zones. These services not only allowed the pioneer to feel less isolated, but also encouraged big business to stretch out its arms to the West.

When the word "gold" flashed across the land, the elusive dream appeared once again before the eyes of the struggling settler. Now was the chance many were waiting for, the real chance. In 1848 gold was discovered in California and would-be miners rushed to make themselves rich even though they had little knowledge of mining. It was not long before big business, with its capital and know-how ran out most of these independent prospectors. But just ten years later, more gold was found in the hills of Colorado. Once again families were coming from all over—this time with the slogan "Pike's Peak or Bust" written on the sides of their covered wagons. With the miners came the farmers, and soon small towns were emerging along the trails.

Colorado was considered to be Indian territory in the 1800s. The Comanche and Kiowa Indians and later the Arapaho and Cheyenne tribes (who were in Boulder County at the time of the westward movement) had moved north and south for generations, living off the buffalo and taking only what they needed from the land with the least amount of disturbance possible. When the settlers arrived they brought with them a basic difference in philosophy toward the natural environment. The Indians had a respect for the wilderness that was completely contrary to the thinking of most pioneers. In fact, even the United States government encouraged and supported the concept of working the land by passing various bills in Congress that gave land freely to those who tilled the soil and raised food. It was the opinion of the newcomers that not only should this natural resource be worked, but also that those who did the work should own the land.

The following are some of the recollections of the descendants of these pioneer families who migrated to Boulder County many years ago. They retell the handed-down tales of their forefathers and recount their own experiences.

Covered Wagons

Grandmother was thirteen years old when she come across the plains to Niwot, and she and her sister walked about all the way, I guess, drivin' the cows. When they come to the South Platte River, it took 'em two weeks to cross it 'cause they had to take the wagons all to pieces ... The water was high; the cows had to swim. Part of 'em didn't get out till they got way down the river. [The family] had come from Switzerland in 1852 to Missouri. So this was '64 then. Mother was just a baby. [Carl Knaus]

My great grandfather, Joseph Harden, was born probably in the very end of the 18th century and fought as a drummer boy in the War of 1812. He started west ... with seven children and his wife and got as far as Paris, Illinois. His wife died. He spent about a year or perhaps a little over in Paris and then married a widow, Elizabeth Macintosh, who had four children of her own. They started west again in a covered wagon. When they got to Boone, Iowa, Mrs. Harden had become pregnant, and he left her with the small children, took all the ones who could help him and went on to Boulder, Colorado, where he homesteaded. ... Then he returned to get his wife. ... My grandmother arrived when she was two years old in 1859. [Charlotte Seymour]

In 1864 [my grandfather] and his brother and another man walked out here from Iowa. They came behind a wagon train and drove the loose stock. [Wanda Burch Armstead]

My grandfather was born at sea. They had thought that the mother would carry her child until she was in the United States, but three days at sea the baby was born and the mother died. So foster parents took him but let him have his own name. ... My mother and father both came with covered wagons, and my Grandfather Smith came here in 1864. He was fifteen years old. It was during the Civil War. The doctor told him he had tuberculosis so he came out here for that. [Irene Smith Lybarger]

I'd grown up with people who were pioneers in ... Colorado, and they'd have to hunt and fish to live, you know. I grew up with a whole generation of people that migrated to Colorado right after the Civil War. [M. Helen Carpenter]

My father ... left home [in England] at the age of thirteen, stowed away on a boat to Boston, walked across the United States, got to Central City, was a hard-rock miner. [Howard Higman]

My grandparents, yep, Lafayette Miller and Marie Miller. They came across the plains in an ox wagon, ox team. 'Course there was a whole caravan, you know, they come [by] ox trains in them times, they couldn't come by one [alone], had to organize and have a whole train for protection, you know. ... I think they always had a scout, maybe. Then I think, too, some of 'em in the train maybe had been west before, and they knew the routes, you know. [Ralph Miller]

[Edward D. Steele] came to "mend his broken fortunes" as he put it. He bought a mining claim at Gold Hill and worked it a while but didn't make any rich strike at all. … He worked for a number of years there, and then he went back to Wisconsin and brought his family back here to Colorado by covered wagon … in 1865. His family consisted of his wife, Phoebe, and three children. John D. Steele [his son] was my father, and he was only two months old when he left Wisconsin. His mother contracted typhoid fever on the way and nearly died but managed to survive; however, his older sister—she was nine years old—had to tend the baby. She fed him by saturating a piece of cloth with milk and letting him suck on it. …

Like all the other pioneers, whom I met out there (and they weren't called pioneers, they were called old-timers) they were all good story tellers. This was something that happened to men who were out in lonely places, sometimes two men would be out alone for months at a time. They didn't have any newspapers, very seldom did they have any books or magazines, and certainly they didn't have any modern means of entertainment like we have—radio, television, motion pictures—so they used something that is as old as man's communicating with man, telling stories of adventures. They had adventures out there in that new country. [Forest Crossen]

Shortly after they arrived here Grandfather got [typhoid] fever and passed away … leaving Grandmother with three children and no friends, very little money and no way to get back home. … Some people living in the area along Left Hand Creek by the name of DuBois—a rich family—took her in, kept her for a year or so. She bought a homestead relinquishment just east of Mountain Mesa, and she managed somehow to survive and keep her family. … My father eventually bought the homestead from her and raised his family there. That's where I was born. The original house is still standing, built in 1866. Mother said she was the first white child born in the St. Vrain Valley in 1869. [Andrew Steele]

My grandmother and my father came out from Kansas in the covered wagon, and grandmother wouldn't leave her flowers behind. … We still have some dwarf iris that she hid in her dresser drawers, because she just couldn't leave everything behind. [Gertrude Tower]

They were pioneers, and they were tough people. They had to be tough. [Robin Arnett]

The old-timers … dressed in buckskin, full beards and long hair, by god, they were men, no doubt about that. …

Rolling West

There was a whole stream of covered wagons of people moving [from] Kansas, Nebraska looking for new homesites, and, of course, ... the only way they could cross the [mountain] range was Rollins Pass. Well, it was pretty good going until they got to the foot of the pass, and then they had to double up their teams to pull their wagons. They had a lot of hardships on that trip. ... Oh, it was a beautiful country in the early days. When I was a boy I used to ride across there and the deer and the elk and the antelope were so thick you couldn't count 'em, you'd miss your count on 'em. Oh, it was a beautiful country then in the earlier days before the settlers came in. [Martin Parsons]

I remember [him] about when they first homesteaded that place. [He] remember[s] seein' a whole file of Indians cross the creek right along there. He watched them, and they watched him. They rode right along by. That must have been in the early 1870s. [Joseph Malcolm]

The latest [Indians to] have occupied the Boulder Valley ... would be the Arapaho/Cheyenne, and they traveled together. The Arapaho/Cheyenne were in bands, and in the 1700s they split. The northern Arapaho and Cheyenne stayed up in Wyoming and Montana, and the southern Arapaho and Cheyenne came down to the Boulder Valley and Denver. ... They were the last people here when the gold miners came in 1858 into the Boulder Valley and settled. [Jean Kindig]

Niwot was named after an Indian chief, Niwot—Left Hand. ... One time my grandfather was plowing and Chief Niwot came and said, "Wrong side up!" [My grandfather] was plowing the dirt up and [Chief Niwot] said, "Wrong side up!" He didn't want him to plow that nice native land. He wanted to save it for the wild game to feed on. So they intermingled with the Indians an awful lot. ... I think there're some Indians buried in the Niwot Cemetery. [Ruth Dodd McDonald]

One mile and a half north of our present ranch building there is an ancient Indian campsite. There are twenty-seven tepee rings a half mile west of the old Gilbert headquarters buildings. The largest of these tepee rings is seventeen steps across, in other words about fifty feet in diameter. There are twenty-six smaller ones arranged in a somewhat orderly fashion around this one central tepee site. By tepee rings I mean the rocks that were used, big rocks, boulders that were used after the eighteen-feet-tall tepees were erected. Some of them were not quite as high. And the buffalo hides were skillfully placed all around the lodgepoles that met in the center and were tied with a rawhide thong. ... Tanned buffalo robes were thrown all over this casing, or form, or skeleton of the home. In a matter of about fifteen minutes these Indian women had a home. [K. K. Parsons]

In Other Words

The early geologists found so much sandstone in the high country ... that they were looking for the vein. ... The archaeologists looked at it and found that native Americans were bringing those slabs with them to grind food, to process meat. They were flat, just like the sandstone slabs. ... These people would carry it with them, you know, if they went up to Wyoming and back around, because they'd have to process their food. Let's say they came with family groups, even the men might have processed their own food ... but usually the women did it. [They] came up to the high altitude, and then when the fall [came], and the hunting season was over, they'd leave [the stones] because they knew they could come back to the Boulder Valley and get more Lyons sandstone. [Jean Kindig]

[The Indian camp] was located a couple hundred yards back from a wonderful spring that brought life to the Gilbert Ranch holdings. ... Without water the land was useless. He who controlled the water controlled everything. The Indians had established this fine camp not too far to carry water but far enough back so that the wild game coming in would not be frightened away along towards sundown and at sunrise. What a wonderful wintering ground for the Utes and the Cheyenne. ... As the great Ogalala Sioux warlord, Crazy Horse, said, "The winds of time erase all memories but not entirely so." The Indians that lived here north of us and four hundred yards south of us with their campsites and all left little. They left the earth as they had found it. [K. K. Parsons]

In the fall ... the early settlers used to go out on the plains and hunt buffalo. They'd lay in their winter supply of meat—more than just the winter, because they dried the buffalo meat into what they called jerky; that would keep almost indefinitely. It just required soaking it up and cooking it. It probably was not too palatable, but it was nourishing. [Andrew Steele]

They came to Valmont where at that time [in 1874] there was a stage. ... They stopped there ... and my father, who was Joseph W. Phillips, had the job [of] shooting the buffalo for the railroad men to bring in meat, so that they had meat all the time. He would go out and work alone. ... He shot buffalo around Boulder. ... He would tan the hides. ... He had a flintlock [rifle] that he liked. It was an old gun that his father had, but he later had a forty-five Colt. ... He shot buffalo with that flintlock rifle. ... [He hunted] on horseback. [Hester Phillips]

I've heard the old-timers talk about buffalo wallows around on different farms. It would be just a half acre in a spot, it would be kind of wet, kind of clay kind of stuff, and they said, "Well that's an old buffalo wallow where the [animals] would get in there." It seems as though in the summertime they'd get in there and get that mud all over them, and the flies wouldn't bother them so much. [Evan Gould]

Rolling West

My mother was injured in a buffalo stampede in eastern Colorado. The buffalo were coming toward the wagon. She was ten years old. She fell off of the wagon, and a wheel ran over her leg. While the leg was never short, it was a good deal smaller than the other one was. Grandpa evidently grabbed her. It killed one of the oxen team that they were coming with. So they had a milk cow that they were leading, and they had to put the milk cow in with the oxen then to come on in to this area. [C. Clarence Waneka]

My father has told me things about the early days here, the wagon trains that would come in, you know, and not one of [the travelers] had a dollar. All they had was a little slab of bacon and maybe a little flour. God, they'd work for any price, you know, to get a little money and get some grub to go on. [Martin Parsons]

You could still get homesteads in Colorado [in 1918]. ... We came in a covered wagon drawn by two flea-bitten gray horses that were named for the president and the vice president, which was Wilson and Marshall. ... I don't remember anything outstanding about the trip. ... We had a tent and a wagon, because there were four of us, and on the wagon ... there was a water bag, which was made of canvas and hung outside where the air cooled the water and kept it cool, because it was a little ways between towns. ... There was a box on the back of the wagon that was called a grub box where the food was carried. My mother and I slept in the wagon, and my dad and my brother slept under the wagon or in a tent. We cooked along the way. My mother had a little iron dutch oven, which she'd set on the rocks piled around the fire. ... You could make biscuits ... and stew and things. So that's the way we got along. It took us about three months to get to Colorado [from Texas]. ... Women didn't wear slacks at that time. ... When I was little I guess my skirts came down past my knees. [Jerrine Sylvia Crosslen]

Well, we cooked on the ground out in front of the wagon. It seems my mother and my sister ... done the cookin' and us men took care of the horses and things like that. ... We would stop for the night. The men would build a fire out on the ground, and the women would come out there. ... They had a certain amount of stuff that they would get out of the wagon to cook with. It was like a chuck wagon. ... We had three of those wagons. ... My father and mother and the girl and us small boys rode in the first wagon and drove in front ... My uncle and his wife and two girls and one boy rode in the next wagon. Then there was another wagon behind that with two of my cousins, the oldest boys—one of them was about eighteen—and three of my brothers rode in that wagon, too. ...

We'd turn the horses loose at night to let 'em graze. ... We tried to sleep in the wagons at night. ... The women and the girls would get behind the spring seat in the front. ... [We] would put the spring seat out on the ground to eat ... there was lots of beddin'. The family and the girls would sleep on there. ... We didn't sleep outside cause it was rainin' sometimes. ... Some days it was rainin' all day. ... They had two or three frying pans, and they had a dutch oven. It was cast iron about six inches deep with a lid on it. That's what she'd cook her biscuits in; cook 'em right over the fire ... boil coffee in a bucket. [Robert Jones]

It was a holiday in that little town, and the only way they traveled was on the mail carriage and so we had to get to this carriage [which] took us to Naples, and the boat took us from Naples. The women ... around me ... were all crying—a little girl like that. They were all worried about me, you know, but both brothers were with me. They were happy—being boys—but we got to Naples, and they took us to the place where you take the boat. They put me in the cabin with two nuns on the first class, and my brothers they put them in the second class. My mother and father were already [in the United States. My brothers were] ten and twelve, and I was eight. They put a big sign ... that said, "As these children can't talk English, ask them if they are hungry." ... We'd show them we had a sack full of bread and salami and cheese and stuff like that, you know, so they'd all laugh at us. [Gentina Moschetti]

I was born in ... Colorado ... in a covered wagon ... on the tenth of December, 1893. In those days a covered wagon took the place of a trailer house as it does today. People traveled in them and lived in them. ...

My mother's health was bad so they came back to Colorado in the end of the gold rush in the mountains and went to Eldora. My folks run a boarding house in Eldora there in 1897. ... Then they moved out to a farm east of Niwot. [Crain Caywood]

Immigrants

[Germans from Russia along the Volga River] had a chance to come in here and somehow or other it got [back across the Atlantic] that they could come to America, and they could work in a [sugar] beet field. Dad wasn't here more than two years. He was a laborer. About the next year [he] saved enough to buy a farm. You see one person would come over here and help the other. My mother left her brother and all her parents and didn't know if they'd ever see them again. [Jacob Schlagel]

The thing that impressed me about my family ... is the remarkable thing that happened with my dad and mother, who could not read nor write nor speak English, and reared twelve kids. Six young ones in Italy and six in the United States. [Henry Amicarella]

Well, the economy [in Italy] was so bad, they were literally starving. So [my family] came over here to find better days, better times, better things, which they did. My father came when he was about eight years old I guess. My mother was maybe six or seven. She came over with her two brothers and that's a long story: [Bauldie Moschetti]

A lot of these young men came in as laborers and later became bosses, superintendents and prominent men in the business way in the communities. [Isabel Mayhoffer]

It was rough, and you didn't dare to talk German on the school ground 'cause you had to stay in after school if you did. [Jacob Schlagel]

There was a screwup at Ellis Island. [My family] couldn't speak a word of English and the story goes that the immigration officer wrote down Daxacher as the name although it was Dexter, and [my family was] afraid to change it for fear they would be deported or some darn thing. "Daxacher" was on all the deeds ... until we got married and finally we got everything changed in 1956 or '7. [Rodney Dexter]

You see, the house we lived in was provided by Ralph [Bixler]. We didn't have to pay rent or electricity or anything. We just lived there. I think my dad was getting thirty-seven dollars a week, and he'd work on the farm. We had everything we needed you know. [Roseann Ortega]

I worked on a farm for five years before I came [to Boulder]. I couldn't find work in Boulder very good. When you can't talk English it is hard to get work. [Elna Craig]

My father came to Hawaii first. ... Neither [parent spoke any English]. ... They more or less stayed within their own group and, you know, that's no way to learn a foreign language, but I guess there was enough [Japanese] in the area; they could get by. ... We had summer school then, and they taught the Japanese language there during the summers for the kids. ... See once they started public school, they'd pick English up and then they'd lose ... what was the native tongue. ...

As far as I know, in this area at one time there were ten to twelve [Japanese] families, you know, but that's about the limit. ... This was back in the twenties. ... Little after the twenties, see, they weren't able to come. You know, they stopped them from immigrating. [Jack Miyasaki]

At that time [in 1902] ... it wasn't against the law, they could come [from Mexico], see. ... So they came, no trouble. [Teresa Alverez]

The farmers were generally Swedes, and we used to have kind of a Russian colony. What became of them I don't know. And then out east of here you know they are nearly all Belgians. [Harold Stevens]

Erie was a town composed of Englishmen, Welsh, Scotch, some Irish; my father-in-law was French. Then later on we had some Italians and Hungarians, Romanians. So it was quite a mixture of people, very interesting. … Most of them just came straight from the old country straight to the coal mines. [Cecilia "Sallee" Gorce]

Coal camps and mining towns. Mostly Italian, Slavic, German people. All neighbors in that town were very closely knit. They would help one another. They would help people [who were] sick and unable to work. … Everyone got along well. No one had much, but nobody missed it, because they never knew what it was. [Bauldie Moschetti]

We always hired the Italians from Louisville. We did have a house for them, and they stayed out there, because they didn't have the facilities to go back and forth into Lousiville, you see. We supplied their house and their water. They did have a home in Louisville. [Mabel Andre Thomas]

The Japanese came in here and raised everything, you know. And we could go down [to their farms] and like pick a bushel of tomatoes. It was a lot cheaper than going to the store and buying it by the pound. You could pick it yourself or buy it already picked. [Bertha Hartenagle Schott]

'Course farming back there [in Japan is] not like here. Actually they only had maybe two or three acres. … We did vegetable farming at that time. … Mostly cabbage, tomatoes, pickles, … onions. Then we had some sugar beets, too. You know, back in them days sugar beet was pretty widespread in this area. Then it just all went out. Oh, we raised about twenty acres of sugar beets and then the rest was vegetables, some alfalfa for rotation purposes. … We used to hire a lot of Mexican, Spanish people for help on the farm. Then to-ward the end there, see, my brother did the marketing, and then I did the getting the order out each day. That's the way we did it. … We had labor houses [for the Spanish-speaking people] except for like during harvest season. I used to go to Lafayette, and then get a bunch out of Lafayette. They used to just come and like chop onions, mostly piecework, pick pickles, chop onions, but for year-round help we had labor houses. Usually they stayed year-round. There wasn't much for them to do in the wintertime, but we used to just pay them so much just to keep them so we had them in the springtime. … They were [USA citizens]. [Jack Miyasaki]

[The Mexicans] came in and worked the crops and hoed the beets. They used to top those beets by hand; they hoed those beets by hand. Those fields would have twenty-five or thirty men, women, and kids out there. As soon as they was big enough to swing a hoe they were out there hoein' those weeds out of the beet fields. They didn't have cultivators and that stuff like they do now. They didn't have farm machinery. It was all done by hand. [Jack Rowley]

ROLLING WEST

They were on the move looking for jobs. Some came ... to Boulder, Lafayette, Erie, Louisville, and Longmont. They came to work in the coal mines. These mines operated only in winter. In summer they went wherever they could find employment. Some miners stayed through the summer if they were skilled in other capacities. ... Trainloads of several families contracted by sugar beet companies came from the San Luis valley to work in the fields. As they moved, they brought with them many of their practical survival skills so that when the question of the Depression came up most people felt very fortunate. They suffered no hunger, perhaps a little cold. [Jessie Velez Lehmann]

A crew of hay threshers and their mechanized threshing devices departing from a field. A child posing in the foreground, Louisville, 1909. Photo by Ed Tangen. Carnegie Branch Library for Local History, Boulder Historical Society Collection.

CHAPTER TWO

DIVIDING THE LAND

Migrants who followed their dreams were encouraged to venture westward by the Federal government through its Homestead Act of 1862, and the subsequent Timber-Culture, Timber and Stone, and Desert Land acts. These land-giveaway bills allowed the head of a family to own land with the only price being that he or she work it. The most-cited in the following quotations is the Homestead Act. One hundred sixty acres of land could be owned by anyone who worked the land for five years (or who purchased it outright for one dollar and twenty-five cents per acre). At the end of the five-year period, the owner was said to have proved up on the land, and he or she was given a deed of ownership. In fact, land was so easy to come by that if a farmer found his fields were no longer fertile, he could simply move further West.

Between 1870 and 1900 the population increased five-fold west of the 100th meridian, which cuts through the Dakotas, Nebraska, Kansas, Oklahoma, and Texas. Millions of acres of virtually free land were acquired and developed. By 1900 the best land was taken. After the 1866–1888 boom of the immortalized cattle drives from Texas to the northern plains, towns began to grow and cattle ranches emerged. Ranch and farm houses built from lumber began replacing the older sod houses, whose walls consisted of sod and turf piled up like bricks. Beginning in 1874 barbed wire was sold commercially and the age of fences dawned, bringing with it range wars between those protecting their property and those who fought for an open range and water access.

Once a parcel of land was delineated, the work began. Barns, houses, and deep wells had to be built and daily chores of raising livestock ate away at the time needed to plow the land and produce crops. Farm mechanization, which began in the 1830s with the reaper, the thresher, and the steel plow, was a welcome addition to any farm. The land was feverishly worked with little regard for soil erosion. Federal control of the way the farmer was to plow his land (e.g., the Soil

Conservation Act) did not come about until after the 1930 Dust Bowl years when the Kansas/Oklahoma/Texas area lost a major portion of its topsoil to winds. This and other natural disasters, such as droughts and grasshopper invasions, added to the constant stress of the struggling farmer.

But it was not only nature that was working against the farmer. The railroads were allowed to set high and varying rates across the country for transporting produce, thus depleting profits for the farmers. In protest, the settlers banded together to form the Granger Movement in the 1870s, which resulted in the 1887 Interstate Commerce Act that controlled and equalized rates throughout the country. There were finally enough migrants in the West to make their complaints heard in the East.

＊┅ ㄷ◆ㅌ ┅＊

Homesteading

Some of the land that was sold real early … was actually just traded. One parcel of land up here on Gunbarrel Hill was traded for—a hundred and sixty acres—was traded for a fine, old, double-barreled shotgun and some of that land sold for ten, fifteen and twenty-five dollars an acre. It was relatively low-priced at that time. This would be in the early 1900s. [Howard Morton]

They stopped at Golden, Colorado to begin with and thought that they were going to stake a mine, but my grandfather knew nothing about mining so they came on up this way. He bought forty acres out west of Longmont. [C. Clarence Waneka]

In order to get homestead rights, the government gave you the right to come in and file on a piece of land. My grandfather filed on the first quarter—that is a quarter of a mile wide and a mile long—which run from Baseline over to the Louisville Road. At that time you could only take a hundred and sixty acres. They later raised it so that you could take three hundred and twenty. Now that was the original homestead of Marie E. and Lafayette Miller. You want to remember, too, that there wasn't a tree in this part of the country only those that were on the crick. They settled close to the cricks for two or three reasons. One was water for their cattle and the other was that when they were close to a stream there was generally surface water. Now I have the distinction of having two grandparents that settled two towns in this part of the country. My grandparents on my mother's side settled the town of Superior. [The other was the town of Lafayette.] [Frank Miller]

The government had opened up a lot of land for homesteading. They'd give you a hundred and sixty acres, and you had to put one hundred and fifty dollars on it and stay on it one year, and then you got title to it … Now that was in 1918, see, that was not so long ago. [Edna Morrato]

Well, you had to live [on the land] five years to prove up a homestead. We raised a lot of potatoes and had this whole field in alfalfa. We had a milk cow and a few chickens. … You had to live [on it] five years before you proved up. You had to have two witnesses and go to Denver to the Land Office and show if you were the same person and honest and everything. [Elna Craig]

[A woman] could have had a homestead if her husband died or somethin' like that. [She couldn't have a homestead] if she was married, not if she was married, no. … About half of the homesteads [in Colorado] had single women livin' on them. [Robert Jones]

It depended on how many [acres the homesteaders] wanted, mostly, or how many they thought they could take care of. Grandpa homesteaded a hundred and sixty acres, but they could homestead as much as a half section, two hundred and forty, or six hundred and forty, which was a whole section. Most of them homesteaded a small section. They had to prove their citizenship for one thing. Now of course we had lots of people coming in that didn't have their citizenships. So they would put a claim on the land that they wanted, a good deal like in later times [when] they would stake a claim in the mining area. Then if they didn't work that claim within a year, or start proving up on their farm, it would be taken from them, and they would start out with another claim … They gave up a lot of their life to get here and some of the hardships were incredible according to my grandparents. [Irene Smith Lybarger]

You had to improve your claim and make a home out of it. You had to plant trees, you had to plant orchards, you had to have machinery and you had to have buildings put up and the cattle sheds for calving time to drive the cattle in, and you had to have everything like that. [Cecilia "Sallee" Gorce]

One was a timber claim. In a three-year length of time you had to have so many live trees growing on your half section of land or quarter section of land, and when you got that many trees growing, then you got that section of land deeded to you by the government, same as though it was a homestead only it was called a timber claim. [Frank Miller]

My grandfather came here in 1861 at the age of four, I think it was … I guess he homesteaded. He settled. He squatted! He gained title to quite a lot of land around here … I don't know why he came here, but that first winter … there was no place to live, but there was a cave along the Coal Creek. He spent the winter there. …

They had to stop in Kansas and leave the family there. Grandpa built a sod house for them, and he came on out here then to live. Two years later [he] went back and got his family. Times were hard. [A sod house] didn't sound good to me and still doesn't! [C. Clarence Waneka]

The buildings were made of sod and adobe. ... Men took a special plough and ploughed up the sod then took a shovel and cut this fresh-turned sod into two-foot lengths and laid it up as we would lay bricks today. They did what they had to do. They had nothing else. [K. K. Parsons]

At that time they just kind of built log huts for the time being till they got settled and all, and then they eventually got lumber someplace. ... Lot of them you know were sod houses ... The grass and the clay together. And made it real—not too wet but wet enough so they could have it so that it'd stick together, you know. Then I think they plastered it with mud on the inside of the houses on these sod houses, you know. No doubt they were warm—warm in winter and cool in summer. I think. I never lived in one but I just presumed they were. ... They probably wouldn't o' had more than one window and one door. [Ralph Miller]

Walls of dirt. It was just dirt all the way around and a big pole all the way up to the top. Cottonwood tree was cut out. The dugout was seven-foot deep, and then we laid a cottonwood log on the north side and one on the south side and the west side and laid a big log right through the center there to hold up the roof. Then we put a lot of poles across there for rafters and then have small willow trees and things to fill up the cracks so the dirt wouldn't go through. The willow trees would be about six inches deep, and then we'd hook a team to a scraper and scrape dirt across on top of that and drive right across that with a team and dump the dirt on top ... and so the water would run right off. ... It was like a little hill. ... There was a dirt floor. [Robert Jones]

The house was a grout house, which is two walls of logs with the space in between filled with rubble and stone. ... We had the first dairy farm in Colorado, and behind the house was a stone structure over the irrigation ditch, also a very early water right—we were always sure of water—and it had benches in it which kept the cream, butter and dairy products cool. The house was a Dutch type, a long sloping back, steep roof in front and then straight down and a small stoop in front of that. [Sarah Brillhart]

The old part of our house ... is old rock construction and the walls are two feet thick. A lot of it [was] just laid up with mud, not cement. ... It doesn't sway in the wind. It's warm in the winter and cool in the summer. They used very small windows when they made these houses. ... I know our house is over one hundred years old. It goes back into the 1880s, early '80s at least. [Joanna Sampson]

There wasn't a stick of wood or anything. You had to haul everything to [the house]. You see in olden times when people went on homesteads, a lot thought that they could build houses. But there was nothing, no nothing. We hauled all our lumber for the building of my mother's house. [Sarah Brillhart]

I tell you that was the coldest house I ever lived in in my life. We had to sit around the heating stove. To keep our meals warm we sometimes had to put them on the stove so they would be even warm. ... I don't think I was ever as cold in my life as in that cabin. You just couldn't heat it up. [Alma Scohy]

It gradually settled up, you know. A few years time the county was all settled up. When we went there, there was probably ten families in the county. When we were there five years, there were a hundred families in the county. [Robert Jones]

Ranching and Farming

Ranching

[Doc Bills] lived in his latter years up Gregory Canyon. He had sort of a dugout. ... I was trailin' cattle in those days from Denver to ... around Hayden, and the old Doc had a cabin there. The back end of it went into a hill, and then he had a log front and ... one of my steers ... put his two front feet down the old man's roof on his cabin. ... The old man came runnin' out of the cabin, and he scattered those steers all over the country! ...

A cowpuncher was gettin' top wages when he earned thirty dollars a month, and his board. ... When we had nearly a thousand head, why ten miles a day was a pretty good day's drive. ... We had 'em graze in the mornin' for a couple, three hours, and you wasn't makin' much mileage then, you know. ... Then we'd bunch 'em up and put 'em on the trail. ...

They fed pretty good on these outfits. ... They'd kill a yearling, you know, and we had fresh meat every meal. It all depended on the cook. ... It was a life that I wouldn't want to live over again. 'Course we had lots of excitement. ... We generally had pretty good cooks. ... He used dutch ovens mostly, and when you got a piece of meat fried in a dutch oven you had all your steaks beatin' a fryin' pan. ... about an inch thick. ... A cup of black coffee was good enough in them days. 'Course we all had sugar, cube sugar, you know. ...

In Other Words

Oh golly, Charlie Temple, I've often thought, well he was kind-a what you'd call an ignorant man, you know. He just could write his name, and that was about all. But god, when it come to knowin' a cow, by god, he knew 'em from the foot to the horns. [Martin Parsons]

Probably the most interesting ranch, which is long gone, was the Ed Kohler Ranch. ... That was where they corralled in the springtime before they went to the top of the world with their cattle. Thousands of cattle. They branded a great big circle, as big as a washtub on the ribs of their cattle and in the middle of the circle was a large *K* that one could read from horseback a quarter of a mile away. The cattle were raised for meat and not for the hides. ... The hides were pretty much ruined with such a large brand. When they went to the tanneries, the Kohler ranchers didn't worry about the size of the brand; they wanted it so they could read it. [K. K. Parsons]

Cranson's brand, that was my grandfather; he had two brands ... that was taken out in 1881. ... One's a *J* with an upside down *C* on the top. ... You had to keep 'em up you know, pay so much a year to the county you took 'em out in. ... They were dropped after he died. I've got the certificates. [Edmund Darby]

To people who live in Boulder today it is impossible to imagine, as they go to the mouth of the west entrance of Chautauqua Park, that in one man's lifetime there could be such a vast change. Today that is all Open Space, but I can well remember the Kohler herds in the spring stretching from Eldorado Springs clear to Chautauqua and with the twenty or twenty-five Kohler cowboys gathering these cattle and moving them ... up toward Flagstaff Mountain. The trail that these thousands of cattle took still winds down below the highway that takes you to the top of Flagstaff Mountain. You could see it a mile away. It looks like a wagon road or a freighting road. It was made by thousands of cattle, and it was a sight that I wish I had preserved. They were still making that drive as late as 1944. They were still driving those thousands of cattle in the spring clear up fourteen thousand feet where the cattle summered. It was a joy to see the lead steers going around the bend disappearing beyond Flagstaff Mountain with the cowboys two miles back. It took all day and into the night to move them, and they kept them moving constantly. They went up what today is known as Magnolia Road and on up ... beyond the Moffat Tunnel through the mountains ... to the top of Corona Pass, and that's where the cattle summered. ...

For years and years and years each spring when they formed a trail herd of about eight hundred mother cows and the baby calves and bulls, they would leave the Hummel Ranch early in the morning and with their daughter

20

riding in the lead and a few of the neighbors helping guide along the sides, they would guide these ... cattle up here to our ranch and open the gate and turn them out. ...

On a September night in bygone years we would hear cattle bawling, and we would jump up and run out of bed and run down and open the corral gate for we knew that the Hummel cattle were coming from their summer range. It was storming when we heard those cattle calling in the fall. We knew that summer was over in the high country. The first storm had come and the old lead cows that had made the trip summer and fall fifty miles to the summering grounds were bringing the herds home. We miss that. [K. K. Parsons]

At shipping time you drove [the cattle] at night, because it was so hot in the daytime. They had spent all summer puttin' that weight on, and you didn't want to run it off so you drove very slowly seven miles into town to the shipping yard. When the freight train came in you drove the cattle in when the cowboys and cowmen and farmers were shipping. The freight came in with stock cars. The men sat around and made a campfire and put the coffee pot on. 'Course the first thing you always do when you stop long enough, you build a fire and put the coffee pot on. You put coffee in there. You'd just pour the coffee in and then you would put water in almost to the top and let it boil until it was strong enough. They said the way you could tell whether it was strong enough or not, you dropped in a horseshoe and if it floated, the coffee was ready to drink. [Cecilia "Sallee" Gorce]

Transportation here was all by horse and buggy—saddle horse. Many a time I've ridden a saddle horse to Denver. Leave home at two in the morning, ride into the stock yards. They would have a cattle drive ready. I would leave the stock yards at seven or eight o'clock, and then we would drive the cattle home. I was about twelve, eleven, somewhere around there. ... You didn't want to stay in a hotel over night because that would cost you a dollar fifty or two dollars. You didn't do those sorts of things because of the cost. [Frank Miller]

I used to ride with him [Homer, her husband] and take out the salt box for the cattle, putting Alice in front of me on the saddle. It was quite an experience. Once in a while some of the cattle would get away from the herd that was supposed to be in a certain place. One time we had a young bull that insisted that he was going to leave his herd of cattle and go to another one. He was kind of vicious about fighting, and Homer asked me if I could help him by putting two ropes on the animal and then we worked him out of there. ... We finally got him out, shut him in a barn and the next morning he was gone. It was a hay barn with big doors, and he had horns. The door was laying on the ground the next morning, and he went right back where he was. We had to go get him again. [Irene Smith Lybarger]

The old man finally built a little fence around his place so the cattle wouldn't get out on his roof! [Martin Parsons]

You had to have two miles of fence, posts ten feet apart and the holes dug two feet deep. Then you'd drive a team of horses with a spool of barbed wire on a pole with two cross pieces. It unwound as you drove the horses along. ... to the other end. And then you stopped, turned them around, started back the other way. Two men were coming along stretching the wire and shaping the fence. Then you came back the same way. As you got back there they stretched the wire. You went around the corner pole and then you went back the other way. Four different times on each half mile. ... It was hard work in the hot sun beating down on you, but you had to have that fence. You had to have cross fences to fence in the wheat field to keep the cattle out, and you had to have a calf corral. ... [for] weaning time. [Cecilia "Sallee" Gorce]

More or less it was just barnyard fencing at the time and the rest of it was more or less open range. [Rodney Dexter]

We all had six-shooters. I remember I had my first forty-four Colt when I was about ten years old. All of us had one. I remember the first gun I ever had ... I traded to my brother for a colt so I had me a horse to ride. ... My other brothers, as soon as they got to twelve or fourteen years old they would hire out to ranchers to drive cattle from one place to another ... Sometimes they would be gone for months at a time. [Robert Jones]

They'd nearly always go to bed, I would say around nine o'clock, and then they were up about five in the morning. ... Everybody went to bed at the same time and got up at the same time, and we always ate together. ...

Breakfast about six in the morning and dinner always at noon between twelve and one. We called it supper in the evening between six and seven. ... All three meals were large meals, because the men were working. [Nell N. Jones]

We got [up] early. ... We had to get up early, milk our cows, get ready, walk to school, walk home, milked the cows, got the eggs, fed the chickens. My dad always had pigs and cows, chickens, turkeys, geese. We had a job. ...

There was no fun, always work. Our family, there was twelve of them and times was tough. We all had to work ... That's all they knew was work. [Louis Varra]

I remember [my grandmother] used to tell me that even before she had gone east to school, in the morning when you got up, your shoes would be still wet from the night before and very hard because they had been drying in front of the fire, how there were never any pretty clothes to wear because you had to work all the time. [Charlotte Seymour]

I was the oldest of nine, and I took care of the children until I was old enough to go out in the field. Then I went out to the field to work. We had about thirty to thirty-five cows, and I'd milk my third of them, go pack school lunches and get off to school. We enjoyed school. ...

Usually we'd get the chores done. I'd help milk about thirty-five cows, and we had to get it done. We'd start milking again about four o'clock in the evening to get it done before it was too cold. [Irene Smith Lybarger]

I guess there was no U.S. inspection in those days. Us kids used to just cry when we seen [the man who bought calves] come around for fear Dad would sell one of our little calves. Once in a while he did. [Bertha Hartenagle Schott]

We had the Holsteins for milk. We had to have a cooler tank so that the milkman could drive right up and take it out of the cooler tank and put it on his truck. No inspector. They didn't have to wash the cow's udder or wash the cow off or anything like that. They just put 'em in the stall and milked 'em, but you had to have the cooler to keep the milk cool—to cool it quickly. And all it was was a tank of cold water. ... My mother traded butter for groceries. [Mable Andre Thomas]

[My dad] milked cows and delivered milk in a horse and wagon. All us children did. My mother had eleven children. We delivered about three hundred quarts in the morning and about that much at night. Then we'd go to school. That is why none of us got a chance to graduate, because we quit school when we were rather young. I quit school in the seventh grade, my brother in the sixth grade, and my sister the same way. We were doing the milking, and we just couldn't get homework done, you know. ... We would milk in the morning, my little sister and I, and we wouldn't get done until nine or nine-thirty in the morning. We'd turn the horse loose. Well, we'd tie the reins around the buckboard and right there on the south edge of town, and she'd take the wagon home, see, with the milk bottles. She'd know where to take it. And we'd go on to school. We was always a little late. And then, of course, at night you didn't get through until seven-thirty or eight o'clock at night, and you didn't feel much like doin' homework. ... We milked cows by hand ... I'd milk about twelve, maybe fifteen. My mother separated the surplus milk and made butter and buttermilk. Usually on Saturday we'd deliver our milk. Then we'd come back, and she'd have all the butter ready, and we'd go back out and deliver butter. I was nine years old and my sister was two years younger. It seemed like everybody worked. [Klubert Warembourg]

They would milk cows and sell butter, and my aunt would take butter to Magnolia to sell. My grandmother walked all the way to Central City and sold butter. She'd walk at night because it would be cooler for the butter. ... They had old wagon roads that would take ore and I think there was a road all the way to Central City. ... And of course Central City at that time was much larger than Boulder. [Ara Kossler Yager]

After 1912 we used to deliver eggs and butter by the pound. We had one of those old churns, you know, you'd bounce up and down. We'd spend all day Friday printin' butter; we had the print on it. ... Then we'd wrap it in paper and then deliver eggs along with the butter. [Elwood Barber]

Farming

We had chores to do. In the harvest time we helped to hay; we helped to shock. One year I helped my brother with a patch of beets. I topped those beets. I run the stacker horse, and Annetta ran the buckrake. My dad did the stacking. The three of us did all that. Of course, we had to help with the laundry. We had to do our ironing; we had to clean our rooms and that most kids did. In the summer time we would have felt a little upset if Dad had hired someone to work out there in the field, because we all liked to work out there with the horses. ...

It wasn't bad [running a stacker horse]. She was pret' near the oldest horse we had, and she knew just what to do. All you had to do was go ahead of her carrying the reins and then back her up, and that was it. She was attached to the stacker to dump the hay up onto the rack. The buckrake is a piece of machinery. You have a horse on each side with two-by-fours; then at the front there is a rack of teeth. They must have been twelve or fourteen inches [long], and there must have been twelve or fourteen teeth. You run that under the shock of hay and bring it back ... onto the stacker. ... Then you lowered it [with a lever] and set the hay on the stacker teeth ... then went on and got another load. The stacker horse would pull that up and dump the hay onto the stack. [Mabel Andre Thomas]

Two acres a day with five head of horses, that was a good day. [Jacob Schlagel]

I started at age fifteen pitching hay. That was twelve hours a day from six in the morning until twelve and then from one to seven. In the morning you'd get up about five o'clock. I worked for my uncle. I tell you one thing, you got pretty hungry when you come in. You didn't need a diet or anything. [Jacob Schlagel]

DIVIDING THE LAND

First we'd cut the wheat and shock it and then put the wheat into the threshing machine. They pulled a cook shack with them. We just had to feed our own men, those that had to help Dad and Uncle Jake get the crop in. ... The men would sleep in the barns, and then they'd have their cook car. There was a lady that went along with it, and she'd cook the meals. [Bertha Hartenagle Schott]

We didn't come back home each night. Her brother and I worked together and we'd take a couple of quilts, and we put that on top. Take a bunch of hay and make a little pile, you know, and lay this canvas on the bottom, and then you carried a couple of pillows. ... The hay was soft. I'll tell you what, you slept! You didn't need sleeping pills. And if you slept in the hay loft, no one smoked there. That was a must. [Jacob Schlagel]

There was a great shortage of horses because of the war, and they bought the horses and the mules so that they could take them overseas and have equipment to fight with. That was in 1918. My husband had his call but didn't have to go. It was really hard times. He was breaking the oxen in order to have some equipment. My uncle knew how to break oxen so they made some oxen yokes like oxen had to have. I think there were sixteen in the oxen team. ... Oxen are called oxen when they are broke to work. That's why they call them oxen. They have the ox yoke. ...

Mother came here from Ohio with an oxen team. They were strong and once you got them trained that they should follow each other, like they would have a lead team, a base team. When you got them trained, why those in between would follow them. But you had to get the lead team to go where they was supposed to go like plowing a field, they would go into the furrow that they had just plowed, and that's why they called them oxen, because they used an oxen yoke. [Irene Smith Lybarger]

The altitude is about seven thousand, five hundred feet so they raised a squaw corn ... for their chickens and even for corn on the cob. It's a lower growing corn and a faster maturing corn. The ears are much smaller than regular corn. ... It was the Indian corn. They kept the seed from year to year. ...

The corn fields, he would ... harrow it down and then he ... had a corn planter. It was a long thing with two handles on it and you'd stick the corn planter into the ground and with a downward motion you'd push it in like that and you'd pull the handles out. It would let the corn out. ... We had [a cultivator] but Daddy never used it for corn. I guess he thought he couldn't get enough weeds out. We always had to hoe it by hand. So we'd hoe ... what would be maybe an acre or two of corn. We'd hoe it by hand. ...

25

I think all of them [were] potato farmers. They grew potatoes. Even I can remember my grandparents, grandmother, that was one of their main crops that they sold, was potatoes. I remember some pictures of my grandmother when they farmed the lake property. ... They would have potatoes four and five inches long or maybe even six—huge potatoes that she'd be holding in her hands that they farmed on a little piece of property they had. ... My dad had a plow pulled by two horses that was a plow that you flipped. You would go to the end of the row and then you'd flip it back and it would plow the same way. ... You'd put the potatoes about twelve or fourteen inches apart ... I would imagine we planted five acres of potatoes. [Ara Kossler Yager]

They would come in with their wagons, their trucks, weigh the trucks full, dump their [sugar] beets in a hopper. There was a funneled hopper. It had a belt, and it would take it up to the top of the little house on the top where they would be screened. The beets would go out the side and drop into a railroad car. ... Then all the dirt that was on 'em would fall in another little hopper underneath this building, so when you dumped your beets you waited till they went up the belt, over the screen into the car, and then you pulled underneath this little building, pulled another lever and you got your dirt back. So you took your dirt back with you and weighed it back. All you were selling was the beets! [Charles Waneka]

'Bout all the farmers had to have a little cash crop to help pay for their places. That's what my dad figured on. Beets. 'Course he had milk cows but his cash crop to pay the interest on his payments on these was beets. My dad, he claimed he'd never got the place paid for if he didn't have beets. He even figured that he could make money by havin' less hay and goin' out and buy hay so he could have the cash crop from the beets to make his payments. ...

Dad used to have a house for beet workers. We had a family that lived here on the place for years and years. Their name was Calvo. His name was Frank, and they had a big family. They were our beet workers or hired help. Then in the wintertime when there wasn't no work, why he would work in a coal mine till it was time in spring to start thinnin' beets. They lived up there, raised their family. Him and Dad, 'course he couldn't talk much English. His wife did the talkin'. They never had one squabble, one fight, and Dad let 'em live there in the wintertime and never charged 'em no rent or nothin'. They had a regular spot where they could raise [vegetables]. They had a little farm there. They put up, themselves, just a lean-to shed to have a goat and a cow. Every year for awhile at this time of the year, Mrs. Calvo would have her baby.

DIVIDING THE LAND

She seemed like she got pregnant about every year for awhile and during beet season she'd be out toppin' beets until she'd have the baby. Then about two days later she'd be out toppin' beets again, and the baby'd be out in a buggy out in the field. She was a very rough woman. [Frank's] job was just to do beets, and then 'course in the spring when it was time to clean the corrals, why then Dad would go up and get him. Dad would pay him by the hour or whatever the wage was then. Every time we had him to help us, he got paid extra. [Elden Hodgson]

A dollar was a dollar in those days. We didn't think anything even in my time of going to help build a house or going to help do some plowing. The going rates a lot of times was about fifteen dollars a month and sometimes less than that for a man to work on a farm from sunrise to sunset and get fifteen dollars a month and his board and room. That was the way wages were. Money wasn't as necessary as getting some food, some clothing and so forth. [Frank Miller]

Oh yeah. We had terrible dust storms in the thirties. Real bad. Then after that, you know, they started to strip farm, and that kind o' helped. Instead of havin' all that open land at one time ... That helped the wind situation quite a bit. [Bertha Hartenagle Schott]

We had two or three bad years. ... [The grasshoppers] were really bad. I mean they'd eat the curtain off the wall if they got in the house. That's not a joke. Some of 'em got in our old bunk house down there, and they actually ate holes in the curtains on the wall. ... They stripped all the trees and ate the bark off all the lilac bushes. We done a lot of things tryin' to kill 'em. The county sold bran, banana oil on it to attract 'em and poison 'em. We'd spread it early in the morning and go back the next day and the ... ground would be covered with grasshoppers. ... They got to smellin' so bad after they started decayin'. You wouldn't think a grasshopper would put out such an odor, but I can remember the terrible odor we got from the dead grasshoppers. ...

Gus rigged up a deal on buckrakes where he put a piece of tin on the buckrake and made this tin drop down into little tanks made of water heaters cut in two. ... He put oil in these water heaters. Then he'd hook a team on the buckrake and drive it through the field and all these flyin' and hoppin' grass- hoppers would hit this tin so they'd slide down into the oil, and then, when he got to the end of the field, he'd take a screen and screen out the grasshoppers and put 'em in a pile ... and go back to the other end. He bucked grasshoppers for several days. I can remember watchin' him burn them piles. ... All of us would be out lookin' for crankcase oil to put in these tanks. ...

In Other Words

I can never remember clouds as people have described. They just were there, period. I never did see them comin' in. I never seen 'em leavin'. I just seen 'em all over. They just were here. I never seen 'em migrate as they claim they do. It just seemed like we just had grasshoppers, period. [Charles Waneka]

I remember one time [my grandmother] told me … she saw this black cloud, and it was the grasshoppers coming just in swarms. She rushed in the house and got some rugs to throw over her tomato plants. She felt that at least she could save that. They may not have any crops, but at least she was gonna save her tomato plants. After the horde of hoppers passed by, she went out and the rugs had been consumed. Anything that was organic, those hoppers were gonna clean up. [C. Clarence Waneka]

Migrant laborers and their children in a field of sugar beets, Niwot, 1908. Photo by Ed Tangen. Carnegie Branch Library for Local History, Boulder Historical Society Collection.

Miner and coal car in tunnel, Alpine, ca. 1912–1913. Carnegie Branch Library
for Local History, Boulder Historical Society Collection.

CHAPTER THREE

DIGGING FOR COAL

Not all migrants were suited for fighting with the elements and the rail-roads. Because Colorado offered more than just fertile topsoil, many pioneers were able to try their hand at digging out the vast resources of coal that were discovered beneath these fields. But this occupation also was riddled with conflict.

Coal mining required an enormous overhead. Large companies in the East sensed a profit and immediately stepped in to dominate the industry. The owners of the companies were interested only in monitory gain, and consequently the rights of the individual workers were forfeited. As the industry developed, the miners began to protest their harsh and unsafe conditions. Before 1898 men worked sixty hours a week in coal mines. This was changed by 1916 to fifty hours and forty hours by 1938. These hours were spent in the darkness of the earth at great risk to life for a meager wage, most of which was paid in scrip that only could be used at the store owned by the mining company. The companies would not tolerate complaints from their workers and as a consequence, some of the most renowned labor disputes erupted in the coal industry.

In 1890 the United Mine Workers of America was formed, and in the 1920s, under the leadership of John L. Lewis, this group became the strongest union in the United States. Meanwhile, in 1905, a radical Labor organization called the Industrial Workers of the World (IWW), also known as the Wobblies, emerged to counteract the conservative policies of the existing labor movements across the nation, primarily the strong American Federation of Labor (AFL). Its goal was to establish one socialistic organization for the workers of all industries, instead of the capitalistic, conservative system of the AFL. Wobblies were after sweeping social reforms and used strikes and slowups for bargaining power. Eventually the IWW dissolved when many members joined the Communist Party.

During this time there were numerous mining strikes in Colorado. One of the most devastating was in Ludlow in 1914, where twenty-one men, women, and children were killed. The nation became so outraged that the government was forced to investigate labor conditions in the coal mines. Eventually, working conditions, wages, and hours were improved and funds providing pensions, medical care, and death benefits for families were established. Although these caused immense improvements for the miners, theirs still was a strenuous and dangerous profession.

As with ranchers and farmers, miners seemed never to give up. They coped with the difficulties that were dealt to them and continued on.

⊷ ⚌◆⚌ ⊶

Hardships

Now in those days a saloon was every man's club and a great deal of news was passed back and forth there. Miners found jobs and mine owners and superintendents found hands. [Forest Crossen]

That's about all the miners did, was work in the mines and go to the saloon at night. [Thomas Kerr]

[These miners were] all nationalities. Mr. Gabriella was Italian. … Where we lived, a little further east, was French Town. What is now our pasture was full of houses. Actually there was a bigger population in Marshall than there was in Boulder at that time. … The Irish and the English lived more west on Old Marshall Road. Their saloon down there, they didn't allow anybody but the English and the Irish to drink at their saloon. There were those kinds of racial prejudices. … There were lots of bars [for the others to drink in], so there was no problem! Mr. Gabriella told me at one time that on the weekends the kids used to roam up and down the valley watching the fights. He said that you'd hear, "Fight, fight, at Binello's [Saloon] there's a fight," and the kids would all run up there to watch the fight. Then there'd be a fight way down on the west side of town and he said, "By the time the weekend was over, we were all tuckered out." I suppose [this was in] the early 1900s. That community has been there such a long time, because coal was discovered in Marshall in 1859. …

The worst part about the ethnic problems … was that these men couldn't speak English, and they couldn't read English. When they would post signs, safety signs and instruction signs in the mine, the men couldn't read [them], and when the foreman said something, they couldn't understand him. This was part of the reason the fatality rate in the coal mines in the State of Colorado was the highest of any place in the world for many years. [Joanna Sampson]

The men must have come first, and then when the women came … they lived right there in the [coal] mine. It was so cold, that they would have to hang up canvases to try to keep the wind out. … Timothy Moon, who was my husband's great-grandfather, ... was born in a tent house. ... There were a lot of tent houses in Lafayette. ... There was wood about three feet up, a dirt floor and then canvas nailed down, batted down over the roof. ... Grandma said it was very comfortable. Her dad despised it. He thought it was terrible that his daughter was livin' in [what] he called ... a rag house. ... She had the two children while she was in that tent. ... It had two stoves. ... Even the Mitchel Mine out there had tent houses, and they used them for bath houses for the miners. [Blanche Moon]

No, I went to seventh grade, I got to seventh grade, and I didn't whip it so I quit. I've been workin' ever since. The only mine I ever worked in was over here at the Columbine. [Jack Davies]

I went to school until ... I graduated out of the eighth grade, and then I went to work in the mine as a trapper. ... Open the doors, you know, keep the ventilation in the mine. [Lawrence Amicarella]

It was none of it safe. ... I done that up till '40. You didn't do nothin' but load coal; that's all you did. ... All you did was shovel. That's all you had to do from the time you started in the morning till night; that's all you did. You'd be bent over all day, but it was high enough to where you could stand up, you know, if you wanted to rest. Why, it was about ten feet high. [Jack Davies]

Usually [you were paid] twice a month. ... At the Columbine we got forty-four and a half cents a ton for loadin' coal. If you got sixteen tons you was a good loader. ... You had to have ideal conditions to load that coal. ...

Your pay didn't start till you started loadin' coal. You loaded coal by the ton. You wasn't workin' by the hour. You was workin' by the ton. You got paid so much a ton ... You had a snap on the end of the car. You hung your check with your number on that snap. When it went up the shaft, the weighman up there took the check off and credited it to your account. [Richard Brown]

Mostly loadin' by hand. That's what I started doin' with [my dad], but I didn't like that. That shovel got too heavy for me! [Frank Miller]

When I first went into the mine, you just wore a cloth cap with a carbide lamp. In later years you used your electric lamps. ... You used carbide in it and water. ... One filling would last about two hours, and then you'd have to refill it with carbide. It had a little water in there, and it would drip down on the carbide and make the light. Had a can for the carbide; had a can for the [black] powder. [Richard Brown]

You had to do your own drillin.' Puttin' the powder in the hole, shootin' the coal down. They had a machine. They called them the machine man. They'd put a cut underneath that was about [eight inches] deep and about eight foot underneath, and that way when you'd shoot it, it would have a chance to break down [as it fell]. They'd shoot it with black powder at that time, but they don't do that anymore. ... Years ago when they was usin' that powder you couldn't go in the place right away 'cause it was full of smoke. [Frank Miller]

Then I went ridin' rope, and I was ridin' rope when I quit. ... They had an incline on a forty-five [degree] grade. ... The coal was up here in another layer. So they had it made so that they'd send down seven cars at a time. The seven cars comin' down would pull the seven cars up. ... Then there'd be one man [who would] put 'em on a rope and send 'em down to me. When they'd come down to me, I'd hook the rope on seven empties and give them a bell and ... send them back up again. Every time I'd send seven up he'd send seven down. This was for moving the coal within the mine. Then they'd bring the load up on the cage. Sometimes the rope would break—why then "that's all she wrote." All you'd done was to get a blow torch and start cuttin' the cars off. [Jack Davies]

The most dangerous job I ever had in the mine was ridin' rope. ... You rode the back end of this car down an incline. ... You had one foot on the steel rope and the other on the bumper of the car. You rode this rope down to the parting ... the loaded cars go on one side and the empties on the other, and then you would uncouple the loads and couple up the empties and ride the front end of the cars comin' up. Sometimes the cars would get travelin'—the engineer would let 'em get goin' a little too fast, and they would just about fly down there, and you'd just wonder if you was goin' make the bottom or not. But ridin' rope was considered the most dangerous job in the mine. [Richard Brown]

The accidents here didn't mean nothin'. They thought more of a mule. One time I was a mule driver, a mule skinner, and the mule got his foot caught in a switch and these folks felt so sorry they all cried. If I'd got killed no one would have said a word! [Lawrence Amicarella]

Mules were very much in demand. My grandfather had a team of mules and the government bought the team and paid him a good price for them. [Irene Smith Lybarger]

[The mules] knew when it was quittin' time, and they knew when it was lunch time. And if they'd been used to haulin' one car and you put two on, they'd hear that second one click, and they'd just stand there; they wouldn't move. Around four o'clock they were headin' for the barn. They had a big barn right close to the bottom of the shaft that had all stalls. Give 'em water, oats, hay. A lot of them [the skinners would] bring up in the summer time. [The mules] couldn't get their eyesight for a while bein' down there for so long in that dark. But they knew when it was quittin' time. Them dumb mules. [Thomas Kerr]

DIGGING FOR COAL

Went to work one morning and the [coal] mine exploded. And there was nine, wasn't it, that got killed down there? Joe Jaramillo, the mule driver and tender. He's still down there, buried. I think there was about nine mules that got killed, too, wasn't there? He was bringin' the mules out in the morning when they had the explosion. [Louis Varra]

That explosion in the Monarch occurred in '36. ... They shut the Monarch down after that. ... Oh, yes. I've seen a lot of them come out of the Industrial that was dead, and I'd be workin' on the bottom of the shaft when they'd bring 'em out. Mostly cave-ins. [Thomas Kerr]

[You had little lunch buckets.] Carried water in the bottom, lunch in the middle, and pie on the top. You ate your pie when you went down, so if you get killed, you already had your pie! ... That was a miner's custom. ... That was your only water. You had to protect that. You were hoping the driver didn't get drunk and take your water. The driver drove the mules to pull the cars of coal. [Richard Brown]

They was just gettin' a little bit nervous down at the mine, and I said time to quit 'cause when they start gettin' nervous, I'm superstitious. My father was killed in a mine. ... Well, my sister Lucille and her husband and my father and my brother-in-law [were also killed] ... Mother says, "Dad, aren't you going to go to work today; don't you feel good, you don't want to go to work?" He just kept piddlin' around and piddlin' around. And she said, "Well, you got to go and pick up your riders." He said, "I'll go, Mary." So he went, but he didn't come home; he was killed. And my sister, Lucille, she was in an auto wreck. My sister's husband did the same thing as my father, just dilly-dally, dilly-dally; he didn't come home. When they start gettin' a little bit nervous then it is time to get out. 'Cause that's dangerous down there. [Ruth Davies]

My husband worked on an electric machine that cut the coal. My father loaded coal. They used to shoot the coal down. The coal fell down on my father and smashed his foot so he had to have his leg amputated. My husband went to step over the machine and fell right into the machine. It cut his leg from the ankle clear up to the knee ... He was in the hospital from December 11 until the last of February in 1902. ... It was terrible. ... It got so bad we finally had to have it amputated. But he got along fine with his artificial leg. [Sarah Brillhart]

They don't like women to go down in the mine. They say every time a woman goes down into a mine there's a death. But there was a bunch of us that went down one time, and I didn't like it down there—it stinks. You can't walk on the ties 'cause it's too dark. You don't know where to step. You're liable to fall and break your neck. I don't know how they ever walk down in the mines. It's terrible. It's an experience, I'll tell ya, and I never want to go again—never. [Ruth Davies]

Miners that had black lung [disease] ... had to prove so much time that they had worked in a mine before they could qualify for black lung. Of course, the black lung was a problem for all coal miners and for many, many years they didn't have pensions. It wasn't considered a pensionable disease. It wasn't even considered a disease. [Joanna Sampson]

Unions

My dad was a miner for sixty-three years. My dad came here in 1895. He was embroiled in the 1910 strikes here. No union. ... They treated the jackasses better than the miners, lets face it. ... In 1908 the Western Federation of Miners was taken over by the United Mine Workers. And in 1910 there was a big five-year strike. It was on for five years and nine months. They didn't gain much. Wages them days were two dollars and eighty-five cents, but they did gain to three dollars and twenty-five cents. Then the strike was over in 1915. That strike caused an awful lot of disharmony between the operators and the union. [Lawrence Amicarella]

I moved to this house in 1910. It was the 1910 strike. The weather was terrible. The snow was up on the fences there. And we couldn't come up in a wagon or anything else so they brought me up in a sled here. I moved up in a sled. We were so scared, you know, the militia came in. ... We slept in the cellar, my stepmother and me and my three sisters, we slept in the basement. Nobody knows what we went through in that 1910 strike. [Hannah Evans]

During the strike of 1910 to 1916 we had a window shot out at our house so we had to go to the basement to get out of the line of fire ... I can remember when my dad was told that he had to check his guns with the army, and that he would get them back as soon as the strike was settled. Approximately two years later he did get them back. [John James]

IWW, International Workers of the World, [or] *I Won't Work*. It was really good. ... They'd sabotage the work, not to the extent of wreckin' it but to slow it down. ... They'd go to work and not produce too much ... Instead of goin' on strike, don't produce. ... And I think they had a good philosophy there instead of goin' on strike. [Elmo Lewis]

I didn't approve of the IWW and still don't. We always considered them radicals and leanin' toward Communism, which I don't have any love for ... Solidarity was their byword. [Richard Brown]

Digging for Coal

My fathers and brothers belonged to the union. I'm a great believer in the unions. The unions used to help people a lot. When my husband worked at this other mine, the company would cheat on the weight of the coal, so the miners in the union would hire a man to weigh the coal, and that's what my husband did after he was hurt. They went on strike in 1909. [Sarah Brillhart]

Almost all of the old coal towns I know about have different ethnic parts of town: Louisville, Lafayette. This was sort of deliberate on the part of the company a lot of the time, because when they'd go out on strike—if say the English and the Welsh went out on strike, then they'd bring in scab labor of ... probably Italian or Greeks. So there was a language barrier. So these guys couldn't get together and really say, "Yeah, the conditions are awful down there. We need to do something." Companies were pretty astute about using these types of techniques. [Joanna Sampson]

Red scarves were a sign of the union miner. It was probably one of the first before we could afford suspenders and buttons and T-shirts miners always carried little red handkerchiefs in their pockets. When the were in a union, they wore them around their neck and they were labeled rednecks because of that and were proud to be. Isn't it strange how words that we honor get turned into negative things when you're a working man. [Gary Cox]

We had a five-year strike. ... The worst part about it ... when [my dad] died, the union was short on money, and they cut my mother off. She had three kids to raise and I was six years old; my older sister was eleven. Pretty tough. The only way she could do it was she took in ironing ... and washing with a washboard. They worked for so much money and that's how we lived. And then my brother and I, we used to empty ash pits and I had a job down in the poolhalls ... the people was good to us, can't complain about that. ... They hired me to clean spitoons. ... You either worked or you didn't eat. It wasn't like it is today. ...

The 1910 strike was a lot worse than the Depression for me. That was pretty rugged. [Elmo Lewis]

They come on strike in 1910. My dad never went back to work until 1915—five years. That's when they had all that trouble. They brought the cavalry into Superior, and they stayed there for a couple of years just to keep peace while the company got scabs to work in the mine. There was a few shootings. The scabs did come down. They'd get thirsty, and they'd come down to my uncle's saloon and a lot of them didn't make it back to the camp. You'd find them on the railroad track. They said they probably got drunk and a train run over them, but I think somebody hit them and put them on the track ... rough. ... Then in 1927 that's when the IWW called a wildcat strike. They were kind of radical. Dad told us, "We're goin' to go on strike, but we were not goin' get one of their cards." We still got United Mine Worker cards. That's when they had the shooting over at the Columbine Mine, I think there was about seven killed over there that morning. ... They had the militia over there and these young kids, I think they had been drinkin' in the wash house all night so when the demonstrators came over the next morning the minute they come through the gates they opened up with their machine guns. My brother was over there, but he got behind one of them camp houses. [Frank Miller]

I moved to Louisville in 1924. I worked at the Columbine [Mine]. I came back to the Columbine in the fall of 1927 when the Wobblies come in. When the Wobblies come in I went on strike like the rest of the boys. ... Well the morning of the massacre—Jimmy James and I, we'd been in Denver all night foolin' around. We'd been to a dance and one thing and another. That morning we got home around four o'clock. 'Course they had guards at the mine, the strike was on, and they wouldn't let Jimmy in. I was escorted up to my dad's place. ... I could see all this activity at the mine office. And, oh, around five o'clock or five-fifteen you could see these marchers, you know, the miners, they came in from the Erie side on the north gate, I warned the people what was comin' in there was goin' a be hell poppin', because I could see the machine gun nest under the water tank, and I could see the man with the high-powered rifle. Well they didn't care. They said they couldn't shoot the American flag, but that didn't make no difference. And in just about a half an hour all hell broke loose and they killed six—right in front of my dad's place. The sheriff come in and they arrested me and a fella by the name of Mike. They turned me loose the second day. I couldn't get a job back after. They told me there was no work for me that I was a Communist. ...

Another thing in my life was the big coal strike in 1927. Ninety-five percent of the people working in the coal mines came out on strike. There were a few fellows who were still working in the Columbine Mine. We used to get up at four in the morning at the sound of the trumpet so that we could go out on the picket line. Some of the coal operators would give us coffee and donuts. On November of 1927 we went to the Columbine Mine to march around the camp with the American flag. But when we tried to go through the fence, they had it electrified. So we crawled under the fence. As we were going down the road near a tank that they got their water from, they began throwing tear gas bombs at us. We were told not to even carry a knife so that they could not say we had started the trouble. But as we approached the water tank, we saw all the machine guns lined up for action. Then Captain White gave the order to aim. All the miners started to run back, and he said, "Fire." There were six miners killed and thirty-some wounded. The American flag did not mean anything to the so-called National Guard. They shot holes through the flag, and when some of the injured had a flag thrown over them, they beat the injured that were under the flag with the butts of their guns. [John James]

I just sat on the bed when a bullet come through one window and out the other on the corner of the house. I looked outside the house, and you'd think someone was plowin' the ground up just where the machine gun bullets was hittin' about ten feet from the house. These miners all rushed into my dad's place, and my mother she took the sheets off the bed to wrap up the wounded. These thugs, they come up to the house. ... We had a fella ... run the state police and he was a thug, in fact he was a guard down at the Cañon City Penitentiary. He was leadin' the group, and they was all drunk. That's when the Rocky Mountain Fuel Company let all the officials out and Miss Roche took over. From then on Miss Roche said that she would recognize any organization that was affiliated with the American Federation of Labor. And that's what started the United Mine Workers of America on its feet again. [Lawrence Amicarella]

Josephine Roche signed a Union contract, which was unheard of at that time. There was to be no Sunday work. When they needed coal, Josephine used to come out and crawl up on the rock pile—she always wore knickers and boots—and she'd say, "Now men, we need the coal. Will you work Sunday? We would like to have enough [men] to work. If you don't work, there will be no discrimination." And almost to a man, they agreed to work. She lived in Denver. She never asked some stooge to come out and ask us to work, she always come herself. She inherited [her position] after her father died. She was not responsible for the Columbine Massacre. ... She was very unhappy about it. [Richard Brown]

In the fall of 1927 Miss Roche got over to the mines. See, her dad was a big stockholder, and he was anti-union. Miss Roche came there, and she give us a talk. She said she would sign a contract that had ... to do with the American Federation of Labor. So we all joined the union, and I worked there quite a while. ... By 1933 they all joined the union. [Lawrence Amicarella]

There used to be a pool hall in town. We used to call it the League of Nations. See, the town settled with the Welsh and the English for the coal mining. And they'd have strikes and [the companies] would send in strikebreakers like Bulgarians, Hungarians, Italians, Czechoslovakians. And when they come in and saw the condition, why they'd join the other miners, and they'd go on strike. [Elmo Lewis]

In Other Words

The coal mines had been important economically, … and of course, with the freight trains being more numerous than ever the coal miners were all exempted from service and the coal miners were doing very well. Shortly after the war, within twelve months of the surrender, the dieselization of the motor power on the railroads was almost complete and that, of course, had a very adverse effect on the coal mines. There were at least eighteen of them running, and by '48 I don't think any of them were operating. [Clyde Boyle]

The entrance to the Puritan [Mine] was all guarded. They had a fence there and they had a water tower. You came into town, into the little camp, they called them camps, and … each miner had a little house, and then the commissary was like a big grocery store. People didn't have cars in those days so they had to buy everything at the commissary from clothes to whatever. They were paid in scrip. … The money for the groceries and stuff were just taken out of their checks so they had no opportunity to shop around or get anything anyplace else. [Cecilia "Sallee" Gorce]

The company store, you know, until Miss Roche got it, you worked—you traded at the company store. Before you got your pay they checked off. When I started working at the mine I didn't get no United States money, I got scrip and to cash up some money I lost twenty-five percent. My folks done and everybody else done the same. Well, I started at Rocky Mountain Fuel in 1916. I was thirteen years old. And before I got my pay—I got fifteen cents an hour—they took out somethin' that I didn't get like oil for my lamp, or carbide, see. The store took theirs out first until Miss Roche come and said that the people didn't have to trade at her store unless they felt like they had to. … She authorized the store to give us credit until the Rocky Mountain got on its feet. And she says if we was gonna leave or needed the money we could have it. But she was in pretty bad financial state. [Lawrence Amicarella]

[The grocery store was] privately owned. My brother-in-law owned it, but they checked off their bills at the office where they got their bills. Boarding house was first, bath house, bunk house, then the store. That's how they got their money—got it in scrip. [The doctor] got his three dollars a month to treat the family. Dr. Cassidy. He come to the camp every day. [Albert Chaussart]

My father-in-law used to walk to Lafayette [from Erie]. He got up at, I don't know, some ungodly hour in the morning and walked to Lafayette to work in the mines. They didn't have any showers or anything like that. They came out of the mines dripping wet. Walked home with frozen clothes, and Mom had a big hot tub of water waiting for him to take a bath. They had to sharpen their own picks and furnish their own equipment to work in the mine. [Cecilia "Sallee" Gorce]

DIGGING FOR COAL

[The bath house] had lockers and benches where you kept your clothes. They changed from their street clothes to their mine clothes, and then in here was the shower room that had a bunch of showers. All the miners took a shower before they left for home after work. Come here in the morning, change clothes, get your mine clothes on, then at night when you got off from work, go in and take a shower. [Louis Varra]

All it was was one big room there where they had their showers and everybody was in that one big room there where the showers were. [Albert Chaussart]

I can remember my mother had a boarding house. ... The table was always set. It didn't make any difference who comes, she had food for everybody. She kept cheese and crackers ... and bread puddings. ... These people would come and they'd stay. They didn't have any money to pay; they'd give her ... their jewelry. Well, it had no value at all, it was nothing, but that's how they did it. ... It was for these coal miners that would come in. Most of them would come and they had no families. They were here by themselves. [Margaret Gibson]

The old miners knew where the shafts were underground so they put those old houses where they weren't undermined. That's about all out there that isn't undermined. Of course, we've got fires in Marshall Valley, too, the coal mine fires ... The fires have burned well over a hundred years. ... Fires are common in coal mines. Often a fall of coal, as it falls, will strike off sparks which then ignite the coal. ... There are stories of stills exploding in old mine shafts. ... There is a story, too, of during strike times miners soaking a carload of coal with kerosene and putting a ... light lamp on top of it and pushing it into the mine so it would catch on fire. [Joanna Sampson]

I'm retired and I'm glad of it because there was a very dangerous and a very hard work in that coal mine. But I was just lucky I got [through] safely. [Rick Martinez]

Them days, when it was cold in the winter time, you know a little foggy, you'd see fires. Fire come out of the ground that high and smoke. ... You could see the flames. In them days you could see it blazin'. ... Years ago they didn't use slack coal at all. ... So instead of haulin' this coal out and dumpin' it outside, they'd dump it in a room that they had already dug out. They'd put a big pile of it in there ... and, of course, it got moisture and air to it, and spontaneous combustion started. One time, if I'm not mistaken, they cut that ditch open in there. Was goin' to put the fire out, and they just made [the fire] a hell of a lot better! [Byron Shanahan]

*A man panning for gold in what is possibly Left Hand Creek near Rowena, 1908.
Photo by Edwin Tangen. Carnegie Branch Library for Local History,
Boulder Historical Society Collection.*

CHAPTER FOUR
MINING THE MOUNTAINS

Hard-rock mining was the antithesis of coal mining. Once a man became a prospector, he was hooked for life. The hope of finding a float—mineral particles carried away by water—and tracing it back to unfathomable riches was ever present. In reality, most of the time the prospector was reduced to digging out riches for an eastern company like his brother in the coal fields. As with coal, hard-rock mining was too costly and complicated an enterprise for most individuals to make a living out of it on their own. Prospectors often were not equipped with the proper machinery or expertise, but nothing kept them from searching "on the side." There was always a chance of finding that lucky rock, which was secretly harboring a fortune in gold, silver or tungsten. If he was lucky enough to find a lode, a prospector would usually stake a claim, name the mine (often with a humorous name), sell it to a large company, take his earnings, and continue prospecting until his money ran out, at which point he would start working for a big company once again.

Despite the allure of wealth, hard-rock miners were far from safe when they entered the earth. Coloradans were lucky in that most of their mines were dry, because water caused erosion, was costly to drain, and often dissolved the supply of precious metals in the rocks. Also, the dryness caused less of a risk to the men when they were timbering—building support structures. Careful attention was given to this construction and to the proper ventilation of the shafts. In a typical mine, large buckets, which were attached to a hoist above ground, were used to carry miners down to where they could begin their work. Drillers drilled holes in the rock walls for the blasters, who packed the indentations with dynamite. The powder was then lit and the miners hurried out of the shaft, counting the number of explosions as they went. Muckers—men who dug out ore and waste from the mine—began their job in the rubble left from the blasting. The ore was then sent to the mill, where the precious metals were extracted. In the early 1890s, cyanide was discovered as a way to remove gold and silver from rocks, and once the public heard of this method, mining tailings or dumps became a haven for fortune seekers who found riches that originally had been discarded.

The value of gold and silver fluctuated with governmental controls, causing variations in the monetary returns received by mines and subsequently, miners. The value of tungsten, however, was directly related to demand, and the mountains of Boulder County harbored perhaps the greatest known supply of it in the entire world in the early 1900s. This precious substance was used for hardening steel, thus allowing the manufacture of high-speed tools needed in the production of weapons. World War I brought value to tungsten; the end of the war caused its demand to decline sharply, and by 1920 other deposits of the ore were discovered around the world. Boulder County no longer held the monopoly.

Even with uncertainty, hard-rock miners continued to work the mines, and to this day gold, silver and tungsten can be found in the mountains of Boulder County.

The Hard-Rock Miner

Most dyed-in-the-wool metal miners wouldn't even go under a roof that a coal miner will go under without any thought. [A hard-rock miner] is just afraid of that. The formations in a coal mine are such that it'll make a metal miner afraid of 'em. ... The coal miners apparently have no more casualties than a metal miner [because] they're used to [the mines] and they know what to look out for, [whereas a] metal miner gets

Well, you know they have a saying, "If you can't grow it, you have to mine it." [Richard Rubright]

under those [formations], he doesn't know what to look for. [Paul Warren]

I would say a prospector is a miner that doesn't want to mine. He wants to find something new, you know, something nobody else has tampered with. And he probably would find something new. He might mine it for a little while—that is sink the shaft or drive the tunnel in or something like that. But he would soon get itchy feet and want to travel to new ground, and then he'd become a prospector again. ... People got an idea they'd come out here and just dig a hole anywhere, but that ain't what they did. They used their heads, and they would go up streams, up gulches and whatnot. ... That's what the prospector did. Find something that somebody hadn't found before. To my way of thinking there is still lots and lots of ore in our mountains that hasn't been tapped. Lots of it. ...

Mining—I don't know whether you'd say it's profitable or not but people could make a living at it. My father had a love for mining. It gets into a person's blood if you start when you're young. It's awful hard to give it up, 'cause it's exciting. You have ideas about making a fortune. Very seldom that happens, but some people are lucky, you know, and work hard at it and the whole bit. But he liked to mine, and I started mining with him the year before I got out of high school back in 1932. [John Jackson]

Oh heck, I started puttin' in underground before I started to school—handlin' dynamite, oh, about five years old, "mucking." See Dad was leasin'; had his own claim down there and then would go work it at nights and on weekends when he wasn't workin' somewhere else. 'Course, by gosh, I was down there helpin' Dad, and I was probably in the road more than I got anything done, but I done my best anyhow. Packed the dynamite, slit it with a knife, put it in the hole and Dad would tamp it, but he never let me use a cap for fuse. He always handled that. [Ralph Yates]

I started in the mine when I was in the eighth grade in 1916. ... I went to work as a trapper ... opened the doors, you know, to keep the ventilation in the mine. [Lawrence Amicarella]

I first went to work as a top man [at seventeen]. ... We used buckets, and we'd have to dump the ore or muck—waste—into the cars out of the bucket when it came up. ... Then, of course, we graduated and went on into the mines, run machines and timbered. ... There was only one mine up there that used the cage [to get down into the mine]—the Conger—the others were just buckets. There were incline shafts and they went down on skids, see, and you rode them down. That's the way all the transportation was. [Charles Perkins]

Well, [to sink a shaft you] go straight down and you drill holes and blast it, and then you get down there and then muck up. [You shovel it] out into a bucket, and then it's pulled up to the surface and dumped ... [The shaft] is lined and timbered. [Charles R. "Binks" Rugg]

Many of the mines had shafts. ... And the miners would ride down [on a] ... bucket for hauling up dirt or ore or whatever. ... The miner would stand on the rim of the bucket and hold the cable to get down into the mine, and they would hoist them out the same way. If the mine wasn't too deep, they'd put ladders in at the side, but not normally. The ladders were used for just a short distance. ... Then they had a bell at the top of the mine with a wire that went clear down to the bottom of the mine, and they had signals. The miner down at the bottom would pull that wire and that would ring that bell to tell the engineer [who] was operating the hoist what was coming up. So many rings would be certain things coming up on the bucket, and so many other rings would be other things coming up— maybe just the miners coming up; they'd have a certain signal for that. So whoever was operating the hoist would go very slowly when somebody was on the bucket. Sometimes there were two or three of them on the bucket coming out of there, and he wouldn't dare go very fast. It would kill them. [Charles Snively]

Used blasting powder, machines. 'Course in the early days before they had machines we had to use our hands. It was all hand work. Most of the mines up here were developed by hand, you know ... They finally graduated, and they got the machines ... When the machines came in o' course the hand work just naturally went out. [Charles Perkins]

I felt sorry for the old hard-rock miners. When they had the old drills, they didn't have water in 'em. 'Course it was just kickin' dust down, and they all got silicosis and died of that. Called [the drills] *Widow Makers*. [Joseph Malcolm]

And they drilled into these mines, of course; they drilled and blasted the ore down and hauled it out. Rocks, sometimes, with no ore in them. They'd just blast and haul it out, and they'd have maybe two places to dump the ore after it got outside. They'd wheel this thing up one place if it was just rocks ... They'd lift the back of that car up and open the other end of it—the front end of it—and dump that out on what they called the "dump." And then they'd wheel it down and put it back in the mine. Maybe the next load might be ore-bearing rocks. They would run that to a different place and dump it. Then they would haul the ore down here ... in big freight wagons. They had one smelter here in Boulder, as I recall, maybe two. There'd be a road up to the dump, and they'd fill this freight wagon up, and sometimes that would have six to eight horses on it to pull the heavy weight out on a little narrow road that you would be afraid you were going to fall off of if you rode along in the freight wagon. Some of them would think that they would pick up some of the ore. You could tell sometimes by looking at it if it could contain ore of some kind ... And they'd maybe pick up a fair-sized rock and crack it to see if it had anything inside that looked like ore. Maybe they would get fifteen, twenty, thirty, forty pounds and send it down here to an assayer to assay it to tell them what it had in it. Then if it looked like it had enough in it to work it, they'd go pick the stuff off the dump and send it down. Maybe the dump hadn't been worked for years. That is, the ore came out of a mine and [was] put on this dump but nobody had paid any attention to it, maybe it was too low a grade of ore, they felt, or something of that kind. They didn't want to go ahead and send it down because it wouldn't be valuable enough. Well, maybe one of the miners wasn't doing very good or something so he just had it assayed, and if it assayed good, why he'd just work it himself, maybe one person. [Charles Snively]

Dangers

There were a lot of tunnels drilled into the mountains, you see. Sometimes they would send out for my dad to check out a certain mine. And if it were a tunnel, he'd go in with what they called a prospect pick: a little bit of a pick device that was sharp on one end and like a hammer on the other end. Some of those tunnels were unsafe, you might say, in certain areas, but he could tell by tapping the roof of the tunnel if it was safe to go in there. He'd tap the roof of the tunnel and listen and say, "Well, this is perfectly safe here." But he'd tap somewhere else, "No, that rock might fall down so you better go the other side and see what that's like." And the tunnels were, I suppose, six feet high, something like that and maybe four or five feet wide. They had tracks that went in there—you might call them small railroad tracks. They had cars, steel cars, that you'd push in there and fill them with ore or whatever it was. When they'd give the signal, same as they gave in the shaft to the outside, they'd pull them out, sometimes with horses. But lots of times the miners would just push them out if the mine was level enough ... They'd step up on the back side of them and ride out with them. There was a little brake they'd work with their foot, and they'd ride out with the ore or whatever. [Charles Snively]

We used to have a wagon. ... We'd go up Boulder Canyon at that time gettin' our dynamite, right on the main road. ... Then we moved to an International truck, hard rubber tires, chain drive. It was comin' down one day and the boys got ta goin' too fast ... and went off into Boulder Crick. The driver ... just went flyin', boxes broke open. Not a one went off. Powder won't go off; it needs ignitin'. But we had a lot of incidences. It was an interesting life. [John Valentine]

There's gas in these mines, too, you know. Have to watch out for that. So we take a lantern and light the lantern, or you can light a carbide light. Carbide light, when you get to that place, why, it will go out. If you

Oh, we were what, ten, twelve years old, somethin' like that. We used to get a big bang out of the mill up there. At that time it was just shut down. [There were] cars there—mine cars—and some of them had brakes on them, hand brakes like on the old railroad cars, you know. We would laboriously push one of those darn things clear up to the tunnel, then we'd get on it, and we'd come down that track. ... It was a big deal. We'd play in that sand that was below the mill there and that had cyanide in it. There was enough in there that you could play in it all morning, and then your hands would be just as smooth as could be. There was enough acid in there yet to eat the, you know, to eat your skin. And Granddad would give us heck for that, though. [Sanford Wagner]

haven't been in the mine very long, we light matches. That match don't burn anymore, we get out. Then we have to go to work and put air down the mine and blow it out, see. It's quite a job to get that out, too. It takes quite a while to get it out of a big mine with lots of tunnels and stops in it. But there is a laughing gas; they call it a laughing gas. That was when I was working over at the Poorman [Mine], and they was openin' up a mine there, you know. Had steam power there at one time. Those guys came up out of that mine just in time. They just laughed, laughed, laughed; boy, they just couldn't stop laughin'. That's why they call it laughing gas. I can't think of the name of that darn gas, but it will kill you after awhile if you stay down there long enough. ...

Then you got uranium pockets in these mines in places. See, a little uranium is always with especially silver ore and lead ore and stuff like that. That will kill you quicker than anything. If you drill a hole in that and then shoot it [with powder], why that gas stays right in there, you see; it won't go out. That pretty near got me one time—right along over here about five miles west. You can't smell it. I was working down there, and I could feel I was gettin' dizzy a little bit. So I crawled up the ladder. There wasn't anybody else but me down there. I had to crawl the ladder, about forty foot to the top. I got to the top, finally. ...

My grandpa Walter ... died at a very early age because of a mine accident, and all of his sons, except my father, died of miner's puff, miner's silicosis, miner's consumption whatever. [My father] didn't work very much in the mines. [Albert Walter]

If somebody got hurt in the mines, ... you just didn't work. But people were always takin' care of the family, see, nobody got hungry and this and that and the other. [Joseph Malcolm]

Rewards

When [the miner] was starving to death for a long time and then hit the high-grade, oh, you know how you'd feel. You bet your life. They'd get excited, and they'd really have a ball, you know. Some of the fellas made some pretty nice fortunes. ...

This fine old silver mining camp [Caribou], which for many years was the leading silver producer of Colorado, it produced twenty million dollars, up until the demonetization of silver in 1893 when the U.S. government withdrew its support of the white metal. [Forest Crossen]

Only thing you had to have money for was to live until you hit the ore. If you didn't hit it, why you'd eat dry pancakes; lot of them fellows was really disappointed. Worked for a long time, thought the ore would be ahead. They'd drive to it, and then when they got there it wasn't there. You'd be disappointed, just like any other business. You think it's going to go and then it don't. And you work all hard and deprive your family of a lot of things, and then when they get there, why the ore don't run like they think it should. They'd think it was going to run maybe a hundred dollars a ton, and maybe it'd only run ten dollars. They'd just be mislead someway, you know. ... Gold ore is pretty hard to judge unless you assay it all the time, where tungsten is different. ... After you've mined it a little bit, why you [can] pretty much tell what it is worth. [Ernie Betasso]

'Course the million dollar 'Tater Patch, two and a half million dollars they took out of that finally. The Ward District—six and a quarter million in gold out of it. Big figures look big, but look at all the dead work that has been done by individuals that tried to make a stake, trying to hit it rich, never got even grubsteak out of it. Just a hole in the ground. That's what they would [come] up with. Some of them several hundred feet deep. New York, mainly. Big money. They'd get some fast talker; they'd go back with a few pieces of paper and kind a finagle the figures to make them look good, and well they'd sink a few thousand here, there, and another, and he'd come out here and stick most of it in his pocket and do a little bit of diggin' and then go back with another big s*piel* and get some more. They finally got laws so they can't do that anymore. ...

[Dad] was one of those guys that always went and done all the work, the dead work ... He'd get ashamed of himself and be in debt for powder and fuse and everything else, and then he'd take a day's pay job and get out of debt. Somebody else would take the lease for two or three rounds; they'd make a little stake. Dad was that way all his life. [Ralph Yates]

When we went to workin' in the mines and places like that we only got paid ... once a month. ... Just once a month. If you [didn't go] to work on the first of the month you didn't get paid till the tenth of next month. [Charles Perkins]

When I came here it was mostly gold mining and in 1914 when the war started it was all tungsten. ... It's a really heavy ore, it's a heavy grade. [Harold Stevens]

Yeah, see they used tungsten for hardenin' rifle barrels. That'll keep the rifle hard during extreme heat, and everything else they knew at that time would melt, like if a rifle barrel didn't have tungsten, it'd melt, you'd shoot it so fast. [Ralph Yates]

That was the boom days in the tungsten fields during the war, World War I. [Delores S. "Dee" Bailey]

Mountain Towns

I remember during the tungsten boom the rag towns grew up around here overnight. And one particular one I can remember. I went to town. ... There wasn't anything when I went down. Came back that night and there was several tents and a store and a pool hall doin' business. Over across in the daylight I can show you over there on the June claim, there was a whole city over there. All tents. You can live comfortable in a tent. Oh, yeah. They would … put a board floor, and then board them up probably four feet or such and set the tent on there. And all you have to do to warm a tent is light a match, and if you want a bigger house, get another tent. [Ernie Ross]

There were mines all over the town. You had to watch. Some of them didn't even have anything over the top of them. At night when you'd go to the dances people would watch very carefully that they didn't step off the road into a mine hole. We were taught from the time we could talk to be very careful about the mines. But now they are trying to get them all covered up, I understand. [Charles Snively]

Well, Mama was borned here in 1885. … [Her family] was up here quite a while before that because her mother run the boarding house where my brother lives right now. There was a big boarding house there, and Grandma Miller-Shaeffer run the boarding house there. Grandma waited on the tables. [Maude Washburn Wagner]

Craig's Grandma Washburn run the boarding house down there at the Good Luck Mill, that's where my house is now. Yeah, there's a boarding house there at that mine. Every mine of any size had a boarding house to it. Women run it, and the old men worked the mines. [Ralph Yates]

Oh, they were good old men. If they were married, they generally batched up in the mountains and their families lived in town. After the tungsten boom started, why we had what used to be our old hog house. We had cleaned it out and the men slept up in the upper part. My mother fed them. I used to have to bake the cakes, and we always fixed them a lunch to take to the mine. Each one had a big lunch bag with a … pail, and it had compartments: one for the dessert, one for the sandwiches, one for the coffee, a cup to drink out of after the bucket was warmed. [Gertrude Tower]

When I was a boy, god, Magnolia, Salina, Gold Hill and Ward, by god, people come in here, miners, you know, from other places, and some of them weren't miners—wanted to hit these new gold fields, you know. Well, they just had them overcrowded with men. Some of 'em didn't have a dollar, and they just had a hard time gettin' along. There was a class of people in this country at that time if you didn't have the price of a meal, and you went in and told 'em so, they never let you go away hungry. You don't find those kind of people today. [Martin Parsons]

The operation continued until October of 1942 at which time the government passed an order closing all the gold mines in the United States. This was because they wanted the men and the material to go into the copper, lead, zinc and iron mines instead of in the gold, which was of little value for the war effort. [Clyde Boyle]

If I could start to mine tomorrow I would go—at seventy-six years old. I think that everybody that spent enough time at [hard-rock] mining would tell you that they would go back and try it again. It's interesting. It's different every day. You learn something new every day. It's hard work. [John Jackson]

Teachers sitting on steps of the State Peparatory School, Boulder, ca. 1888.
Carnegie Branch Library for Local History.

CHAPTER FIVE
LIVING IN THE CITY

Many towns grew overnight in the West, some of them as tent cities until building materials became available. As the settlements developed, they became richer. Salaries disappeared quickly when the farmers and miners came into town, either through the purchase of goods needed at home or the stress reliever at the corner saloon.

The early townspeople quickly built hotels, stores, and saloons, which in turn led to the appointments of firemen and lawmen. Small, family-owned businesses that catered to the needs of the community's population thrived. Local newspapers became important sources of advertising and information for events such as births, deaths, and social occasions. In 1886, the first linotype machine was used commercially, allowing the operator to set about 150 characters a minute, certainly an improvement over the old system of setting type by hand. Boulder County has its own story about the significance of newspapers to the development of a town. It goes something like this: The settlement of Valmont was larger than Boulder City in 1860 and was growing fast. In 1866, the *Valmont Bulletin* began circulation. Several men from Boulder City did not like this competition from a nearby rival town but had no printing press to start their own newspaper. One night in 1867 they managed to lift the printing press from the Valmont office and move it to Boulder after serving the editor of the *Valmont Bulletin* a number of strong drinks. Valmont's population subsequently declined and Boulder City's exploded. Could it have been because of the transplanted the newspaper?

As towns grew larger with migrants from all walks of life, an unfortunate prejudice often developed against those whose race was different from that of the majority. As early as 1866 the Ku Klux Klan (KKK) was founded by former Confederate officers as a social group and soon evolved into a clique set on terrorizing former slaves. The Klan disappeared in the late 1800s, only to reappear in 1915, this time directing its thrust against Jews, Catholics, radicals, and foreigners as well as blacks. In 1925 Boulder County finally rid itself of klansmen in the government when legislators and voters united and turned against the KKK.

Citizens were helped in their banding together by an inexpensive means of communication—the United States Postal Service. With the opening of the West, clerks began sorting mail on railway cars. They would drop the sacks of letters at towns as the train passed through, many times without stopping. As soon as roads were built to ranches and homes, the Rural Free Delivery Service (1896) began delivering mail to those who lived in the country at no extra charge. Not only were townspeople and rural settlers able to exchange information by mail, but also immigrants in the new towns were able to keep in touch with the loved ones they left behind.

Businesses

That Sunshine was a busy little camp in the early days. By golly the stores was busy and [the] saloon. Then the next camp was Gold Hill, and by golly she was a ripsnorter, too, when everything was goin' good. … Gold Hill had quite a number of saloon bums. By god, I can see their faces, but I'll be danged if I can recall the names. [Martin Parsons]

There was gold, copper and what they call sulphite now [in Sunset]. We had over a hundred men workin' up there. They had two hotels, two saloons, grocery stores. [Charles Perkins]

Sunset had one saloon, Copperrock had a saloon, Wallstreet had one, Salina had three, Crisman had one, Summerville had ten, and Nederland had twenty-eight. That was the years between 1872 to 1903. [Delores S. "Dee" Bailey]

So then mines were booming—the whole town up there. Oh, we had twenty-five or thirty men in the hotel alone. Boarders, you know, miners. Probably two or three hundred. Miners and families. We had about, oh I think there was about forty or forty-five kids in school. The school house is still there. …

He run the hotel for years up there till the … boom that went bang like these mining camps do. See, all of them, Wallstreet, Salina, Gold Hill, all of 'em went bang, you know. We just lived then on road work, and my dad and I worked the mine just a little bit. We had the hotel then until about 1912 when the dang thing burnt down. Went clear to the ground. The other hotel burnt down several years before that. The Sunset House as they called it. It was right along side of us. We saved the Columbine Hotel, that's m' dad's, but the other one burnt clear down. [Charles Perkins]

The windows, we thought they were painted on the front and the back. Come to find out they were so dirty, and they were beautiful glass windows and all we had to do was wash them with paper. So then … we remodeled the hotel. … And people couldn't find a room. My dad, when he'd rent rooms out in that thirteen room hotel, he wouldn't put the "no vacancy" sign up unless he had rented the swing on the back porch and the couch in Joe's office. ...

The hotel had those beds that went clear to the ceiling. ... And every room had a thing for the wash basin and the pitcher and the soap dish and then the pot under the bed. ... They all had to use the same bathroom; they had big tubs. And see, we remodeled and put in private baths. We had double beds. My dad used to rent a room, and there'd be two beds in a room—two double beds—and people would come to rent a room. He'd say, "Well, you have to share this with another man." And they'd say, "Well I'm not going to share a room with another man; I don't know who they are." "You'll do that or you'll sleep in the street." My dad was Irish, and he could get four men sleeping in that one room. He had them all friends by the time they left. He was really marvelous. [Edna Morrato]

They had two stores at Sunshine for a while. And years ago they had several bars up there. And it had a paper at one time. [Charles Snively]

There was a blacksmith shop. ... I used to love to go past that as I was going downtown and watch the blacksmiths shoeing horses and making horseshoes. Hearing the pounding of the hammers on anvils and seeing the red-hot metal that they shaped. [Franklin Folsom]

When I'd get to go to town about twice a year with a skinner, ... there was probably at least one, maybe two blacksmith shops, and that was my pet place to hang around. ... I think I was about twelve years old before I ever shod my first horse. [Ernie Ross]

The [Longmont] blacksmith's name was Johnson, and his son was named Alex. He was crippled with a double hump on his back, but he always used to be Santa Claus at Christmas for us at Potato Hill School. So we liked him very much. [Irene Smith Lybarger]

They had a blacksmith shop over there, and Steinbaugh, ... He helped more doggone farmers here. ... He helped my dad on certain things. He even helped me, you know what I mean? ... If you didn't have the money ... he'd lend it to you ... and you'd pay so much back. ...

He was really good to Genny and [me]. We wanted to build onto our house here, and we didn't have the money. That's when Cindy was comin' into the family [so] we needed to build a room. I went over there and told him, "I need to build a room, and I just don't have the money." 'Course they had the lumberyard then. He said "What are you talking to me for? Get across the street and get what you want and pay me when you can ... so much a month and do what you can, with no interest." He never charged us one dime of interest, and that's just the way he was to us. And he was that way to my dad. 'Course I guess a lot of people tried not

55

to pay him back or was takin' their time; he would get on 'em—you can't blame him for that. [Elden Hodgson]

Well, it was just a little town, had a grocery store and a lumber yard. Had a poolhall, and I guess, there was a barber on duty once in a while—not all the time. Old man Bittner run a barber shop in the Grange Hall, what is the Grange Hall up here, for a good many years. ... He barbered in there. [Clarence Conilogue]

The town [of Boulder] was a mining-supply town, it was never a cattle town. It was partly agricultural, I think partly due to my grandfather, but he was not at any point interested in mining. He rode about the country a great deal, planting trees as he went. [Charlotte Seymour]

There was a great big mill there and we loved staying there in the summer time and the mill as I remember was very, very noisy. Oh the machinery ... you could hardly hear yourself think in the vicinity, but its a funny thing, in the middle of the night if the machinery would break down and stop, everybody in the village would be wide awake because the noise was all gone. [Anabel Barr]

Boulder had a lot of other industries. ... We had a big flour mill on the corner of Twelfth and Walnut Street. There was a fella by the name of Bentley who had a little watchmaking store right next to where Potters was on Pearl Street. He always had a clock in the middle of that window that was supposed to be the correct time. A fella, who was an engineer at the mill here, stopped and was looking at that clock. Old Bentley came up and thought he was interested [so] he said, "Mr. Peterson, can I sell you one of those clocks?" He said, "No, I'm not interested. I'm the engineer over here at Rowland's Mill, and ... I check the time of your clock every time we open and close. ... " Old Bentley says, "That's funny, I set my clock by your whistle!" [Harold Stevens]

*M*en were the ones who sold the hardware. The only woman on the list of employees ... was the bookkeeper. And that lasted for the whole of my family owning that store. [Jane Valentine Barker]

The famous Valentine Hardware Store, which was just the center of Boulder, we never went down the hill that we didn't [go there]. It was a social event, and the clerks were the same people who spent their whole life there. Mr. Valentine ... was just the greatest guy in the world, very popular. [M. Helen Carpenter]

John Valentine, Senior, a very large, interesting man, was sort of an angel for all the miners in the area, and had been for a long time. ... He was doing a thriving business of selling black powder, or dynamite to miners who were still hanging on hopefully thinking maybe they'd hit that lode. There were a great many miners around Boulder ... coming to Valentine's to get [supplies]. [Clifford Houston]

LIVING IN THE CITY

Valentine's Hardware used to have a logo, a heart, and it was the heart of Boulder, and truly Valentine's was the heart of Boulder. Everybody, men, particularly miners, always shopped there. Whatever you wanted you could get at Valentine's Hardware. ... Some of the displays ... a very talented clerk in that store made. He used, once a year, to make a big display in the window, and he used only the stuff that was in the store. A mop might be a head of hair. ... Everyone went over to look at what was going on because it was an artistic display, very ingenious. [Elizabeth Wiest Farrow]

You just did everything at Valentine's. On the outside wall, on the east side, they had painted a whole map of the whole [county]. ... It was a tourist attraction. We all loved it. I never went down the hill that I didn't look at it. It was a part of Boulder that we all loved. [M. Helen Carpenter]

Saturday night, when the miners ... [would] come downtown, the women would go shoppin'. [The miners would] come in and sit by the old—we had a furnace with one pipe up. The heat come up from the coal, and they'd sit there, and they'd dig more mines, and they'd tell better lies than all the fishermen. But we got acquainted with them, and one would outdo the other. ... On Saturday nights we'd stay open to nine, nine-thirty, ten depending on how the stories were goin'. We didn't do much business. We had a bunch of loafers there. ... We used to have a lot of fun in there. ...

[My dad] always said, we're here to serve people. He says any store in town can have a saw like we have or a hammer, but we've got to give 'em a little better service than anybody else. And another theory that he had: he says, "We'll sell somethin', and it doesn't prove good. ... They bought from us, therefore we're responsible." We built our whole business on that philosophy. The customer's right, although you may know in your heart he is wrong. [John Valentine]

There were four weeklies at the time and one daily. ... [The *Camera* became] a daily on March 17, 1891 ... In 1892 my grandfather became editor of the *Camera*. ... Ball and Johnson who started it thought they would use more pictures than were being used in most papers at the time. That's why they chose the name *Camera*. They found that it was terribly expensive and didn't use as many as they thought, but the name stuck, and it's the only paper of that name in the country. [Laurence Paddock]

There is a little story [in the newspaper] about a prostitute in Boulder, and it said, "Topsey's At It Again." Now you wouldn't be able to put that in the paper now days. And it goes on about how she had been makin' her livin' and got picked up for bein' a prostitute. It says her mamma had done it, and she's always done it. It's the only way [she] knew of makin' a livin', and there's no way she's goin' get out and wash and cook for anybody. She's goin' to continue makin' her livin' that way. ... Topsey made front page with that little headline that she had. [Delores S. "Dee" Bailey]

One thing I remember so well, when there was extra special news, they'd send the news boys out, and you'd hear them calling in the night, "Extra! Extra!" We'd rush out and get a copy and know what was going on, 'cause, of course, there were no radios or anything of that sort. [Louise McAllister]

Boulder, to my way of thinking, used to be a much more pleasant place in which to live, because you never had to worry about anybody entering your home, thirty, forty, fifty years ago. A lot of people didn't even know where their keys to the house were, and they would go out and leave the house unlocked. Nobody would worry about a thing being touched, and it never was. [The population of Boulder] stayed around 20,000 for years [including students at the University]. [Charles Snively]

Segregated Neighbors

There was a period of prosperity. … Whatever you could do, somebody needed to have done, and it didn't matter what color you were, if you got the thing done that they needed to have done. … This was before 1870. … There was at least one [black] cowboy and … two horse trainers. … There were many musicians. Generally, people who had some musical talent were able to make a living. [Charles Nilon]

We who [were Negroes coming] from Cripple Creek, which was perfectly wide open, found that Boulder was absolutely closed. There was no place we could go. The important thing that came about as a result of Oklahoma and Texas practically owning Boulder—we called it little Texas and little Oklahoma at that time—was that there was no employment for Negroes, absolutely none. The Negro man was either the shoeshine man in the barber shop, if he felt like he could stand the degradation of that. It was ten cents a shine; if he didn't get a tip, that's all he got—was ten cents. If you got a tip you had to act simple-minded, you know, like you see sometimes on the movies, entertain the person who was there above you. Most of the men would refuse to do that. The other job that the men could get was on the railroad. [Ruth Flowers]

Most of the Boulder black population of 1880 until 1900 and beyond had menial jobs of some kind and in [most] households, husbands and wives both worked. [Charles Nilon]

The women could get only two jobs and that was washing and ironing or working in the homes. I washed and ironed my way all the way through college, but it wasn't a very pleasant task. The important thing here is that our men who couldn't find work had to, of course, leave Boulder, and many of them did go to Denver. [Ruth Flowers]

Prejudice was always present in Boulder. … Boulder, during these years, had the good and the bad mixed together. … Black people continued to come to Boulder. That meant that life in Boulder was better than it was in some places. [Charles Nilon]

Living in the City

It was absolutely impossible for you [if you were Negro] to get any house, rent or buy, except in what was called a little rectangle. … When we came here and Grandma tried to find a place to live, they told her that all Negroes in Boulder lived between Nineteenth and Twenty-third and Goss and Water [streets], which was four blocks down and, of course, we were on this side of the tracks, you know, the wrong side of the tracks. You couldn't buy on the other side. … It wasn't a ghetto. It was a very small piece of land, but it was not a ghetto, because everybody owned his or her land, and they tried to keep it up with pretty grass and painting houses. Everybody had a garden and one or two people … had cows. [Ruth Flowers]

Really … I don't think we had too hard a time. We got along with the whites, and they got along with us. They would come down to the house. … We had to make our entertainment. … We made roller skates … We'd get out at night and play under the street lights. They had a man who would come down [there at night] and light the street lights, and we were out there playing hide and go seek. … As I say, we had an enjoyable life. … It was really lovely. [Helen Washington]

There was prejudice here against the Mexicans. … Those people were pretty much supposed to stay to their own. As long as they tended to their own business, well, that was just fine, you know. No problem there at all. When they come up on Main Street, they were supposed to come up there, buy whatever it was they wanted and then go away. So that was prejudice. [Jack Rowley]

The town decided they needed a swimming pool so they built one. Now, of course, many people in town were of Mexican descent, and they helped with the work and this and that and the other, and their taxes helped build it. Well, then there were some people in town who looked in [at the pool]. There's Mexican children swimmin' with their children, and they thought, "Good lord, this cannot be; this is not right!" They had a big argument about it, and they filled [the pool] up [with dirt]. Believe it or not they filled the swimming pool up. Isn't that ridiculous? [Joseph Malcolm]

Kids used to make fun of me because I was a Mexican. … If you had to take a lunch and you took a tortilla, well, you hid so nobody would see you eatin' a tortilla. It was kind of embarrassing, you know. [Sally Martinez]

We were ashamed to show our lunch. We had these brown sacks, and my mother used to make pepper sandwiches. … Here these other people would have these beautiful sandwiches … and our mouths would water. My brother and I and some of the Mexican kids that were friends of ours and Filipinos … had to get away from the schoolhouse and go to the side of the creek to eat our lunch, because we didn't want to be embarrassed. Isn't that something? [Henry Amicarella]

Only group that I knew that came in there was the Ku Klux Klan in the first part of the '20s. My first experience with them … one Sunday night we was in the

59

[community church], and here they came in all hooded up. Scared us all to death. And they went up to the front two by two. ... Then the big mojo came in and said somethin' to the preacher, [who] gave them some money. He came out, and they turned around and went out, too. There was nothin' dangerous ... It turned out to be nothin' but a political organization. Well, we had a governor that was [a member of the] Ku Klux Klan. When he died ... there was hardly anybody at his funeral. [Elmo Lewis]

Everybody forgets. I remember what a big thing in the state of Colorado the Ku Klux Klan was. I'm thinkin' of the 1920s or so, and I can remember ... outside of Lafayette and Louisville, out there on the old highway there was a big gathering and a fiery cross, oh there must have been five- or six-hundred Ku Klux Klan out there. I understand they were not very popular but powerful in state and local politics. I can remember one time bein' at church with my mother. All of a sudden there was a horrible quiet, and here comes four or five Ku Klux Klan people walking up the aisle. ... They all had white robes on. You couldn't tell who they were. [They] threw a roll of money, you know, on the thing and turned around and walked out. They had a whole roll of money, bills for the church. ... I think it was more power politics than anything else. [Joseph Malcolm]

In Boulder the Ku Klux Klan was very powerful at that time. They had parades on Pearl Street and burned a cross on Flagstaff Mountain and so on. ... My father never joined the Klan; many people did in Boulder. [Franklin Folsom]

They used to come to Louisville, some on horses [with] flares, and those poor ethnic old European women would all rush to the cellars scared to death. It was terrible. [Peter F. Zarina]

[Louisville] used to belong to the Ku Klux Klan when Miss Roche took the mines over. She hired supervisors from this town, and they all belonged to the Ku Klux Klan. They made it tough for the people up at the mine. You, know, Columbine was a big camp. There was, what, six- to eight-hundred people who lived up there? ... These guys here in town, they had the preference, because supervisors here, they belonged to the Klan. And they give the preference. The people from Erie that belonged to the Klan, they had the privilege of being the best. The Klan didn't believe in foreigners, you knew that. One time they got after me. ... They sent me a letter from Erie, not signed. They wanted to meet me at the Erie cemetery. I knew what it was all about. I knew a bunch of [Mexicans] in Denver that went out with me, oh there was eight carloads of us that went out. You know what happened? [The Klan members] even put their fires out, because they seen these cars come in. [Lawrence Amicarella]

Streets and Sidewalks

I can remember the sidewalks. We had wooden sidewalks and many a tragedy occurred on those sidewalks, such as when I lost a quarter down the cracks, and some kind man took up the board and got my quarter. That was a lot of money for a child to have in those days. Then we had the dirt roads with mud knee deep. I can remember when they put a concrete walk in in front of our house. That was quite a fine day. [Mabel Edmondson]

'Course everybody walked where they went, them days. Everybody had a saddle horse around, or a combination team and saddle. But if they went any-where most generally walked, never bothered to fool with the dang horse. I've been out more or less on my own, lone-wolfin' all the time, trappin', huntin', fishin', always by myself most generally. [Ralph Yates]

We just walked. We just walked. We just plain walked. [Della Friedman]

All [of the town of Noland] was there [when I was a boy]. Boarding house and all. The old post office, the old stores, the old buildings. ... I don't think there was other than maybe two or three of those old stone [-cutting] people that lived up there—bachelors or something—but you know that's a funny thing. Those people lived in Lyons and worked in Noland and walked up that hill every morning, worked eight to ten hours a day and walked back that night, and that's a long walk across that mountain. ... They were a hardy bunch. [Glenn Tallman]

Horse and buggies, and streets, oh brother. This is the main route to the canyon and the ore wagons used to come down—six-team ore wagons and the dust they could churn up was absolutely unbelievable, and tally-hos used to go back and forth. Whenever my mother couldn't think of anything else for me to do [she'd have me] go and dust the front room. And there was always enough dust. ... My earliest recollection of the sidewalks along here was that they were wooden, long planks. [Elizabeth Wiest Farrow]

I can remember the condition of the streets when I was a child. Oh, there was mud up to your necks sometimes, it was awful. The only nice part of it was in the summer time when the weather was dry. There was always a little ditch water running up and down the streets, you know. It was a lot of fun to make dams and put boats on them and so forth. I don't know now where all that water came from, but it ran down every street that I can remember—had a little ditch running down the side of it and it was so much fun to play in. [Anabel Barr]

The streets as far as I can remember were so muddy, ankle deep at least when it was wet—ankle deep. Wagons. ... I can remember ore wagons with four, some-times six horses depending on the load the wagon was carrying. [Harry Goldberg]

I came here in 1911, and ... when I came up to Pearl Street ... the town looked a good deal busier than it does now. Of course, the streets were not paved then, and some days it was incredibly muddy. When the horses would trot up and down the street they would splash mud up on the store windows. It was quite a little hick town then ... and also the streets tended to be wider than they are now. They had kind of a smart city council, and later on when they paved the streets they widened all of the city sidewalks five feet so that business people would have more snow to shovel, and the city would have less, you see. Saves a lot of money that way. [Harold Stevens]

Another campaign I remember was keeping the streets clean, particularly men spitting on the sidewalk. Women wore long skirts so to keep the ladies' skirts clean we would do this and that. [Elizabeth Wiest Farrow]

Mother did tell one quip about going downtown. ... She said the mud was ankle deep in spots, and if it rained they put planks across so that you could get across the streets. [Frances Bascom]

I can remember the hitching posts along the highway. People used to come to town either in buggies or riding horses or walking. ... There was only three blocks in town that you could sell spirits. [John James]

The very first traffic signal in Boulder was at Twelfth and Pearl. It was a sign on a stand, which the police would turn to "stop" or "go" during busy times of the day. [Louise McAllister]

Mail Delivery

Yes, there was a post office in one of the stores. ... The postal department had buggies. ... They had a horse and buggy that came down and picked the mail up from the train. The train carried all that. [Charles Snively]

Well, didn't they call the one that went straight through and didn't stop at Niwot, wasn't that the *Flyer*? [Evan Gould]

Yeah, they always called it the *Flyer* 'cause it flew through. [Beth Dodd]

Yeah, and it had a stand out there, and they hooked the mailbag to it. The guy stood in the baggage car with what was like a cane, and he would hook that as they went by and drag it in. Then he threw another bag out. Sometimes it would be down the track quite a ways. [Evan Gould].

The mail came in on the train. They threw off the mail and picked up the mail, whatever they wanted to go. They had a special catcher along side of the railroad track that they hung those sacks on. It was just a bar sticking up in the air with two arms on it. One arm was coming out this way, and another arm down below it. ... The mail sacks had a ring in each end of the sack. ... They'd stick it on out there next to the track. They had a catcher on the side of the car. ... The train would just go through and that catcher would catch that mail. They'd grab it up and take it in the car. ... Nearly always they'd stop at Niwot at ten in the morning 'cause somebody was gettin' off or on, and they'd just boot the mail out there on the track. I don't know who took it over to the post office. Well, nearly all the time they would be goin' so fast that thing sticking out would just grab that sack just like that, right in the middle of it ... and take it along with them. And, of course, they had it on both sides of the car so they could pick up mail on either side of the track whenever they wanted. They had to know when the train whistled whether they were coming into Niwot or not so they could be ready to get their lever out there and grab the sack. It was in operation until, oh, I would judge, probably 1930. About that long. [Clarence Conilogue]

They used to have a post office up there. I think that was about in '23, and then they closed that post office. ... [When the post office closed, the mail came] in a truck like it does now. I carried mail when they closed that road. My younger brother and I carried the mail from—we had to go and gather it up down below if there was any. ... Well, I rode a little pony from Sunshine over to Salina, over the hill ... the reason we did that, the road from Sunshine into Gold Hill would drift [with snow], and they couldn't keep it open. ... It was after I got out of school. Fifty dollars a month. I split it with my brother. Picked up the mail at Salina and then we had to deliver it all around Salina. It wasn't only snowy, it was cold. One day it was thirty-eight below zero. My brother wasn't helping me; he had pneumonia, and he had to stay in most of that winter. It was so cold, I put the mailbag on my horse, and I walked to keep from freezing. It was cold, but I was tough, too. [Dorothy Burch Walker]

I can remember grandpa every morning around ten ... getting the horse and buggy and heading out to get the mail, and during the winter he had an old beaver-skin cap that he wore and a bear-skin coat and an old buffalo robe that he would throw over his legs to keep himself warm, then a muffler over his face and these great big old gloves like they wore those days and it was always a picture that you would remember ... for the rest of your life, and of course, whenever us kids got a chance to go to the mailbox with grandpa we went. [Howard Morton]

When we carried mail, anyone that wanted anything brought up, we would take it to them. See they didn't have groceries in Nederland when we first started there. There was a little drugstore and a few groceries, but you couldn't go down and buy meat the things like that. We used to take that up. Boxes to different people, and we were allowed to charge a fee for taking these things besides the mail, and we could also haul passengers, too. So we used to carry men back and forth between here and the mines. This was the Star Route and we worked under contract and not as employees of the post office. [Ruby Roney]

Yeah, they did have a little store and a post office up here at one time, but it just carried a few things. But our mailman used to be good that way. If you wanted him to bring up somethin' he'd bring in hay to feed the cows or chickens—different from now days, [when] you're just lucky if you get a stamp! [Delores S. "Dee" Bailey]

Members of the Seventh Day Baptist church on sabbath school outings in the mountains riding in hired stage coaches and picknicking, ca. 1892–1900. Carnegie Branch Library for Local History.

CHAPTER SIX

TRAVELING FROM PLACE TO PLACE

Migrants could come West on the famous trails, many of which were built by the government to encourage migration. Those not coming in their own wagons often took a stagecoach, which was costly and slow. By 1869, however, the Union Pacific Railroad linked up with the Central Pacific making a transcontinental line and offering a form of transportation that was fast and relatively inexpensive. Only three years later, two railroad lines came into Boulder City: the Colorado Central and the Denver and Boulder Valley Line. Once in the city, a passenger could hop a streetcar or an overhead electric trolley, which was the chief mode of transportation within cities and towns before the automobile.

As the railroads and streetcars became more popular, road care declined. Maintenance grew slack. No one seemed to mind until the bicycle craze hit. Transportation changed radically in 1880—the same year that Billy the Kid was killed at the OK Corral—with the invention of the "safety bicycle." When the price of this two equal-sized wheel device came down to an affordable eighty dollars per bike, everyone wanted to own one. Riding was not easy, however, because the streets were in disrepair. Bicyclists pressured town and state governments to improve the roads; in fact, they fought for hard surfaces similar to those being built in Europe. By the time the craze peaked in 1896, the citizenry coveted individual transportation and smooth roads. The United States was ready for the "Model T." In 1893 the first gasoline-powered vehicle was invented, and by 1913 Model T Fords were produced on an assembly line, making automobiles affordable for the average person. As the number of people who owned cars increased, the demand for paved streets grew. By 1924, national highways spread across the country competing with the railroads for travelers and migrants.

Horse Power

You see, in the early days, they didn't take the water out of the river, ... and they had a stage stop over there. Sometimes they had to take people across in boats. It's hard to believe, but they did. [Edmund Darby]

There's an old tree as you go out of Erie on the north side of Erie with a big limb hanging over. My father and I was coming along there one day ... and he was tellin' me—and these old timers used to whisper some of these stories almost, when you were out on the prairies, because I couldn't decide whether he had taken part or somebody's family had. But ... a man murdered a couple up at Golden; stole what they had, stole their horse. The vigilante committee had wind of it. They caught him at Erie, and they hung him to the tree. That limb is still hanging down there by Erie where they hung this fella. They didn't hang him for murderin' the two people; they hung him for stealin' a horse. Now that was how important horses were at that time. [Frank Miller]

Stage stop and hotel? Well, that was put there by Tommy Jones as a stage stop and a hotel for the people coming through here. And he was their first man. ... probably was the first building in Valmont. It was, I forget how many rooms, it had in it, but least ways it was accommodation for stages, and ... he run this stage hotel and boardinghouse and like that. [George Sawhill]

They had a stagecoach out south of you know where Stern's Dairy used to be. They had a stagecoach [stop] there. The stage would come up from Denver from Sand Creek out to there and stop, I suppose they'd lay over night, and leave there and go on to St. Vrain about Berthoud or Loveland, the next stop. ... I think [it came through] either once or twice a week. Maybe it wasn't quite that often. But they had a ... station there for quite a long time. ... I remember my grandmother tellin' once about the military, the cavalry came through, and they stayed overnight. ... I remember her tellin' us she stayed at the kitchen range and baked a hundred pies for them militia men. A dollar a pie. As fast as she could get 'em made. She grossed a hundred dollars a sack [of flour]. I remember that so plain, she used to tell about it. [Ralph Miller]

Us stage drivers, we didn't have to pay for our meals at all, 'cause wherever we went, why, our passengers went with us, you see, so us drivers, we didn't have to pay for any meals. [Martin Parsons]

Before Longmont started to really growin' there was a little settlement there named Burlington. And then the stages and everything came from there directly to Boulder, and so they had to cross Gunbarrel Hill over here. The sayin' is that the road was so straight and the two tracks like a double-barrel shotgun [that] it was called Gunbarrel Hill. [George Sawhill]

All I know is the same story Bill Harmon told about watchin' the stage come over the hill right where [Highway] 287 [is] north of Lafayette:

They had a horse change-over about where the Davidson Grange is, and they'd run their horses as hard as they could, but as they came up the hill over here. ... When they hit the top of the hill over here Mr. Harmon told me that the most thrilling thing that he had ever seen in all the experiences he had all his life was when the driver raised up, threw the bullwhip, snapped the horses, and hollered, "Hey," and they took off on a dead run down that draw. [Frank Miller]

Bill was sittin' alongside of a granary watchin' this young fella shovel grain into a granary and an airplane went over and he said, "You know you young guys get a kick outta watchin' those planes." But he says, "It's nothin' compared to when I was a kid." He said, "We'd go up to the top of the hill there and watch the stage come over the hill and as soon as the driver hit the top, he'd pop that snake over that six-up and go like hell for the station." [Charles Waneka]

It's awful steep, gets awful steep up in there. Well, the wagons, hauling lumber and all that coming down that zigzag road down into Gregory Gulch; that was awful. They would have a cable on to heavy pines, and let themselves down on the cable. And another way they drove wagons over those steep roads was ... they'd put timbers through the spokes in the wheels so the wheels would just drag all the way down. The brakes wouldn't hold and horses couldn't hold them back. So they just used timbers through the spokes of the wheels, and the wheels couldn't turn so they just dragged the wheels all the way down. ... I guess the horses did [panic] sometimes, and I know they had a lot of accidents. They'd be hauling lumber, and it would get so steep their whole wagonload would slide. I tell you the pioneers had an awful hard time. [William Herzer]

And of course sawmills were all along the foothills and back into the mountains. ... [My father] and my grandfather hauled lumber down the St. Vrain Canyon. ... They didn't have a road in there. They had a cable bridge and the cables were fastened to the huge rocks. They would bring the lumber down over those bridges, which would freeze in the wintertime. They had to put ... a pole ... across from one wheel to the other. ... It acted like a brake. [Irene Smith Lybarger]

Well, the road was so damn crooked you couldn't make six [horses] pull straight ahead, you know, but you could make four pull straight. If you add on six head you had to hold the lead back, and they wouldn't ... make these short curves. It was really too dang short for *four* horses. They didn't give a damn about the horses in them days. Just so's they got through, that was all that was necessary. [Martin Parsons]

[My great-grandfather] built a toll road up Boulder Canyon, and I think it was … fifty cents a wagon, twenty-five cents, horseback. … My own grandfather, he collected the money. It was no hard job. He just sat there and held out his hand. [Robin Arnett]

See, the road wasn't there like it is now, just a one way road here. … There was no cars them days here. You know in Boulder Canyon, it was straight up. That road wasn't there alongside like it is now. Four hours with a horse and buggy, yeah. [Elna Craig]

But you could ride down to Boulder, the freight wagons were running most of the time. You'd just get up with the freight wagon driver and ride to Boulder. We'd come down about once a year, is about all we got to Boulder. We'd take in a show and go different places to eat and things like that is all we did, and then we'd ride back up. I assume it took a couple hours, maybe, cause it was about seven miles, yes it would probably take that or longer, I don't know just how long. But pulling those heavy freight wagons, that was pretty hard on the horses, you know. They didn't go very fast. [Charles Snively]

They put another man on and instead of goin' up Sunshine Canyon, he went up Boulder Canyon, like a damn fool, you know, 'cause there's a lot of travelin' holdin' him back. By god, he got up to Four Mile, and here come another rig down Four Mile. By god, I don't know how it happened, and he didn't either. He said it had been so damn quick that him and his mail cart went off the road and killed one horse. Well, then's when they put me on, you see. Well, I never had no horses killed, but I've been in some pretty tight places. Always a lot of excitement on these mountain roads in the early days. [Martin Parsons]

Martin Parsons [was an] old cowboy around Boulder that used to drive stages up the Boulder Canyon up to Gold Hill, to Nederland, to Eldora. … Every night he would take his horse up Flagstaff Mountain, all the way up to the top, and check the fires and all that and stay up there while people are fryin' hamburgers and eatin' out. He'd make sure the fires were put out, and then he'd ride back down Gregory Canyon. He lived over on Bluff Street. He did that all summer. … He was really interesting. … I used to ride with him some times. I had a horse, and I'd go up there and listen to him. He'd sing songs to the people having picnics up there in the summer. Tell awful wild tales, and they'd believe him. I don't know how many of them are true. [Frank Streamer]

Anyway I rode up in one of those stages, and they didn't have sideboards, you know, those old buggies. Those old stages had four or five seats in them, and they had probably four horses anyway. But anyway, on the way up there the roads were so bumpy, I remember. I rode up on the front seat with the driver and over those old bumpy roads. He was carrying supplies up to that hotel, and they had big crates of eggs. They used to have about twelve dozen or more [in each crate]. There was two or three of those in front of one seat, and I remember one of those big crates of eggs bounced out, and a wheel went over it on the way up there. [Ina Gerry Wild]

We come in the buggy with two horses. We'd get up, oh, around four o'clock in the morning and come to town. ... It took a long time, you know, to come that eighteen miles when it's so rough and everything, you know. There was hardly any roads at all, there was just barely enough to get by. You'd have to watch to see if there was anybody comin' and when you was goin' around a turn ... to see that they didn't, you know, run into each other there with their horses. ... I was seventeen years old before I come to Boulder [from Nederland] ... and stayed over night. [Birdie Mather]

The road at that time down to Boulder, was very narrow and very steep and on the way back [my mother] would have to stop two or three times and let the horses rest, which didn't matter 'cause we had lots of time in those days. [Ruth Specht]

You know they had that what they called the Switzerland Trail [Railroad] here? Well, that went right up Boulder Canyon, and that scared the horses, you know. And the people that were freighters that hauled the ore from the mines with their four- and six-horse teams, they'd get scared you know those horses, and oh boy, ... it was awful. [Birdie Mather]

In 1909, [we] went by buckboard when we was kids. ... We went to Boulder to buy things. ... The best thing I can remember about Boulder is the clank, clank, clank, clank of horseshoes ... brick streets. The streets around town even way late in the '20s, the outskirt streets of town were just dirt. Now they're all paved. ... The inner streets there I remember they had brick for a long time. ... I remember in them early days horses more than automobiles—old stables. [Elwood Barber]

When I was quite young there were no automobiles that I remember at all. People traveled entirely by horse or on foot. [Franklin Folsom]

We didn't have a great number of paved streets [in 1920]. ... They were still meeting the trains with horse-drawn cabs. I know we went from the depot to the hotel in a horse-drawn cab. [Lois Huston Baum]

Rail Transportation

That brings me to the railroad here. The railroad tracks went up Water Street, which is now Canyon Boulevard, from what is known as the Y, which is about three miles down. The trains coming from Kansas got to the Y and then backed into Boulder. ... They then went out the right way. On the other side of the station were the electrified tracks. Those tracks ran between the old field out here and the armory, which is up there on the side of the hill. It was a little Interurban made up of two cars, and it ran on a cable—ran from here to Denver by way of Louisville, Lafayette, Broomfield, and Denver. [Ruth Flowers]

When the railroads first came through, that was something. They tell the story about Deke goin' to town to see the train come through and here it come a smokin' down the road ... and somebody says, "Well, Deke, what do you think of her?" He says, "It's great, but I bet the [engineer] can never get 'er stopped." It pulled into the station, and he says, "Well now, Deke, what do you think of her?" He says, "Well, I bet the [engineer] can never get 'er started." And when it pulled out he says, "Now, Deke, what do you think of 'er." And he says, "I think it's a hell of a thing!" [Frank Miller]

They had one running every hour to Denver. ... Overhead trolley, you saw pictures of these 'lectric trolley cars haven't you? We used to call them the old Interurban. We rode 'em many and many a time. ... I used to drive my horse and buggy up to Louisville and leave it at the livery stable. Take the Interurban and go into Denver to the show. The late Interurban left Denver at eleven o'clock and we got out to Louisville at midnight. We'd go get our horse and buggy and drive home from Louisville. ... Everybody in the country did it at that time. That's all you had a goin', boy. [Ralph Miller]

The Interurban was a system run by large cars, electrically powered, operating on tracks, which the Colorado and Southern and Union Pacific used. The cars were large like the passenger cars on trains, and they looked very similar, but they had the parallelogram-type trolley that picked up the electricity from the overhead line. ... The streetcar system in Boulder ... was operated by the Public Service Company. It had cars running along tracks on the middle of the streets in Boulder. The track was a narrow gauge, then the standard gauge used by trains. ... But it was also ... electrically powered. The cars looked altogether different. They could connect with each other and make trains, but they usually ran just separately. ... Before 1925 the streetcars were abandoned, and the tracks were paved over. [Roland Wolcott]

Boulder itself was full of electric cars. The town had, I would say, at least a dozen streetcars. ... They were tiny streetcars that were very popular with people. ... The streets were dirt streets, and when it rained for very long the streets tended to get a little muddy, which was offset by the community putting on a thin layer of oil on the dusty streets when they were dry, so one had the benefit of semi-paved streets running along the side of little, cute railroad tracks that all lead eventually up University Hill and ran several courses around University Hill. A favorite occupation of the students in those days during the winter when Twelfth Street hill. ... became frozen over, was to run along side the street car ... and pull the trolley off the overhead wires that gave it its power. Then the little streetcar sat there utterly powerless, unable to move, which gave the students a great deal of glee. ... I don't think they ever helped to get the trolley back on. [Clifford Houston]

We had streetcars instead of buses. When you got to the end of the line they would simply reverse the tops of the seats and simply go back the same way, 'cause they were not able to turn around. [Louise McAllister]

It was quite a pleasure to ride the Interurban, and, of course, there was no pollution whatever 'cause it was electric. It was in the early '20s when they abandoned it. ... That was progress. The trains had to go. [Marguerite Sherman]

I wish they had [the Interurban] now. [It ran] every hour, and it was real fast. [Hugh Smith]

The Switzerland Trail Railroad. They tore the rails out when I was a kid. Ma says she rode it quite a number of times. It was built to haul ore from the mines. Then they run—in later years—a spur over to Ward to haul ore, but by that time minin' was through. Then it stopped at Glacier Lake. They had a big lodge they started there. When they built the dam they had a spur down to Nederland to haul the concrete. [Charles R. "Binks" Rugg]

The narrow gauge line was called the Switzerland Trail, and it went up the Boulder Canyon. ... For a period of years there was a flourishing tourist business; there was a lot of sightseeing and excursion travel along that line. Glacier Lake and Mont Alto were favorite places for people to visit for their pleasure. [Roland Wolcott]

My mother ... used to ride that train up in the mountains for picnics— the Switzerland Trail. ... it washed out in 1917. ... After the flood washed it out it was never rebuilt, because the silver boom had come to an end about then. [Mildred Tanner]

Bicycles and Automobiles

High wheel bicycle. ... it was one of the first. Eighteen hundred and some that [it] was produced to ride. ... It was a little trick to it. Maybe a little more than riding a bicycle today. The way you got on and off ... was from the back, and you stepped up on a step, and you got on. You had to be in motion to ride it. ... It wasn't bad ridin' on the pavement and all, but I always thought, boy, ridin' on the cobblestone on the streets ... and the bricks—it was a little trick. I read where they used to have races on these high-wheelers, and I imagine it was quite a thrill to those who could race 'em at that time. [Lyndon Switzer]

I can remember puttin' together a bicycle. I'd pick up the parts. I'd go down to the old city dump and round up some of the parts and maybe buy one or two and put me together a bicycle. [Samuel Altman]

We paid twenty-five dollars for an old Model T. ... We drove that thing for a couple of years and sold it for twenty-five dollars again. [Dorothy Allen Greene]

It was a Chalmers, and they bought it in Boulder. At that time they would send a man out who stayed two or three days to teach my brothers how to drive the car. So that was much different than it is today. ...

No, you didn't have to have [a driver's license]. You just drove. You didn't learn how to drive. No one told you. You just got in and learned by yourself. No driver's training. [Ruth Dodd McDonald]

We drove out from Nebraska in a Model T Ford. I was thirteen years of age and the only one who could drive the car. That was quite something for a small thirteen-year-old child. [Robert Gruen]

I learned to drive when I was twelve years old. I just learned to drive by myself, nobody to teach me. You didn't have to have a driver's license. It was a gear shift, an old Model T. And one day I was allowed to take the car, I guess I was about fifteen at the time. I had a carload of girls, and we thought we'd take a little joy ride. We went out on Arapahoe, and I bumped into a bunch of cows. I couldn't stop fast enough. It didn't damage the car or anything, but I was scared to death to tell my folks about it. And I didn't get the car by myself after that. [Della Friedman]

Dad must have taught me to drive when I was about twelve years old. He would take me out Sunday afternoon out east of town [to] Valmont ... where there were no houses or nothing, [just] nice big roads where I wouldn't hit anything. And I would drive. I don't believe we were really required to have licenses. I wouldn't be surprised [if] I was in college when that law was passed—you had to have a driver's license. [Elizabeth Graham Demmon]

My father drove the first gasoline-operated vehicle in the state of Colorado. ... He was a mule skinner. ... They put him in this big truck, and they showed him how to start it and everything, but they didn't show him how to stop it. So the only way to stop it, he collided with a streetcar! [Roy Fling]

Budd says, "Whatever you do, don't get this thing out of gear, 'cause you got no brakes." That was the first thing we done, was got it out of gear! We were rollin' down the hill with no brakes. [Evan Gould]

That was a Ford, and my dad drove it up brand new. He used this machine shed, and he drove it up to the doors. We had to push it in, because he was afraid it would go through the other end. We just thought that was quite the thing. And I got so that I could crank it even as little as I was. I didn't get to drive it, but I could crank it up. It had the isinglass side curtains on it for the winter. [Mable Thomas]

Traveling from Place to Place

[In 1922] we came in two Model T Fords, one touring car that my dad drove and a roadster, which my brother drove. And [there was] no paving from Lawrence, Kansas, west, it was all gravel. In those days there weren't motels as we know them today, and they camped out at night. Believe it or not they had bedsprings tied on to the sides of the touring car, which they used to sleep on at night. [Robert Estey]

You probably have no idea what a touring car [was]. There was side curtains that were made out of cloth, and then for the window it would be a piece of formica or somethin', you know. And there was a rod that fit down into a hole in the door, and you'd put that curtain down over it. It would snap up around on the top to close it. When you went to get out you had to unsnap all of that stuff to open the door. But it sure did help to keep the cold out and the wind. [Ruby Jackson]

I remember one time in coming across the plains in a Model A roadster. I had no side curtains. I had a roof, a canvas-top roof, but no side curtains. ... Just in case there were high winds and so forth, I made myself a pair of side curtains out of linoleum, yes, just to shield the wind. ... I had to take whatever came. Rain, if it rained from the side, and the rain slanted in, well, I just sat there and drove the car and got soaked up. It was as simple as all that. ... I made these side curtains out of linoleum, and I poked little holes in there, and I roped these on. ... They were approximately ... a foot square. ... I had them on a bolt ... so if I wanted to look outside all I did was push this up and lean down a little bit and then look out the window, then let it flop back again. That's how I did it. Well, we got a terrific wind from the north while I was going west, and I was on the so-called lee side, and the wind was comin' in from the other side. Well, I'll tell you it got worse and worse and worse and suddenly those side curtains just blew all over the place, and that one on the north just wrapped around my head somethin' terrible. It just blew against me, and it just folded itself! ... Oh, I had to rip that thing out. ... That was the end of the side curtains. ... So then it was just hang onto the steering wheel and keep a goin'. ... Traveling in the Model A roadster was quite a thrill. [Raymond Friese]

I do remember the first car I ever rode in. It was my Uncle Joe's. It was a touring car with a top that could go down or up. Most of the time the top was down. ... Uncle Joe chewed tobacco, and if you sat directly behind him—that memory is very keen. [Elizabeth Wiest Farrow]

I remember the first car I ever rode in. I must have been in elementary school, and of all places this man took us for a ride up Boulder Canyon, and the road was narrow. It was scary, but it was thrilling, because we were in a car, you know. It had sides. It had a little, tiny running board. ... It was an open, touring car. You could see over the edge and see the drop. ... Why you would take somebody up Boulder Canyon to show off your car, ... I don't know. [Elizabeth Graham Demmon]

There are ninety-nine curves from downtown Boulder to my cabin [in Wallstreet], ninety-nine curves … one way, ninety-nine curves. Can you imagine? And if I made a U turn in the road and brought the car into my parking place there were 100 turns. I counted them. Everytime I turned the steering wheel off center, whether it was a real sharp turn or shallow turn, I counted that as a turn. Most of them were sharp those days, oh they were sharp, you know. They would hook around like a fishhook. [Raymond Friese]

The first car that was really any much of use in the canyon was the red Stanley Steamer. It was run by a young German. … [A friend of mine] used to run a little wagon up to Sugarloaf with mules. He had an old Colt gun about so long, and I said, "Bill, we can't load the gun up in the store. I'll clean it up for you." … I says, "Who are you gonna kill?" I was only just kiddin' you know. He says, "That S.O.B, Bob." I said, "What's the matter?" "Well," he says, "I came down the hill from Sugarloaf, and he came a whistlin' and a screechin' in the red steamer of his that's like a fire engine and drove my team into the crick." [My friend's] harness was broken, and his whole wagon was broke. I says, "It won't do any good to kill him." I says. [Harold Stevens]

Oh, we'd go to dances, up to Sugarloaf dances. A lot of times my old Model T, if you tried to go frontwards up, the gas tank was lower than the engine. We didn't have a pump, so we'd back up. One time I backed through Sugarloaf and didn't even know it. Missed the whole town. [Hugh Smith]

We would have all kinds of troubles with Model Ts, because the gasoline would get low. You'd start up a hill, and you'd think you had plenty of gas, but due to the grade the gravity flow became insufficient so you would have to turn the car around and back up the hill in order for the gasoline to flow properly! [Robert Fernie]

You put the car in the garage, and you took the wheels off and put some wooden legs under it. You didn't think about runnin' the car in the winter. It was a different way. There was no Prestone and no snow removal. [Emma McCrone]

He soldered the head on a Model T coupe I had, a 1922 coupe. I got the flu; I just passed out one day when I came home from taking the milk into town. I was in bed about three days. I'd always kept a fire where I kept the car. 'Course nobody knew that but me. The car froze. I had a nonfreezable radiator on it … and [it] froze the car solid. For three days it was cold. A long crack in the head of the motor. Brother John happened to be there when I come to and told him about it so he soldered it for me. Never bothered me again. He sure knew how to solder things. [Elbert "Al" Specht]

We had to be our own mechanics. On Model Ts we got so we could take 'em a part and put 'em together almost in our sleep, because you had to. … Many a time I'd been out late at night goin' to a dance or bringin' my girl home, and something would go wrong with it, and when I'd get through I'd look like a grease monkey. … If it got to rainin' why then the coils would get wet. You'd maybe leave your automobile, and have somebody with a horse and buggy pick you up and take you home. We really had a lot of fun in our lives. [Frank Miller]

For us [things] changed in 1910 when father bought a Buick car, a little white Buick car. It had no cover. It had two doors I think but was a very good car. … When my father came home one day with an automobile cap like they all wore in those days, mother said to me, "Well, it won't be long now." And sure enough, father was getting the [car] fever, and so we soon had this 1910 Buick. He got the cap, and then he got the car. But, of course, if it rained, we'd walk to church. We wouldn't take the car out in the rain for anything! We protected the car. [Jessie Fitzpatrick]

We had no excitement [as children], except my father bought that Ford. But there wasn't any place to go, because they had no roads. [Marguerite Ensz]

I became aware of Stanley Steamers. They became an important item of travel in the mountains. They were so powerful that they could go, well, all the way up to Estes Park. … It could go over sixty miles per hour and used kerosene for fuel. [Franklin Folsom]

The way you went to the mountains in those days, there were these people who had these big, Cadillac touring cars, and they arranged weekend trips. … There were two women in Boulder who ran one of those things, Mrs. Molloy and Mrs. Macleay. … They were wonderful people. … Mrs. Molloy, she was a marvelous driver and great, big, masculine type of woman. … She could have picked up an automobile, I think … and Mrs. Macleay … was just a feminine as [Mrs. Molloy] was masculine. … They were outdoor people and very sophisticated. Although they were women earning a living, which was unheard of in those days, they were accepted by the social life of Boulder—… two single mothers. They ran a taxi business in town in the winter time and then did these mountain trips in the summer. You could ride all over town in a taxi for a quarter. [M. Helen Carpenter]

Mrs. Molloy and Mrs. Macleay used to run that tour service and Mrs. Molloy was just as tough as they came, I'll tell you. There wasn't anybody who crossed her, and if any man wanted to try to out-swear her, he came up short. There wasn't anybody who parked in her parking place. … She was the nicest person in the world, but you just plain never crossed her. [Frank Streamer]

She was a big, tall, tough old babe, and you always felt perfectly safe coming home late at night and having her driving you back up on the hill. [Mary Folsom]

Home of August Clyncke, Dry Creek, Boulder, 18?. Photo by J. B. Sturtevant.
Carnegie Branch Library for Local History, Boulder Historical Society Collection.

CHAPTER SEVEN
HOUSE AND HOME

Early western houses, with no electricity, heating or plumbing, were certainly not the comfortable houses of today, but they did provide a home in which family members could gather. Although the man was the 'head of the house', the woman spent most of her waking hours at household chores: washing, cooking, cleaning. It was the woman's job to see that everyone in the family was fed and clean. Fortunately, technology eased her load as it did that of her husband, especially after society harnessed the working power of electricity.

One of the most tiresome tasks women had to face was the hand-washing of clothes. For them, the invention of the washing machine saved many back-straining hours of work. One of the first mechanical washing machines was patented in 1858. It was shaped like a box and had paddles that a person cranked to churn the clothes in water. It was an improvement over the washboard, but not much. In 1910 an electrically powered washing machine was invented with a hand operated wringer to extract the water from the clothes.

As time went on, more and more inventions eased the housewife's tasks, freeing her to become involved in other activities. Not all inventions were considered an improvement, however. For example, in the kitchen, many women did not want to give up their coal range. They had learned to cook on it and felt food tasted better when cooked the old-fashioned way. But no one could deny the advantage of refrigeration. Except for the loss of the ice man, a person who was a beloved member of the neighborhood, having ice made in a machine in the house was a true luxury. Of course, electricity was not suddenly available throughout the country. Many a family was not able to take advantage of the new technology, but it was a comfort to know that the lives of the next generation would be filled with fewer strenuous tasks and more leisure hours for enjoyable activities.

With the invention of the foot-peddle sewing machine in 1851 by the Singer Sewing Machine Company, and later in 1889, the electric sewing machine, women were easily able to make clothes that suited their new life style. It is interesting that dresses remained cumbersome to wear and hard to clean until the bicycle craze took hold of the country, at which point women shortened their skirts. They simply could not keep their balance on a two-wheeler with a long skirt flapping in the wind. Technological change had an effect on all aspects of everyday life.

The Woman of the House

On her seventy-seventh birthday, I called on [my grandmother], ... and I found her rocking back and forth in her chair in her living room, weeping. I had never seen the old lady weep. ... I was kind of shocked. I asked, "Grandma, what's the matter?" and she said, "Alfred" (that was one of her seven children, the only one that she did not get through college—he had dyslexia) ... Alfred had lost his farm for taxes. And she was weeping about that, and I said, "Grandma, are you sure?" She said, "I'm sure." And I said, "How do you know?" She said, "I bought it!". ... She was a tough old lady ... She was crying because he had failed. [Franklin Folsom]

I have so much admiration for my grandmothers. They left good homes, secure homes, and their families and came all this way. It was pretty rugged in those days. But they liked it after they got here. [Mabel Edmondson]

Yeah, the women had the babies and the men worked! [Albert Chaussart]

No, they didn't help women in those days. Well, women had to do most everything. Men were the "man of the house," and he ruled the house with the pay check and everything, you know. The women worked, and they got along [with each other] okay. They'd see each other, and that's the entertainment we got. Go visit one another. That's it. The kids would play outside. That's the way it was. [Gentina Moschetti]

What made things go was the woman helped the man to make things go. If it wasn't for the woman, you couldn't survive on one of these mountain ranches. And all the women around here were about the same way. [Ernie Betasso]

They talk about the good old days, but they weren't good. It was hard work; it was awfully hard work. [Maude Washburn Wagner]

Yeah, but you lived through it. [Sanford Wagner]

Yeah, we lived through it. We washed clothes on the board, everything else. No, it was hard work in everything you tried to do; it was hard work. [Maude Washburn Wagner]

As we girls grew older we were taught to dust and wash dishes. Each of us had work to do, and we weren't allowed to work together. When we were through we got to play. There were a lot of dishes. Sometimes I used to wish the table would fall over, and they would all break. You're lazy at twelve, you know. [Pearle Yocom]

Care of Clothes

Washed on the board, you know. I think really we had cleaner ways of washing then [than] they do now. 'Course we didn't boil colored clothes, but everything white we had to boil. We had a stick. We'd poke 'em around and take 'em out then and rinse them. Had two tubs of water. You could buy bar soap, five cents a bar, six for a quarter. [Sarah Brillhart]

When we would butcher a hog we saved all the fat and then we would cut it up in small pieces, and mother would render it in the oven. The pieces that came out then would be what they called "cracklings." We would sometimes grind them and put them in cornbread. After we got all the lard rendered out, mother would strain it so that there wouldn't be any little pieces of crackling in it. We used a certain portion of lard with a can of lye—there was always a recipe on the side of the can that told you how to make the soap. ... It took quite a lot of stirring. I know. We had a long paddle that my father made. ... We used a big iron kettle. We sat and made it outside. We used that kettle to heat water and do our washing and to scald the hogs when we butchered. It was a very servicable thing at that time. Then we would pour [the soap] in the pans, and when it got hardened, mother would take a sharp knife and cut it into bars ... Mother would make about fifty pounds of soap at one time. Lye soap to do your washing and ivory soap to wash your body and hands with. All these varieties of soaps [they have today] weren't to be had. [Irene Smith Lybarger]

[My mother] had an old wooden washing machine, and it had a motor on it. She would shave the soap into a boiler on the stove and then put that into the washing machine. And you had two big tubs. One was the first rinse. [In the other] you'd put the blueing that came in a little bag, cloth bag, and you'd swish it around, and that was your blueing. It had to be rinsed twice. In order to really bleach [the clothes], we would have to spread them out on the grass, and the sun and whatever. They would come out this sparkling white. Oh, they were beautiful. You started washing about six o'clock in the morning, and it was out by eight. If you didn't have your wash out then

You didn't consider it a hardship. It was something that had to be done. [Cecilia "Sallee" Gorce]

everbody thought you were lazy. [We did wash] on Mondays and Thursdays. There is a special place to hang the clothes. The sheets had to go on one end of the clothes line, because the sun would hit that, and they'd dry first. [Della Friedman]

Monday wash, Tuesday iron ... Wednesday you clean ... Friday maybe baking or whatever, Saturday was kind of a general cleanup. But that was a religion. Mother was always proud to have her washing out the first ... on the line. Bet your booties. Washing was no easy job. First of all it was getting hot water. ... We had a great big copper boiler that was filled with water and put on the coal stove and then that got hot. There was also a reservoir in the old range and a tea kettle. You started with that and kept filling all these utensils as fast as you emptied them and added to or changed the water and washed on the board and rinsed in ... cool water and then put it through the blueing. You blued your clothes. Wrung them out by hand and hung them up. I've seen them come in stiff as boards when it was cold weather, and there was nothing else to do. ... Always hung out.

[A washboard] had a wooden frame and then it had ten rough grooves that you rubbed the clothes over. We would put part of a tub of hot water in this round tub, put the wash board in there. Rub soap on the clothes and then rub them up and down on the board until we thought they were clean and then rinsed them in another tub and hung them out ... In the winter time we'd have to hang them around the stove. ... We always took pride in our appearance ... We had to iron all our clothes. [Marie Pooschke]

Mother had a washer and a wringer, a hand wringer. The washer had an electric motor underneath. You see, this washer had to be pulled into the kitchen until this big back porch was built. ... Then we got an electric easy washer. You washed, picked the clothes up and put them in a spinner. It didn't work by itself like our washers do today. [The clothes] were agitated automatically, but when that washing cycle was finished, then you had to take the clothes, put them in an easy washer, and it would spin most of the water out. Then you hung them out on a line. That was after the hand wringer. ... You were always warned to be careful not to get your fingers in it. We never did, but you had to feed the clothes. But as I remember, Mom did that. ... I think Mom did the washing, but we had a lady come to do the ironing. Because then all the shirts, all the dresses had to be ironed, and I remember the woman came always on Tuesday, and she ironed all day long. [Elizabeth Graham Demmon]

Some people had what they called the "hired girl" who lived in the home. We didn't have a hired girl. Father took care of the outside of the house and mother took care of the inside of the house. We sent our laundry out. We'd send a huge bunch of laundry, and there was a little woman who would come and get it, take it home, wash it and iron it, and bring it back, for a dollar twenty-five. [Jessie Fitzpatrick]

In those days there was ironing. There was no such thing as wash and wear, of course. Men wore very stiff collars, and they had to be done just right or they blistered. Shirts and dresses and petticoats—and a half a dozen petticoats to boot—were starched. ... You could starch them before you hung them out, of course. But if it was windy or anything of that kind it might whip the starch out. You saw that they were starched and dampened down and got ready for Tuesday. And then you had a hot fire and irons on the stove and the hotter the day the hotter the fire, the hotter the iron and the more clothes. In hot weather there were a lot of summer clothes that had to be ironed. I can remember when I learned to iron. I hated men's shirts and hate them to this day. ... Start with the yoke and do the sleeves and proceed, ... but you better be sure you touched up the collar and the front before you were through and hung it up and hoped to high heaven it would meet everybody's requirements. A thankless job if ever there was one. [Elizabeth Wiest Farrow]

Electricity, Heating and Plumbing

Electric irons helped a whole lot. ... It seems to me that mother's first [electric] iron was when my sister was at least in high school [1915-1920]. And I do know that we had electricity put into the house about that time. It was rather primitive wiring, but I remember when we didn't have those everlasting and eternal kerosene lamps to clean. [Elizabeth Wiest Farrow]

We had oil lamps, and do I remember 'em. Used to have to wash those chimneys all the time. Those black chimneys. All shiny—we had to have them clean. Go upstairs and clean 'em and take em down and wash 'em and fill 'em with oil and take 'em back up again. [Flossie Allebaugh]

Of course, electricity and gas was totally unheard of. We used kerosene lamps for light. And to do the chores the men used lanterns that also had kerosene. They had a handle and the chimney was secure, but they were a hazard in the barns if they tipped over, because then they would catch fire very quickly. [Marie Pooschke]

Originally, of course, in my memory, there was just kerosene lamps and then years ago Dad purchased a thirty-two volt electric lamp. Then we had our own electricity. It was satisfactory. We could run small motors, things of that nature. We really didn't have electricity here until 1941 when the REA

[Rural Electric Association] came in as part of the Colorado Big Thompson Project. [Andrew Steele]

Things were so much simpler then. You know, we didn't have to have so much to enjoy ourselves ... I can remember before the room was wired for electricity, and we had coal oil lamps. We even had an outside toilet. I was born in 1908 so it was probably up until 1914 that they built an addition, and we had an inside bath. [Della Friedman]

One story he told about—I don't know whether I can tell this—about a farmer. He heard this noise. I guess it really happened somewhere. He heard this noise out in his chicken house so the wind was blowin' pretty bad, and he had, instead of a night shirt, he had these old red flannel underwear with the trap door on it and that was loose. He was headed with his shotgun out to the henhouse and his old dog, fearin' for his safety, touched [the farmer] with his cold nose. The gun went off, and he killed twelve of his best hens! [Hugh Smith]

The room was so cold I had to sleep in Dr. Dentons, you know, the [pajamas the] kids use with feet in them. Like long underwear with feet in them, and they were grey. When I would go in—we had to use the outdoor toilets— ... in the covers I had an earthenware thing called a pig. It was round, and it had a little snout kind of like a pig that you filled the hot water in. That got real hot. That would stay all night long, not like a hot water bottle that cools off. So I would put that in the bottom of my bed. I'm so mad I didn't save that thing. It'd be an antique now. [Elizabeth Graham Demmon]

We left our home back there and moved up here to Wallstreet, where mom and dad and us eight kids and grandma and grandpa lived in a one room house with a tent behind, and we'd sleep out there winter and summer. We'd run in and pick up a brick in the winter time and put [it] on a stove to warm it [and then put it in our bed] and that's how we [kept ourselves warm. [Delores S. "Dee" Bailey]

Beyond the living room was my bedroom, and it was cold. I wore Dr. Dentons ... And I would have to go in there to brush my teeth before I went to bed. I'd take the water from the kitchen, pour it over my toothbrush into—I guess you'd call it a slop thing—and it would be frozen by the time I brushed my teeth. Now that's what I lived in. [Elizabeth Graham Demmon]

[The chip box] was your kindling, because we burned wood mostly, and we had a big tank kind of a stove that sat here, and that's where the chimney was. This was partitioned off so that the door was always kept shut so you went to bed with a flatiron and a cold bed. You'd heat your flatiron. If you forgot to bring your flatiron out in the morning, when you came out [at night] to get it on the stove you were in pretty bad shape. [Gertrude Tower]

We had a pipeless furnace. It came up through a big grate-thing that came up between the living room and the dining room. You see, you had to keep your doors all open upstairs. This house was a square house, four big bedrooms. ... Dad was really an early health nut, I guess, because he built sleeping porches on so every bedroom had a sleeping porch. [We slept in the fresh air] and it was cold, but none of us had tuberculosis. Dad was not going to let any of us get it from all these people that had it. [We slept on a screen porch] in the winter, and we didn't have any heat. Later we had windows put in but no heat. It was still cold out there. [Elizabeth Graham Demmon]

In those days you slept on a sleeping porch. I can remember in the winter waking up every single morning when there had been a snow storm, and there would be snow on top of the bed. It would blow into the sleeping porch. ... It was a screened porch, but you were exposed to the cold air. ... a lot of quilts. [Mary Folsom]

When we lived at Sunshine we had what they called a Round Oak Heater. That was the name of the heater, and that was in the living room. You had to put coal in that, of course. It was just hand fed and [you had to] clean out the ashes every morning. And then later they had what they called these circulating heaters that you still put coal in and take ashes out in the morning, but it had a metal thing completely around the stove out, say about six inches from the fire box. Cool air came in the bottom and out the top. They had circulators for years. ...

Many of the houses had what they called a coal bunker, and when they would deliver the coal they'd fill that bunker up, and you'd never pay any attention to it. It automatically fed it into the furnace all the time. 'Course you had to every morning clean out the ashes out of the furnace, but it would feed it until all that coal was gone. It was completely automatic. Whatever your temperature was set, that controlled the thing. [Charles Snively]

[We would] deliver at homes, shovel coal through a window chute. Sometimes if you couldn't get to that window you'd have to get a wheelbarrow and wheel it down there and then shovel it in. Then if the bin got full and you had a little more coal, you'd have to get in the bin and shovel the coal back and make room, you know. It was hard work, oh. [Bauldie Moschetti]

A wood-burning stove and coal. It was just one stove, the cooking stove in the kitchen. It was a kitchen, and you'd walk up the step and that would be the middle room. And that's where I slept. Just a room. And then the other room, which my parents slept in, and I guess I slept with them until my sister was born.

That's what they tell me. I can remember sleeping in their bedroom, and I also remember sleeping in my own room in my own bed. [Roseann Ortega]

We had a rain barrel out at the side of the house, and, of course, mother had a cloth over that so that it would strain whatever the dirt was that came in. ... She had a soap that didn't smell very good. It was a bar soap, and they always said it kept the head lice away. So we washed our hair. It started with mother washing the six girls, and then it started in again with her washing the boys' heads; shampooed hair in rainwater. Our baths were taken in wash tubs in the kitchen. I always accused mother of starting with enough water to wash the baby and by the time I got to it, it was too thick for me to take. The boys took their baths in what we used for a wash house. My father would help them, and mother would help us. [Irene Smith Lybarger]

[Baths were taken] in a common washtub, and they were made out of some kind of pressed paper. ... They were heavy as could be, but I remember those were the kinds of tubs we had. [Birdie Mather]

They didn't have any plumbing of any kind in the house where they lived at all. [Allen Bolton]

No, we didn't have running water until about 1950, 'cause grandma Bailey didn't want no water in here. She fought us head and toe. She had carried water from the crick for all these years, and she didn't want water in this house. [Delores S. "Dee" Bailey]

Our water was about a quarter of a mile from the house, and we carried it in buckets. ... Dad had a kind of a sled thing ... that he fixed with a big barrel on it, you know. ... Every week, why he'd fill that and bring it to the house for mother to wash. ... [We got the water for cooking] twice a day, first thing in the morning the boys carried the water to the house, and I used to, too. ... I used to have one of those five pound pails, and I used to carry that. [Birdie Mather]

Right under the kitchen ... we used to have a pitcher pump there at the sink, and you'd drive water from this cistern up under the sink. There's a well in the back yard about twelve feet deep and lined with stone. They filled up [the cistern] from a ditch. There was some kind of filter out there on the south side as I remember. They filtered [the water as] it came into the cistern. [Allen Bolton]

We had a cistern where we used to get our drinking water. It used to be trucked in from Lafayette with a big truck with a big tank. ... Then we'd pour it in the cistern, and we'd bring it up with a bucket for drinking water and for bathing. [Roseann Ortega]

We had a great big range Mama used, ... had a big water tank on the end ... We all had to [help with the hotel]. We washed dishes, stacked dishes, it was terrible. Wash the clothes. ... We had to wash sheets and pillow cases and towels for all them de*ng* people for nine rooms. ... Miners used the rooms. [Flossie Allebaugh]

Cooking

My mom, you know, had that big cook stove when we lived in Tung- sten, and people that used those are used to those, you know, and when we moved to Boulder she had an electric range. It took her the longest time to get used to that. She kept a sayin', "I wished I had that other stove in here." "Mom, now come on, don't you like this better? You don't have to haul in coal and wood and take out ashes." "No, I'd rather do that, because they cook better." I guess if you cook somethin' you could push it back, let it simmer or somethin' or keep it hot. [Ruby Jackson]

We had a coal/wood range. I still like to cook on a coal/wood range. The food tastes different, and the biscuits are always better in a coal/wood range. I don't know what the difference is, but there is a difference. It's a different heat. It's been a long time since I've had it—a coal/wood cook stove. 'Course the gas you can turn on and off, you know, it's more convenient. [Annie Bailey]

I enjoyed baking in them anyway [cast-iron ovens]. It had a reservoir on it so that I could fill that and [then I] had hot water without using the tea kettle all the time. ... [The reservoir] hooked right onto the side of the oven part. ... The heat then on this side would heat those little reservoirs right there. We used that water for cooking. It was all right. We carried it up from the pump down over the hill. There was a big pump there—a well. [Ruby Jackson]

Ordinarily, mother didn't bake every day, but she baked all the bread we used. We children considered it a rare treat if we had to go to the grocery store and buy some, what we later came to call gummy bread. In those days it was a change. Yes, mother baked maybe twice a week, I wouldn't say every day, and marvelous bread, beautiful bread that I've never been able to dupli- cate. [Elizabeth Wiest Farrow]

[There was] a little ole lady that lived down in a tent just below us, an old black, black tent with soot hangin' down, and she had a little ole stove. Yet you could go into her house, and she'd be rolling bread on this black bed spread, but the bread would be so white when it would come out. [You'd be] just amazed. She always wore a little ole sun bonnet on her head. Always in black, black cap and black gown and black coat, everything was black, and she's the one that taught mamma how to get out and look for the different things [to eat]. ... What berries was good for what, and they'd use those Oregon Grapes; [they] would make the best grape jelly there was. [Delores S. "Dee" Bailey]

We churned our own butter, too. It was a stone jar, and it was kind of tall. It was about as big around as a gallon bucket, but it was tall. It held three gallons. In the top of this lid there was a hole in the center. In this hole we placed a stopper. This stopper had a handle on it just like a broom or something but on the bottom there were two pieces of wood—one went one way and one the other—like a cross. They were on the bottom of this handle. So we raised this handle up and down in the cream until butter came. My sister and I used to get so tired of churning; we didn't like to churn too well. The cream had to be just the right temperature ... room temperature. Then it would usually come quite fast. Then we would take the butter out and underneath would be the buttermilk. ... We salted it lightly. ... My sister would bake the bread. We never thought of buying a loaf of bread. Never thought of it. [Marie Pooschke]

It was hard work all the time all the way through, because we had so much to do and nothing to do [it] with, you see, hardly. [Birdie Mather]

Mother's kitchen at that time, ... the coal stove was on the north wall and the chimney for whatever reason ... went up almost to the end of the east wall. One of the horrors of my life was when we had to clean the stove pipe, because if you joggled that thing when you were taking it down you got soot all over the kitchen and so it was a model of inconvenience. ... So there was a stove and we always had a kitchen table, we always ate in the kitchen, and a cupboard that had dishes and everything else in it. Things were so cramped. ... We would get a ton of coal at a time and at first we had a coal shed ... right outside the north wall. ... I remember when we had a great big snow that time, the snow was up to the window and you couldn't get out the door, couldn't get into the coal shed, couldn't get the shovel to shovel the snow. There was a casement window on the north. Mother opened that ... Helen climbed through on top of the snow to get to the coal shovel. ... The ash pit was right out there also. See, in those days you had an ash pit and somebody had to come in and clean out the ash pit. They had to haul the coal in by wheelbarrow. ... Usually we ordered a ton of coal, which was about twelve dollars a ton in those days. ... We had maybe three tons a winter. Then, of course, you had wood ... to start your fire. Although [some] coals were cheaper, you didn't want them, because they were dirtier and far less economical. [Elizabeth Wiest Farrow]

In those days people always had big pantries, and there wasn't one cupboard in the kitchen. All of our dishes and everything was in that pantry. We shut the door, wasn't anything in that kitchen. Everything was in the pantry. There was a big work table there and big bins that you'd pull out that was down below, you know. A great big one that would hold all of the flour. It must have held a fifty-pound sack. She kept flour in one and potatoes and onions or dried stuff in the other. There were drawers for silver and drawers that opened just like bins for your pots and pans ... all in that pantry. 'Course all up above that counter were just open shelves. [Ruby Jackson]

Food Storage

So our family was quite a rustling family to get food for the wintertime. Dad would take a load of wheat to town to get flour enough to bake for the winter's supply. Then he would take another load to the mill here in town to get money to buy sugar. It took about seven or eight hundred pounds of flour to last us through the winter. As long as it wasn't opened we had no trouble with weevils. [Irene Smith Lybarger]

My dad would just shoot the pig when we got ready to butcher a pig. We'd have a great big pole across two other great, big poles that we'd hoist the pig up on. ... We put it in a barrel of boiling water, and that was the way you could get the hair off the pig. You just scraped it. ... Then they would butcher the pig ... [The smoke house was used] only for the pigs to smoke the hams and bacon. ... They had to be put in brine in great big barrels, and they had to be in brine for so many days before they could be hung up in the smoke house. Then they would smoke them. ... I can remember them starting the fires in the smoke house, and it seemed to me weeks that they smoked. ... They would keep a fire going that would smoke. There would just be smoke in there. ... You'd have to bend to go in the smoke house. It would be maybe five foot ... off the ground. The top of it would have a pole across where they would tie the bacon and the hams up on these poles. ... It was a little stone building with a tin roof. [Ara Kossler Yager]

My mom with deer, I know she could make more dishes out of one deer than most people would even think of makin' out of beef. How they would make the sausage and fry it down. No refrigerators then 'cause no [electricity] and they would just fry the sausage down and pour the grease over the sausage, until they'd made layer by layer, and it was built up, and you'd put it back in what they called the cave. That's where you kept your winter supply like potatoes, and carrots and onions and stuff. It wouldn't freeze back in there. Wanted a sausage, you'd just go back in the grease and pull one out and refry it. [Delores S. "Dee" Bailey]

[The cellar] was back in the mountain. It had a dirt floor, and it had two doors going down into it so that it would keep the cold air or the hot air from going down into it. You'd go through one door, then you'd go down three or four steps, and then you'd go through another door that was really heavy. ... In the cellar when you came in there were big bins on both sides. ... There would be maybe two or three great big bins of potatoes, ... carrots, parsnips, beets, and onions. All the root vegetables would be in sand. ... In the back of the cellar as you were facing it there would be real deep shelves that would hold probably five rows of quart bottles, five rows deep. ... In the center of the cellar ... we had probably a fifty gallon barrel ... of sauerkraut. ... The cellar probably was ... ten by twelve, something like that. ... It had a tin roof on it ... It always had a vent. ...

My mother did can a lot of the meat. The meat in those days was just canned. You never thought about what kind of poisoning you were going to get. It wasn't even put in the pressure cooker. It was baked in the oven and then put in jars. They would be cold-packed. They'd be put in boiling water and boiled for a certain amount of time and then the lids would be tightened. [Ara Kossler Yager]

My mother did lots of canning. I'd venture that during the summer months we canned two to five hundred quarts of food. And we butchered our own beef and our own pork, which my father taught us to help with, and mother would can all this fruit so we always had good lunches. ...

Everybody canned because ... they didn't have any refrigeration for anything so we didn't have any oranges or bananas. We had peaches that were brought in from across the divide. They use cakes of ice to carry them so they wouldn't get mashed. And, of course, pears. They didn't have very many. We raised lots of apples and cherries and raspberries and mother had currants in the garden that she made jelly with. [Irene Smith Lybarger]

My mother would can probably six or seven bushels of peaches, four or five bushels of tomatoes, two or three bushels of pears, and maybe twenty bushels of pickles. [Ara Kossler Yager]

We had a couple of big apple trees, and we'd bury our apples out in the back yard for the winter. We'd dig a big trench and line it with straw and that's where the apples and celery was buried for the winter. ... The potatoes would go into the cellar. ... My mother would can two to three hundred quarts of tomatoes a year. It would be all gone by the summer. [Della Friedman]

The only approach to any kind of refrigeration was the cellar. ... Butter and milk, whatever, you climbed down into there. [Elizabeth Wiest Farrow]

Had a cellar was all you had, and usually you'd build a box in the window in the cellar, many times, with a screen on the back of it. In the winter time it got cold enough you didn't have to worry much about keeping food in this box. They would build them different sized, you know, to fit in the window, and that was in what they called a cellar. Usually something attached to the house or under the house. [Charles Snively]

Ice was something. We always had lots of ice and had ice houses. My father would get sawdust from the saw mills and they would put sawdust over the blocks of ice, and that's the way we kept our ice. [We cut it] from lakes. The ice would probably get as thick as eighteen inches deep, and they would go out and saw it. They would first bore a hole into it, and then they would saw it in blocks and take it off to the wagons and put it in the ice houses. And, of course, saw mills were all along the foothills and back into the mountains. They could get all the sawdust they wanted for ice. I think as I remember, my dad said [that they put] about two inches thick [of sawdust between blocks]. Then they would block one block on top of the other. That way it would keep all summer long. We didn't have trouble with it thawing. When my father delivered meat that he butchered, he used the ice blocks for that. [Irene Smith Lybarger]

There was a big ice house run by Mr. Peterson, Pete Peterson. ... The time to put up ice was on the coldest day that you could find for the reason that if you put it up on a warm day, you got wet. If you put it up on a cold day, why it froze solid and the ice wasn't slick. In order to put up ice ... we had a sled that was twenty-four inches wide, pulled by one horse. The ice was thick enough so that this horse could travel on the ice and we shod it ... [with] sharp prongs on 'em so that when the horse got on the ice he wouldn't slip. ... They pulled this sled down as straight as they could.

... Then they would score the ice. ... It was quite a job to get the ice all scored. Then they would score it crossways about two inches maybe three inches deep. Then they had big hand saws and the hand saws were probably eight feet long with long teeth on them and two or three men would stand there and saw ice. ... Then you had a pair of ice tongs and a shoot, and you would shoot it up into the wagon, and you'd haul it to the ice house shoot it in by shoot put in a layer of ice then a layer of sawdust then a layer of ice, a layer of sawdust. It took a long time. ... We could make maybe two trips a day. [Frank Miller]

A little ... girl came hunting her mother, and she was very excited. She said, "Mother, the iceman has just been to our house, and in unloading the cake of ice from his wagon he dropped ... [it] on his foot." The mother said, "Well, that is too bad. What did the man do?" And this child, who had been brought up in the faith said, "Well, he sat down on the grass and talked to God for half an hour!" [K.K. Parsons]

Johnnie, he ... used to cut ice up on the lake here. They drove a truck out on the ice, and they had big saws. ... They would start the hole a goin' and those big cakes of ice—well probably as big as that table, 'cause the ice would get real thick on that dam. Haul it down to Tungsten and put it up in Ted's Ice House there and cover it all over with sawdust. The ice would hold through the summer till they had to cut it again. Well, he sold it there, too, of course, and kept it in the meat counter where he kept all his meats. I can't remember having an ice box in the home until later on. [Ruby Jackson]

There was a big ice plant right there where the swimming pool is [today] called the Hygienic Ice Company. They made ice in big chunks, and then they sold them from these wagons that went around town. You had a sign that you'd put in your front window if you wanted ice, and [the iceman] would drive up and down the street. If you needed some ice, you would have a sign that said "ice," and you had a place where you put "25" or "50" pounds. They were in blocks and then he would stop on the street. ... I think a chunk of ice like that would last two or three days, maybe a week. I think it was ten cents for a big block of ice. [Pete Franklin]

Plain old icebox. In the winter time we had a cellar. It was just a little icebox that sat out on the back porch, and you'd put your sign out each morning, "Ice Wanted," and he'd come with his old horse and wagon, Hagman was his name. It was a pretty good-sized wagon, and the kids would all run to try to hook a ride on the wagon on the back with the shaved ice. [Della Friedman]

We would have ice delivered to the house, and George Peterson who later became chief of police, he was the ice man. We kids in the summer would follow that ice truck, and he would be very kind to us and give us chunks of ice so we could munch on it. [Dorothy Woodbury]

They delivered twenty-five, fifty and a hundred pounds of ice wherever it was needed, and you'd follow the ice wagon. If there were any little chips in there you could help yourself. It was a big deal. [Elizabeth Wiest Farrow]

That's the old ice card that you used to put in the window. ... Whatever number was up [25, 50, 75, 100] that's what they delivered to your house. You would put it in your window. ... It gives you the instruction here at the end, "An unnecessary delay at each place may make the driver very late at the end of his route." They wanted to make sure that you put the correct corner up so they could tell what you wanted. [Dorothy Woodbury]

Then the man came, and he was out in front in his horse-drawn wagon. He'd chip off the ice and bring it around to the back door and put it in your icebox. You had to have a little container underneath the icebox to catch the water and then usually, like Dad did, he bored a hole in the back porch floor so if the pan ran over [the water] went on outdoors; it didn't fill the back porch. [Elizabeth Graham Demmon]

Fashions

We had a good variety of food. We got a little low on clothes once in awhile, but we had plenty of food. I started sewing clothes when I was twelve years old. What I sold I would give the money to Mama for things like shoes that we needed. [Irene Smith Lybarger]

We shopped at White Davis. We didn't buy ready-made clothes much then. … We bought the material, and then there were seamstresses in town. … She would always be engaged a week ahead for fall and for spring, and she came and stayed about a week—coming and going—and would make up all the clothes for the next season. … You spent most of your time trying things on that week. …

That's one of the interesting changes in our life. You look about the same now whether it's morning, afternoon, or night. But then you didn't. If you went to church, you didn't look like you did Saturday at home. If you went to a party, you didn't look that way. You were dressed up. It was an entirely different affair. You had your party clothes, and you had your regular clothes. Now, you just have clothes! [Jessie Fitzpatrick]

Even if we didn't go to church, why we'd always on Sunday have to change to a different kind of clothes 'cause we'd always have company or go somewhere. [Nell N. Jones]

Men wore suits and ties more then. They were never as casual as they are now, never. [Lorena Ketterman]

I can remember how pretty she looked. She had a pretty black dress with the lace with a high collar with bones. … She made everything. … Long skirt, long lace sleeves and kind of a yoke … of lace. … Beautiful materials. [Alma Leatherman Husted]

You wouldn't think of going to town without a hat on and without gloves in those days. [Nell N. Jones]

All the hats were handmade hats. … Oh, I can remember how I enjoyed going into the shop and selecting a hat that I wanted. … They made them for—everyone was wearing their long hair, you know, and they made hats accordingly. It was after they began to back comb and all that sort of thing, people quit wearing [hats] 'cause they mussed their hair. But before it was plainer. They always had their knots and things, and then you have your hat pins and pinned your hats on. After short hair, there was nothing to pin your hats to. …

There was … somebody nearly always sewing or making something. We had to wear petticoats, too, and we always had to wear two or three of 'em. They would of thought it was a disgrace if you walked out, and they could of seen through your dress. You weren't supposed to, even when you got older, to even know that you had ankles. Dresses were full length. Wash and iron [the petticoats] and starch 'em to stiffen up so that they'd almost stand alone. ...

Full length stockings and nearly always black. I just can't remember when I first saw colored hose. They were thick, cotton hose. [Most of the clothing] was cotton and wool. ...

The way I can remember now, there wasn't colors like there were today. Red and blue was about the extent of the coloring. [Nell N. Jones]

I remember one I had. Mother had made this coat that year. The most beautiful shade of blue wool, and the collar was faced with kind of a rose-colored satin. Then she had made a hat for me, which was a large hat. It was blue, the same shade as my coat. ... It was faced with that coral, too. ... It was so pretty. They were all such pretty things that she did for me. [Alma Leatherman Husted]

The women wore very long skirts, very full and the separate blouses; we didn't have dresses. Everything was more or less separate blouses, and of course, they had high collars and long sleeves but they all had lace on them. ... My mother did sew. All my dresses were made out of the one material. It was a blue calico, and I remember all the same style. [Ruth Specht]

Most of our clothes were long skirts. We didn't dare to show our knees, high-top shoes, and mostly skirts and blouses. Otherwise when we were in grade school if we had three dresses we were lucky, and they were mostly pinafores, below the knee for sure. We wore long hair. My hair had quite a bit of natural curl, and my mother would put it up in rags. When I went to school it was quite curly. ...

That was about the time hobble skirts came in. They fit your hips all right, but they didn't do much for the bottom part because they were so tight. But you took small steps. You were quite a dignified lady with that, and gettin' into that buggy with those was somethin' else. Usually, I had to be helped to get in and get out. There was a little step on the buggy, but it was about eighteen inches high, and the skirt had to be down to the ankle. Imagine getting up there when ... probably the whole width of that skirt couldn't have been more than twenty-four to thirty inches wide. There was no split in the side of the skirt. My idea of wanting a hobble skirt was what my mother thought was awful. She said, "You can't do anything in that." I said, "All the other girls had one so why can't I?" And I had one; I made it myself. But I didn't like it so well after I got it made. I was used to having a fuller skirt. They only lasted about one year. It was a fad. ...

[With hobble skirts] we had to have a pretty white blouse, and most of our skirts were dark in those days. Most of them were made out of wool. Mother washed them. We used a lot of homemade soap, and I don't know why the lye in the soap didn't bleach them out. ...

HOUSE AND HOME

My grandmother knitted. Beautiful knitting. She knitted our mittens and by all means our hose, which I did not like. ... [It was] very scratchy. We wore long underwear, but when my sister and I got almost to school, we would roll our long underwear up above our knees and pull our stockings up, because we didn't want anybody to know we was wearing our long underwear. I often wonder what they thought of the roll that was above our knees. ... Children in town didn't wear the long underwear. ... Mother thought we should have long underwear as well as wool stockings. [Irene Smith Lybarger]

She had a flowing full black skirt with various blouses. She changed blouses but she would always have a floppy black hat. And this one time, I remember,— usually the wind catches you from one direction or the other on our front porch. I remember looking out, and here she was. One hand was on the floppy hat; one hand was trying to hold her skirt down. But the thing that impressed me was that she had the most beautiful green satin bloomers underneath that skirt. That was really wonderful, because I had never seen satin bloomers in any other color than black. Or bloomers made out of feed sacks—flour sacks. Sometimes the flour label was still there. I remember the first year in school that there was a little girl whose mother made her bloomers out of flour sacks, and some of the kids were pretty ornery. ... They used to ridicule her 'cause you could still read the flour sign on the pants. [Mary Hummel Wells]

My mother made all of the clothes, coats and pants too. ... It was all wool cloth. Everything was wool. There wasn't any cotton clothing in them days. She made the shirts, too. [Robert Jones]

Young woman. You didn't cross your legs and you dressed properly. You covered your kneecap and arms. You didn't dare wear short sleeves. You didn't drink or smoke unless you drank at home. Oh no, they didn't have slacks in those days. The only thing we wore next to slacks were bloomers, and that's when you'd take gym, physical ed. They were black satin bloomers and cotton stockings. We didn't swear. Well, I swore a little; you can't take everything away from me!! When we were in school we weren't allowed to wear make up. Of course, they were more strict in a Catholic school. [Della Friedman]

Two women riding side-saddle and a man on horseback, Jamestown, ca. 1905–1910.
Carnegie Branch Library for Local History, Boulder Historical Society Collection.

CHAPTER EIGHT

FILLING LEISURE HOURS

Fashions reflected the changing role of women, who began to enjoy leisure hours because of the availability of machines. This leisure time was easily filled with entertainment devices that were being developed at a fast rate. Thomas Edison, perhaps our greatest inventor, created the phonograph in 1877 and twelve years later the first motion picture. (It wasn't until 1927 that the first "talkie" film was produced.) In 1895 Guglielmo Marconi managed to send radio signals through the air, thus opening the door to the creation of a form of entertainment only surpassed by today's television. By 1915 a telephone service linked New York to San Francisco. People were finally able to communicate with each other faster than through telegrams. One can easily imagine the delight of a family in Colorado speaking with relatives in Kansas over the telephone for the first time.

These inventions were a long time in reaching all communities in the United States. Meanwhile, inhabitants of some areas were lucky enough to have a Chautauqua Park. These were summer schools and later traveling groups that performed at a particular hall and carried information from town to town. The Chautauqua in Boulder, founded in 1898, was one of the few to survive after the movement's almost total demise in 1929 because of competition from radios, motion pictures, and other forms of entertainment.

Probably the most popular form of entertainment were the dances. It seemed that everyone went to the dances whether they could dance or not. On almost every oral history tape when the question was asked, "What did you do for entertainment?" the first response was, "We danced." But like the Chautauqua Parks, even this activity could not compete with the spread of radio, television and motion pictures and eventually dancing became less popular.

Holidays were another excuse to socialize. Probably the most popular holiday was the Fourth of July, which was always celebrated with the much-loved picnic, and surprisingly, May Day was a special day, recognized with May Poles and flowers. Halloween, of course, was a delight for children, who had a chance to aggravate cranky neighbors. Thanksgiving was usually a family affair and Christmas was often celebrated with the neighbors at school programs and in church. The weekly reunions at church were, of course, one of the best ways to keep in touch with "close" neighbors who might live five miles away.

Socializing

In the summer time the children had chores around home. Most of 'em I guess had gardens and took care of the yards and that sort of thing. There was never any summer problem of entertainment with the children. They ran around and had fun without any organization coming in and helping 'em, and I don't think we had nearly the delinquency that we have now. ... Parental supervision, parental authority and pride. The children wouldn't do anything for fear that they would disgrace that home. ... And I think we had more religion among the children, too. Sunday school was an event and had an impression on the children. It was just a home influence and a human relationship. ... 'Course we had some bad children, had some problems then as well as we do now, but not nearly so fundamentally affecting the child. [Isabel Mayhoffer]

Everybody was out to help everybody else, and that was their recreation. That's what they did in them days. They didn't have no money to go anyplace else, to shows or stuff like that. And in them days, why people was more wanting to be with other people. They had time. Now they don't have time. [Elden Hodgson]

The neighbors would come to each others houses to brand [the cattle], dehorn them and things that had to be done. All the neighbors would come. The men would come and then the women would come, and we'd all gather. People done for one another. Everybody thought when somebody was in trouble it was their duty to look after them. My brother went and sit up all night with a little boy that had the flu, and the next day he got it. He was awful sick. You didn't stop to think about those things, you just did them. 'Course it wasn't very wise to do, but ... they always was good neighbors. [Sarah Brillhart]

People in those days were congenial, and they just got along good. We was just all one community, and everything was just all done together. They'd pitch in for somebody who was burnt out or something, why they'd get in and help build them up again. [Charles Perkins]

[My grandmother] also hated house guests, because, all her childhood she never knew when she went to bed where she'd wake up—in a bureau drawer or where —because some caravan would be coming through, and they'd put people up. [Charlotte Seymour]

We really enjoyed the grange. We used to have different get-togethers like picnics and things. And then whenever there's a death in the family we still do that, you know, serve a dinner to the family or whatever they want. [Bertha Hartenagle Schott]

It's patterned after the Masonic Lodge in a way. … [It is] a farm fraternity … patterning it a bit after the Masonic ritual. More or less as a community center [with] mainly an entertainment function back in those early days. Dances. They raised money by dances. O' 'course, later they had square dances, and the grange had a contest for the state. And they still have bowling contests. … But that's merely for social. But it's really a serious-minded community organization, which works for anything that's good for the community or the public. … The idea of Rural Free Delivery was started in the grange. [Andrew Steele]

What did we do for amusement? Well, we worked! You milked the cows, churned butter, washed the dishes. I never thought about [entertainment]. Oh, once in a while we'd go to the Elk's dance, but you didn't have time to get bored. I think we had more fun riding horseback and going on picnics. [Emma McCrone]

We'd go over there and then down to the creek on Grandma James' old place and have a picnic. There'd be probably seventy-five to a hundred people there. We would go early in the morning and freeze our own ice cream over there and have the whole day. Then, of course, we would have to go home and milk cows and do chores. That's the way we had our entertainment was all gettin' together and goin' on a picnic. [Irene Smith Lybarger]

Most everybody in the community [would come to a community picnic] … about a hundred or so. [Amy Sherman Cushman]

We would go to a picnic. Picnics were the big things in those days. All the farmers

And that way as far as the Negro was concerned was that you stay out of our way and we'll see that you don't have any contact with us. … There was no place we could go. … It came as a shock to us, and we had to do something—the young people did—so we formed ourselves in a little group, and we roamed the mountains. I know practically every canyon and every mountain in Boulder because for four years that's what we did. At nights we used to start out about eight o'clock and get to the top of the hill and have what was known as a beefsteak fry, where we fried some meat and put it between bread and had some coffee and [played] a guitar and a ukulele and had a good time. [We] got back home about two o'clock. Nobody bothered about us because, they knew we'd be home eventually. [Ruth Flowers]

and people in town would go up to a picnic, and we would have races by the women. Shoe races—see which woman could kick her shoes the furthest, which woman could drive a nail the fastest. Then these men would have these contests where they'd have an old man dressed (I wouldn't [have been] in it because people didn't live to be seventy, seventy-five years old when I was a kid), but they'd have old men's races. They'd have three-legged races ... and sack races for the kids. They'd always end up with this binding race. They'd bring the grain in in sheaths and they'd have ten to tie. The men who knew how to tie it would take off when the gun sounded, and, oh, they might get a dollar and a half or something for winning that race. [Frank Miller]

Then we'd spend all day up on the mountain dragging down wood for our bonfire at night. We'd build a big bonfire and have marshmallows that we roasted, and it was fun. We were like mountain goats, we'd never get lost or fall, you know. We'd climb anything. [Annie Bailey]

But we all did a great deal of hiking and steakfries up in the mountains where there were either shelters or there were fireplaces that had been put in by the forestry service or the parks department. ... The Royal Arch was one of the favorite places. That's up on Green Mountain. That's much beyond the third Flat-iron. Sit around the campfire after you'd eaten your fill and sing. Most of the boys played guitar, mandolin, banjo and all of us thought we could sing whether we could or couldn't. [Lois Huston Baum]

We did a good deal of hiking in the nearby foothills. No good foot wear then. No back packs. We would wrap our lunch in a pillow case and carry it in our hand or over the shoulder, which is a very inconvenient way to carry things. ...

I had, what I recall, was an absolute idyllic childhood ... My friends and I were free to roam over the area. We could walk up to Chautauqua which had nice playground equipment, more than it has now and without any danger. People were not worried all the time about crime. ... I could walk out my back door, cross some lots and pick up a friend and we could go up on the mesas by ourselves. Nobody was worried about it. So that was quite different. [Marian Cook March]

And in the summer there was always a mountain to climb. We'd just climb mountains, you know, and go on picnics, and we were never bored. I know my grandchildren ask me, "Well what in the world did you do, grandmother, you didn't have TV and you didn't have a radio." I says, "We had more fun than you do! We'd play cards in the evening, you know, and we had games we played. We weren't bored, we had a lot of fun." [Annie Bailey]

Then they'd have card parties. You would pay fifty cents or somethin', and then you could play cards all night. They'd bring refreshments. We really had a good time, I mean they had card tables set up all over ... the main hall [of the grange]. Oh they could play Seven Up or Bridge or ... whatever you wanted to play. [Rosalie Kelsey]

FILLING LEISURE HOURS

Saturday night was the night that everybody went downtown, and everybody else was there so it was quite a social gathering. You may not have gone down to buy anything. ... They stood about in groups at the old courthouse, sat on benches, and on Saturday night or Sunday ... they would have band concerts down there and that was a great event. ... So there it was downtown, of course it wasn't very far down, I promise you. ... All the stores were concentrated between Tenth Street and Eighteenth. Of course, there was no such thing as a shopping center then. There were a few little grocery stores around, but not even a great many of those. In those days you could order your groceries from the grocery store, and they'd be delivered. [Elizabeth Wiest Farrow]

Even [in] Boulder [it] was a big day on Saturday, because everybody stayed open until eight o'clock at night—eight or nine o'clock. ... Everything was open. ... We would walk to town. We were allowed to go to the movies on Saturday, it was a nickel, and we were given a nickel to buy a pop or ice cream cone. That was our allowance—ten cents a week—and we were thrilled to death. We weren't afraid at all. We had to be home at nine at night. [Della Friedman]

... cracker eating and whistling contests. You had to eat three crackers and the first one who could eat three crackers and whistle would win a ticket for next Saturday's [movie]. [Pete Franklin]

But those were the things that we had to do to entertain ourselves. We had no radios, no telephones, only just now and then a telephone. No TV. 'I'm ramblin' a little bit, but I don't know how else to do it.' Not even a picture show for a long time in Lafayette. The first picture show that I saw was in Superior. They had a machine, and they showed a bullfight. They charged us twenty cents a piece to get into this bullfight. They only had one reel. It was the most flickering thing you ever saw, but we saw a bullfight. It was so marvelous to us, you can't believe what we thought about it. They didn't have a second reel to pick it up on, so they run it into a clothes basket. Then they'd rewind it. I think they showed it to us three times, because we just sat there awestruck. If you can imagine, just to see the first moving picture that we ever saw. [Frank Miller]

I can remember the very first movie out. It was Douglas Fairbanks Senior in Sinbad the Sailor. ... I used to love the movies. [Robin Arnett]

The first movie I ever saw was. ... Mary Pickford in *Less than the Dust* ... Isn't it ridiculous the things you remember? [Elizabeth Wiest Farrow]

No, there wasn't any sound. There was the organist, and there was this piano. Oh, it was posh. With the red carpeting and red seats. Mary Pickford. [Della Friedman]

In 1912 I took a job at the old Curran Theatre. I took a job as the janitor, and I learned to run a projector. That's all I've done since then [until] I retired. I cranked the machine by hand; it was before we had a motor on them. The average was five thousand foot reels. They had different music. They had an orchestra part of the time, and then they put in an organ later on. The piano player [played] most of the time, though. We didn't have no matinees then and no Sunday show. We had matinees on Saturday. No Sunday shows so we just had two shows a night—seven and nine. That was a big change when sound pictures came in. Big head-ache, too. At first the sound was on big records [about two feet across] ... and they had a turn table connected with the projector. The problem was to keep them in synchronization. You'd leave 'em, and they'd jump the groove and keep repeatin', you know. It was impossible to get 'em back to be synchronized again. You had to change the record when you changed reels. The big change was when we got sound on film, you know. Then it was all synchronized together, you know. About 1925 I guess. [Crain Caywood]

[The projector] was too complicated for me. ... There was quite a lot of dan-ger connected with it then, because the film was so flammable. [Lois Caywood Graves]

I remember one time they had a fellow come up to show motion pictures. I remember I got in to watch the picture by cranking the thing, you had to crank it at a certain speed, and it had [an] acetylene light, as I remember, inside to project the picture, and it was flashing and all. It was quite interesting. I'll never forget that either, because when you're younger there are some things that stick in your mind more than others [Charles Snively]

Every Saturday there was the ten cent movie. ... I remember if you wanted to see the shoot-'em-ups you had to go to the Isis. ... The Curran Theatre would have a higher class of movie. [Dorothy Woodbury]

'Course in the early days the Curran Theatre had a stage, you know. ... We had mostly vaudeville and traveling stage shows. They filled in with pictures. As I say we didn't have any Sunday shows then. ... The only things we would have on Sundays was Christian Scientist lectures and things like that. Weren't allowed to have pictures. Had to be voted in by the people before they could run on Sunday. ... I think the third time they had an election they got to show pictures Sunday. [Crain Caywood]

I still remember the excitement of having talkies for the first time. The theatres were never open on Sundays in the beginning and when they were open, the ministers in town weren't sure this was quite proper. Some of them would go out and watch to see how many of their parishioners would go to a Sunday movie. [Louise McAllister]

The Curran was originally built as an opera house, it was called the Curran Opera House. We generally showed a movie along with the vaudeville. Not a feature, but we'd generally show the news and a cartoon or comedy. Things like that. 'Course with the travelin' road shows we didn't have that. The vaudeville I think was fifty cents. [I made] five dollars a week at first. It gradually went up a little bit at a time. ...

Glenn Miller played on the stage [at the Curran], you know, at the concerts before he became famous—when he was in school here. Two of my friends were with him and his band. They even went with him when they toured foreign countries and all. [Crain Caywood]

If I remember right, didn't they have a graphaphone? With the cylinders? I think they did ... and instead of being records like we got now, it was a cylinder. I remember the old graphaphone they used to have, we call them phonographs, but they called them graphaphones. It had the cylinder on it all the time, slip right over the shaft. ... A little square box ... with a big horn coming out of the top of it. Yeah, I remember that. [Louis Varra]

We listened to the phonograph. We had a great big Edison phonograph with lots of records, and that's what we listened to ... mostly. Then ... the radio came in. [Ruth Dodd McDonald]

I remember having had a crystal set, and we'd all hang around waiting for the earphones. We'd pass them around. [Hazel Hall]

On the homestead we had a little radio run with a batt'ry, and we had to take the batt'ry to town every week to get it charged. So we had to be very careful with it. My husband used to like to listen to the ball games and fights; I had to be careful when I used it in the daytime so I wouldn't run the batt'ry down. I remember the radio was just comin' in when my mother died in 1925. My favorite program was a family affair, I don't remember the name of it now. It was so good. They had a lot of music. [Sarah Brillhart]

I can remember the first radio I heard. You heard it with earphones, and you were real thrilled. You could get a lot of stations. [Elizabeth Graham Demmon]

When radios first came out why dad had to have a radio, and boy, it was a good one, too. He was afraid all the sounds weren't going to get across red mountain out there, so he had the men get two of the biggest, tallest poles— trees they could find, and he set them in. They must have been forty or fifty feet tall, and [they] put a wire across each of them for antennae. Ruth Dunn and Dick Yates and all of them would sit in the living room where the fireplace was over there in the corner and listen to the radio—*Amos and Andy* and all the rest of those. When Dick was over there ... whenever there was a news report on, he'd go in and turn the radio on. He'd come back out into the kitchen. Mom would say, "Well, Dick what was the news today?" "Oh," he says, "usual thing: murder, fire, robbery!" [Delia Peterson]

I remember standing around the organ, and we'd sing and sing. I can remember singing a lot. We always sang as a family. We had one of those old, old fashioned phonographs, you know, that had a horn through it, and they had little long disc records. We used to record songs, I remember we used to record other hymns that we used to sing all the time. I've often wondered what become of all those old things. [Ina Gerry Wild]

Used for ... one family to another, somethin' like that. If you wanted to talk over the telephone you had to go into town and talk from there to another town. ... We never telephoned in the first ten years it was in the country. I don't think we ever talked on it 'cause we wouldn't go into town just to talk on the telephone. We didn't know anybody at the other end of the line anyway. [Robert Jones]

We used to have a phone, and we could call any of those places [Longmont]. Our first phone. We had that privilege for a long time. We paid, I think we paid a dollar and a half a month for years and years and years. You could call Boulder and these places around. ... [Our neighbors] on the other side of us [were] on our line, but we weren't bothered by them at all. ... Our numbers were purple and green. I think we were purple and theirs was green. ... Then we changed to somethin' else. ... I know we were purple six two for a long time. ... [You'd tell the operator] It was nice to have an operator. ... They were so accommodating and nice. [Stella Lee]

Many evenings during the summer months, most of the women of the neighborhood would be up here playing croquet. Across the street was a vacant lot, the men would be playing horseshoes and up the street across from the school where the light is, we children would be out playing under the light that made circles, if you remember those old-fashioned lights. When we lived here it was called Hill Street. In a year or two they changed the name to Mapleton. Why they ever did a thing like that, nobody knows. [Jessie Fitzpatrick]

I remember when we came down for the Chautauqua on [the Switzerland Trail Railroad from Ward]. I was about four [July 4th, 1898]. I remember we looked forward to that. Mother had us all rest up, you know, and she had her little brocade basque and a little black parasole. We came down to Boulder for the opening of Chautauqua. That was really something. ... The streetcar wasn't running yet. We came up in what they called a livery. ... There were places all along Pearl where you could hire a livery. ... When we wanted to do something a little more grandly, we'd hire—what did they call them—two people this way and two people this way. They were real grand. When we had somethin' special we'd hire one of those and go up the canyon. They were stately. They were beautiful. They were leatherlined; they were lovely. [Hester Phillips]

I remember [Chautauqua] had a lovely playground for children. We used to go up and have picnics and play on the grounds there. Then at night we would go to the lectures. It was an adult education institution, one of many that existed around the country, all of them called Chautauqua after the town of Chautauqua in New York where the movement started. Lecturers would come and talk about all kinds of things. I remember particularly the travelogue lectures. ... There were evangelists who came there. I remember going to hear Billy Sunday, who was the equivalent of our television evangelists of today. [Franklin Folsom]

Dances

Oh it was quite a country, you know, when you grew up with it. We had hardships and everything, but we enjoyed our life more than we do today. We didn't have all the conveniences as we do today, you know. Then we enjoyed everything. We had time to do it. Now we don't have time. The trouble today is people don't know how to have fun anymore. We used to go to dances, you know, every week. We'd have dances four, six, seven miles away, you know. Maybe we'd walk over there, you know. Dance all night. Oh, we used to have lots of fun in that respect, you know. [Charles Perkins]

They built this beautiful big building here in Boulder and for many years they had conventions and a lot of the things in the Chautauqua program. Entertainment and a lot of things. Several of us were chased out of the rafters by the guard up there, because it was a climbable place, and we used to go up in the roof of that building and shoot pigeons with our BB guns. [Pete Franklin]

It was [enjoyable to go to a meeting in the evening]. Heck, you'd live for it from one week to another. I know us kids would; I know Dad and Mom would talk about it. Dances, they'd have their dances down here. They made quite a bit of money off of that, too. [Elden Hodgson]

We used to have kids dances there in the hotel, in Lyons, and I can remember the men would play the fiddle, and we'd dance; we'd have a ball with dancing. That's what we used to do. They'd let us kids have a dance every so often. [Ina Gerry Wild]

It wasn't very far from our cabin where they built the dance hall. They took lumber and took the two-by-fours down and put the lumber on it, and they'd dance on there. There was generally somebody who played the fiddle. That's all the music they had. [Maude Moomaw Beasley]

Whenever anybody gave a party, why everybody was invited. Everybody went. They put up little signs and everybody went. They had an old schoolhouse that my dad had attended years and years ago, and they kept that for a dance hall. I played for several of the dances up there myself—a mandolin and a banjo. [Charles Snively]

IN OTHER WORDS

We danced one Saturday night here, and the next Saturday night was either Wallstreet or Salina in the school houses. And then Friday nights we usually had the dance in Magnolia. Thursday nights there was a dance at the Templeton Dance Hall in Boulder. [Maude Washburn Wagner]

Oh yeah, we had a dance hall down here [in Sugarloaf]. That's all it was for, just a dance hall. Every two weeks—and they'd have them all around all these mining camps—they'd have dances. Well, square dancing and round dancing. Oh, once in a while they'd get a Schottish in there and a few polkas, but most generally it was just fox trot, two step, and waltzes, and whenever we'd get Dick Betasso kind of wound up just right, he'd call a few squares. He was another old miner down there and rancher. ... I can live on a dance floor, seems like. [Ralph Yates]

Esther Yates would play the piano, and at midnight they'd always have supper, and then those that cared to stay would keep on dancing. For refreshments, ... if you baked bread that day, well you brought sandwiches. If you didn't, you baked a cake. [Maude Washburn Wagner]

Then one time we got to the dance and this old building was old, and they had this Mr. Craig. He was a real fiddler, you know, playin' the violin. And the wind was so hard that night they had gasoline lanterns for light. They were swingin'. [Hugh Smith]

The children were just in this one room. We just played. There was no such thing as a baby sitter in those days. They took their children with them. I suppose there was somebody out there watching us, or I suppose we would have gotten into mischief! [Bertha Hartenagle Schott]

We put the kids to sleep all around on tables and things. [Hugh Smith]

There was a bench 'long by the piano, and there would be one, two three, there'd be a dozen little kids sound asleep there, you know, layin' out in the blanket or basket or crib or somethin' else. Yeah, you never picked your coat up without tryin' to shake it a little first to see if there was somethin' in it. [Sanford Wagner]

When I was really small I can remember going down there to dances with my folks, and they would bed all the kids down on the benches around, you know, and I can remember all the ladies would take sandwiches and pie and cake and around midnight they would stop the dancin'. Everybody would fill their plate and sit down and eat. Then the music would start again, and they'd be up dancin' again. ... When the school house was still there they had dances in it almost every weekend. My dad would call the square dances, and he played the piano. There was an old gentleman who lived up the other end of town; his name was Mr. Carter. He was the barber, and he could really play that fiddle. People from all around would come there for dances. [Ruby Jackson]

FILLING LEISURE HOURS

They had dances in the schoolhouse on weekends. I was workin' in Boulder, and my mom said, "Well, we'll have to come down and getch' ya and bring you up to the dance. There's some pretty good lookin' young men comin' to those dances." So I did, and that's where I met [my husband]. He was leasin' [a mine] with his dad … there in Wallstreet.

The dances and all quit about, I suppose, in about 1920-21. Not too long after automobiles. Whenever cars got prevalent, why the community broke apart, after cars got too plentiful. [People] could go other places and do other things. …

The people would bring seats out of their car and make beds back in the corner for the kids to sleep on, and the kids went to sleep. When they got ready to go home they'd gather [the children] up and go home. You didn't have baby sitters then, you sat your own kids. [Gertrude Tower]

[Dancing] was the thing then. … Every weekend. Every Saturday. And then the barn dances. The old Smith barn. And you know, you get started in that darn square dancin', and they keep bringin' in new calls. Every week you gotta learn a new dance. We never did get into the round dancing. I wish we had a picture of when we dressed up that time. We were dressed like eggs or potatoes. And all you could see was our feet, and the body would be the whole tater, and we just had eyes. I wish we had some picture of that. We really had a ball. [Harold Eddy]

Well, I come up for one of their dances, and I couldn't dance, but I could drink, and I got grand and gloriously drunk. … If I wanted a horse (Art had the pasture that joined mine where he wintered his horses) I'd go get one. I wouldn't ask him for one; I'd go get it. He didn't care. He knew the horse would be taken care of, the same way if I had something Art wanted. He'd come and get it. … But that's the way we went. … This time I needed a horse, so I went down to this pasture of his and borrowed a horse (a lot of them were easy to catch, you know, take a little grain, and you can catch them), and I went to the dance. Well, I couldn't dance, but I could drink a little whiskey and bootleg in them days, and I guess I over drank a little. So I started for home, and just had the horse tied out there in the timber, and I don't know where I did pass out. But when I woke up the next morning the gate was open, and the horse was in the pasture, and I was on him, and a little bit cold; it was in the winter. I never fell off that horse, but I sure slept on him the rest of that night. [Ernie Ross]

Hey, do you remember so and so. … Group of guys would sit in here, and they'd say, "Do you remember so and so?" No, they couldn't remember that guy, and they'd say, "Well, do you remember this guy?" No. They'd bring up this woman, Margaret something or other, whatever her name was. You'd bring that name up, and every one of those guys would remember her just down to a tee. I don't know what went on, but the guys all remembered her. [Delores S. "Dee" Bailey]

We walked from that ranch clear over to Rowena, danced all night. I had on a new pair of shoes and they rubbed my heel and I could hardly walk. We walked over there and that was a long way. It was in the little old schoolhouse. [Dorothy Burch Walker]

One time there was a bunch of us up here, and they had talked about—that is my Dad and Mom, Aunt Jenny and Uncle Mick talked about walking to Wallstreet to go dancin'. So us kids thought it would be a lot of fun. 'Course you didn't go on somethin' like that without a chaperon. You had to have a chaperon. There were twenty-six of us but that was all right, you had to have a chaperon. So Grandma was our chaperon; she walked to Wallstreet with us. There's an old trail that goes ... you go over the hill into Wallstreet. ...

You had to do your chores. You didn't go anywhere until your chores were done. That would depend on when you found the cows. Sometimes you'd get them in fairly early, and other times you would have an awful time findin' them. 'Course they'd have bells, and us kids could always tell whether it was Sam Craig's cows or Toots's cows or whether it was our cows or Aunt Jenny's or whose, and 'course they all ran out on the range here. Usually we milked about five o'clock. And we left, I don't know, around seven o'clock, danced till about three and come home. Sun was up. Grandma was the only one who'd stay up till about ten o'clock 'fore she went to bed. The rest of us got the cows in, milked them and went to bed. We couldn't stay up any longer. [Maude Washburn Wagner]

Oh yeah, that's where I learned to dance [at the grange] what little I learned about it. [Evan Gould]

Well, I always thought you was a crackerjack dancer. I always liked to dance with you. [Beth Dodd]

They used to have dances at Hygiene. We were married twenty years before I knew he could dance! His mother didn't believe in it. [Beth Dodd]

We went to Canyon Park. That was right up where Pearl and Arapahoe meet. It was a beautiful building. All open air and it was a *jitney* dance They had this big railing all around the floor—this big floor with a railing all around, and there was ticket takers there. You'd buy so many tickets at a nickel apiece, maybe a dollar's worth. Then you'd go ask somebody to dance, and as you went through the gate with her, they'd take your ticket. [Hugh Smith]

Chivaree

[A chivaree is] something that after a couple are married, then the friends, and neighbors find it out. They all congregate kind a just all with a lot of pans and horns and make all the noise they can. The couple are supposed to have some candy and stuff in the house. They finally let you in, and you get treated to candy. ... So that used to be the main thing, when anybody was married ... you knew you was goin' to a chivaree. ... It was lots of fun. We always enjoyed going. [Ruth Dodd McDonald]

Another habit we had, when a couple got married, we chivareed them. The fella had to push the girl over the beet dump in a wheelbarrow That would not be too easy to do. ... Yeah, I was one of the last ones that rode over the beet dump. Poor Alva would huff and puff like some of them. Funny part of it was, we'd run to try and get away, and we was out of breath when we got there. [Beth Dodd]

That beet dump had another purpose, too. After they got married they had to push the bride in the wheel barrow. That was an established part of the chivaree. [Isabel Knaus]

Russ and Helen got away when they got married. Oh, they was down there in that dang pasture. I went a wanderin' off down there by myself, and I came to kind of a little wash. Boy, I tell you, they reached up and grabbed me and pulled me down in that hole, and then they sat on me. They kept me there for quite a long time and finally Russ said, "Well, it's gettin' cold down here; let's go to the house." So when we got back up there a lot of people had went home, but his brothers—and there was quite a few of them around there—... got a wheelbarrow and pushed them from the railroad tracks clear up to about Sixth Avenue. Up that hill, it was late at night , not many cars on the street, but he had to push her up that hill. [Evan Gould]

Everybody chivareed. When you got married you better figure on cigarettes and candy for the whole neighborhood, because that was one of the social events. [Rosalie Kelsey]

We were married ... during the beginning of World War II ... so they had a chivaree. I don't know where they got the wheel barrow, but I threw Margaret clear up over that wheel barrow. I don't think I could do it today. I'm weaker and she's bigger. [John Dodd]

[A chivaree was held] after they was married. If they went on a honeymoon, after they got home and kind of got settled, why then—when you least expected it. It might be in the middle of the night or towards morning or any time. ... And you'd better have a lot of treats and cigars. There were very few big weddings. Maybe a couple would get married, they'd take their best friends with them, and they'd go and get married and that was it. We couldn't afford big weddings. [Evan Gould]

Nearly every Saturday down the main street, they'd go down the street honking horns, you know and ribbons and old shoes a flyin' I guess that's a chivaree. ... That's today's chivaree. [John Dodd]

Recreation

We had wonderful times in the summer and winter. We had a bobsled. … Streets were cordoned off [for coasting]. It did become dangerous. … At home, tidily winks and card games and we girls played with paper dolls. … We'd get fashion plates down at the dry goods store. [Elizabeth Wiest Farrow]

We used to sleigh ride down Fourteenth Street. That was the favorite place to sleigh ride. It just had the right kind of slope, and you could go all the way down to the courthouse. They'd close off that street so you could sleigh ride. Just on a sled. … The city would pay for crossing guards so there was a guard at each street so that … a car didn't come through. And they would build a fire, so you know, if you got chilled from the sleigh ride you could warm your hands. … Then over on Eighth Street from about Highland down, they used to close that off, too. [Cecilia "Sallee" Gorce]

Well in the winter, the colder the weather the better it was. The better the skating and the skiing—the sled riding. We didn't have skis. It seems we just lived outdoor all winter. We just loved it. [Irvin Demmon]

The time I was growin' up, where the Community Hospital is now, … was a swamp, a great huge swamp. One of our activities was to go down there and find cattails. Cut cattails, bring 'em home and let 'em dry out. Then we'd soak 'em in gas and make big torches out of the cattails and wander around. [George Smith]

There was an old pond about a half a mile from the school, and when we were let out at noon, everybody hurried to eat their lunch and rush down to the pond. It was froze over. Well, it wasn't deep, not more than a foot deep at the most. It was just a water hole where the cattle drank from. … We would go down there and skate. You were not supposed to go, because you wore out the soles of your shoes, and shoes cost money. You were not supposed to wear [them] out skating on ice. But we did. [Cecilia (Sallee) Gorce]

He kept the old mill pond flooded for all of us in the winter time so we'd have a place to skate. … First we [had the kind of skates that you clamped on to your shoe], you know, with a key and then, oh boy, finally got a pair of shoe skates for Christmas, and things were lookin' up. [Ruby Jackson]

They used to put me on the [ore] cart and they used to push me up the … high hill at the Blue Ribbon Mine. … Then they'd all jump on the cart, and we used to go almost halfway to Erie. … Pretty fast going down that hill. [Elmo Lewis]

No skiing. We did go skating. We had these poor old skates that clamped on to the soles of your shoes, and they weren't very good. [Irvin Demmon]

The University used to flood the tennis courts that were located just beneath the women's gym. … It was pretty well sheltered from the sun … so the ice was pretty good down there. That was a wonderful place to go ice skating. [Jane Valentine Barker]

We used to ski down the little valley there where the stadium is. ... We skated on the little pond at the university. ... The wildest ride we ever took was on a set of buggy wheels, buggy chassis. [Samuel Altman]

We could go down Nineteenth Street on our sleds, and we lived at the base of what we called Lover's Hill at that time. My grandfather always took a piece of the fence down, put straw in his back yard so that we would come down the hill and land in the straw. It was a steep hill. [Ruby Roney]

There was a Lover's hill up three or four blocks up north of Pine Street. ... We would go to the top of Lover's Hill and slide down [on sleds] clear to Pine Street. Once in awhile we'd get real brave and go up to Ninth and Mapleton and slide down Ninth Street. But that was a little far away so we usually stayed at Twenty-second Street. Traffic? Well, there just wasn't much traffic. [Irvin Demmon]

Lover's Hill, now Sunset Hill ... and that's where the circuses set up when they came to town. ... We had Barnum and Bailey and Ringling Brothers with Buffalo Bill. I don't know which one Buffalo Bill was connected with, but he came. I remember him with his long white beard and his beautiful white horse going around the ring. 'Course it cost extra to stay for the Buffalo Bill Show. [Frances Waldrop]

Circuses ... put up on Lover's Hill. [They] were real exciting to us. Like when Dee said that Buffalo Bill came, he was such a hero of hers. But I remember I always had to work my way into the circus, and I actually had to water the elephants. I remember that very well. But one time I worked so hard and long, I worked through the noon hour, and when I got home—I had my tickets—but when I got home I was sick. I had worked too hard. Didn't get to go to the circus. I was younger than a teenager. The circuses were fun, but the side shows were more interesting. Of course, we didn't get to go to the side shows. Our folks didn't think we ought to see the fat lady or the rubber man—tattooed man—but circuses were a real thrill to us. [Irvin Demmon]

I can remember the circus being unloaded east of town, and they always paraded through town. 'Course they always had the parade early in the morning. ... The clowns were always so entertaining. ... It was a very interesting time, very pleasant. [Elizabeth Wiest Farrow]

They were Ringling Brothers, Barnum 'n Bailey circuses. ... They always had a parade from where they took the animals off of a train ... right down Pearl Street going to Lover's Hill. The clowns were out and the big wagons that carried the tigers. It was a pretty thing to see. ... They were getting to the circus grounds, but the parade kind of advertised the circus. [Elizabeth Graham Demmon]

Ivy Baldwin was his name. And they had a big cable stretched clear across the canyon way up from peak to peak you know. And he used to walk that every Sunday. One day I was up there when he came off, and he just set down there right on the cable. I asked him what was wrong, and he said the sun got in his eyes and he had to sit down. He carried a pole about twelve or fifteen feet long. He had a hundred dollars every time he walked that [every Sunday]. 'Course a hundred dollars was a lot of money in those days. [Crain Caywood]

Then they'd have card parties and you would pay fifty cents or somethin' and then you could play cards all night. Then they'd bring refreshments and we really had a good time, I mean they had card tables set up all over that dining room, I mean the main hall. Oh they could play seven up or bridge or whoever, whatever you wanted to play. [Rosalie Kelsey]

I'd come over to his place and we had cards; we'd play poker. Not for anything [did we bet]. Didn't even use matches. But we'd play poker for a couple of hours. [Irvin Demmon]

You know they had sewing contests for the grange members and you would make some garment and then you had to model it. …

Oh yes, they had the horseshoe team. … Yes, the men, they had horseshoes. … They used to go to the … Longmont Fair, and they may have competed with different teams over there. [Rosalie Kelsey]

I used to throw quite a few myself. … We'd have a couple of pegs right across the road here, and we'd set out there and throw horseshoes until way after dark at night. See how many ringers we could make at night. [Clarence Conilogue]

They had a regular team down there. Boy, they really had some good pitchers. George Baessler was really a top-notch pitcher. I would imagine he was probably hittin' eighty percent, ninety percent, nothin' less than seventy percent. … They really had a team. They'd meet down there on Sunday afternoon and really go at it. Heaven sakes, I could never hit the peg, could hardly ever see it besides hit it. [Elden Hodgson]

[The swimming pool] had a lot of business because that was one thing that could be open on Sunday. [Mother's] bathing suit was funny looking and Dad's was awful. It was one that I thought Dad would drown if he got it wet. It was so bulky and Mother's was also, but Dad didn't like water much. [Elizabeth Graham Demmon]

Many years I worked at the Hygienic Swimming Pool. … It was built in 1922. … Well, I worked there as key boy and office boy, cashier and sort of the manager for about the next twenty years. I could write a book about the experiences at the swimming pool. It cost twenty-five cents to go there. I remember when I became cashier, people were not using paper dollars, they'd use silver dollars.

... We would have seven to eight hundred dollars in the evening to bank. In silver dollars. [Irvin Demmon]

We had a boat on the creek. ... We'd go down and get in the boat. ... I don't know why the folks let us do it, but they did, cause there wasn't a one of us that could swim. We always went and played in that boat, and they never said anything about it. I never did learn to swim, and I know none of my sisters ever did. ... The boys always swam ... but I never heard of the girls doing it. [We would wear] just our regular dresses [when we'd go boating]. [Nell N. Jones]

One of those things that demonstrates to me the advantage of a friendly, small town. Everybody was in on the festivities. The Pow Wow started in 1934, I believe, as a paydirt pow wow, which was a successful effort to get the mountain people—the miners—and the flatland people—the ranchers and farmers—together in that Depression period where there was little enough to do, and no one had money to do it if there had been. It was a low cost celebration on Pearl Street in front of the courthouse on the courthouse lawn. As I recall that first one was just like a big picnic. Tug of wars between the hill and flat people, and there were produce stands up and down the street. Later on, not much later, the miners had their part of it with rock drilling, which became world-class rock drilling. ... Jimtown, Ward, Nederland, Eldora were all represented. ... They would haul great chunks of Eldora granite, considered by most to be the hardest available, put it on the courthouse lawn—and I mean they were big, automobile size. The single and double jack competition really drew a crowd. ... Later on the valley people had their say when they started the ... rodeo, ... which attracted world-class riders. [D. M. "Dock" Teegarden]

It was in 1936 ... someone suggested, "How about a pow wow between them?" And that is how the name started. ... We started with the parade with the hunter and trapper back in the early days, then the Indians, covered wagon, and the farmers and whatnot. ... After the parade and celebration we had the rock drilling, ... and before we got through we had world champion rock drillers from all over. ... That was quite an attraction for a number of years. Then a horse show started, and that really was when the pow wow went from the rock drilling to the horse show. To begin with we had calf roping. ... The rodeo started and ... increased each year. ... 1940, I believe, was the first good rodeo we had. [Lyndon Switzer]

They'd have a drilling contest where, I think, they'd drill fourteen inches in ten minutes by hand. Then the double jack. ... That's one man turnin' the drill, and the other swingin' that drill. He never missed, if he missed he'd smash the other fella's hands. They'd just whirl this big double jack, that's like a big special built sledge, and this fella was down turnin' the drill. He'd have to keep turnin' and the other was hammerin' ... Yeah, minin' and cowboy. [Hugh Smith]

You didn't have athletic clubs around the mining camps. Those fellas had plenty of exercise! [Joseph Malcolm]

Holidays

May Day was quite a thing when I was a child. All the kids in the neighborhood made little May baskets. We either had little cottage cheese cartons, that sort of thing, that you covered with—you'd crinkle the edges of crepe paper, pasted that on and put a little handle. … We used to go up [to Lovers' Hill] and pick Johnny-jump-ups and sand lilies and whatever little flowers there were. … [Or] we would take some construction paper and weave a little basket, you know. Then you'd put flowers in it. You would go to your neighbor's; you'd ring the bell, and you'd leave the little basket and run away. You didn't expect anything. … And you did it mostly with the elderly or shut-ins or something like that. [Cecilia "Sallee" Gorce]

I remember May Days. There were always children celebrating around the May Pole with dances and with May baskets. I remember with horror one May Day. I must have been either six or seven. What you did on May Day according to my mother was pick flowers and take them to young ladies. Well, at the age of six or seven I wasn't quite up to that, but she insisted that I go out and pick Johnny-jump-ups, put them in a little basket and take them … where a new family had moved in with a nice young girl. … I got out there and dropped this scrunched up little bunch of flowers on the front porch and fled. I cordially hated that young girl—a totally irrational emotion—for years! [Franklin Folsom]

May Pole dances. It was about planting time for the farmers. … At school we did a May Pole every year … with crepe paper. We'd wind the [flag] pole and have a big time with it. [Irene Smith Lybarger]

We had it in the evening, I know. They had a May Pole. Girls had their long streamers from it, you know, and they'd go around, weave in and out … and that was real pretty. … They put up a pole. … All of them came. … There weren't so many people then, and everyone came. [Cleo Turner Tallman]

The Fourth of July we would go to Lyons, because there would be ball teams up there, and we'd have to go and root for our team. So we'd go up there and have a picnic all day. [Irene Smith Lybarger]

Well, I can remember only one [Fourth of July] celebration Niwot ever had. … It was so muddy that day you couldn't hardly walk across the diamond; it was so muddy … I remember Loel Young was pitchin' and I don't know who else was playin'. I didn't play that day, but they had a little celebration here in Niwot. I don't know what they done, it didn't amount to very much I can tell you that, it didn't amount to very much. [Clarence Conilogue]

FILLING LEISURE HOURS

I can remember one [Fourth of July] celebration. They had a parade and in the afternoon they had a terrible hail storm. [Amy Sherman Cushman]

With the horse and buggy it took quite a while, so we didn't have much time to picnic. I remember one Fourth of July we went with my sister and her husband. The wagon, they called it the *Bird's Eye*. It was yellow, and they put flags on the horses ears. We went up Left Hand Canyon about five miles and had a picnic. That was the way people did that in those days. That was their entertainment. [Ruth Dodd McDonald]

We had a Fourth of July celebration on Mapleton. The children in the neighborhood would go around and collect money and bring it to Father, and Father would buy the fireworks. I remember one evening we sat over in front of that house—well, I had Mother's fur coat on it was so cold. Some Fourth of Julys were pretty cold. But everybody collected, and people from all over town came, because this was the only celebration that there was. Father would set off those fireworks, and he generally would have to have a new coat afterwards, because you know how those sparks come down afterwards ... and that went on for years, and years, and years. ... Father had the best time of all. [Jessie Fitzpatrick]

They were all volunteer [fire fighters], and they were kind of like private clubs, too. The outstanding men of the town belonged to the Hose Company. ... It was volunteer first before it became a city organization. ... It involved a lot of prestige to get into the Hose Company, and there was great rivalry. They would have races on the Fourth of July, the Hose Company. These men would pull their wagons and have races up and down Pearl Street. [M. Helen Carpenter]

We had this on Pearl Street; we run the hose races. We connected on the plug of the courthouse. There was four of us [who] ... had a harness on and was pullin' this cart We had a man in front that was called the *spike;* we had a man in the back that was a hose puller; we had a guy up in front that had the nozzle. They'd break that coupling and put that nozzle on and give water. That's when you were timed when that water come out of the hose. It was a great sport. [Peter F. Zarina]

Every Halloween, Mrs. Wickstrom had me get every kid ... in the immediate neighborhood [together], and we had a Halloween party. ... Everybody had to entertain, do something. We played *wink 'em*. ... There were boys and girls. The boys would stand behind the chair, and the girls would sit in the chair. There would be one empty chair. That fellow would try to lure one of the girls, and he would wink. [Dorothy Woodbury]

At Halloween, of course, we all had our pumpkins and went around scaring people. They used to take [an empty] spool for thread and cut little zigzags on it and put a rubber band through the middle with a toothpick and, I think, a piece of soap on the other end to hold that rubber band through the hole. Then you would let that thing crawl up the window. It would make this racket and the house-holder was supposed to be frightened, see, and come running out and give you a piece of candy or something like that. [Cecilia "Sallee" Gorce]

I remember in the fall the community had a big dance, Halloween, I guess. And they took everything out of the school so they could dance ... The next morning ... the kids were helping me put the [furniture back], and that was the day Mrs. Mayhoffer [the new county superintendent] came to visit. So she pitched in and helped us put the stuff back in. [Irvin Demmon]

They took Dave Johnson's cow [up to the second floor of the schoolhouse], and then they took your granddad's, Sam Harvey's, wagon that they hauled sand with. Took it down there and took it apart. Took it clear upstairs (in the school-house) and put it back together. I tell you, kids was just ornery then, they wasn't mean. [Evan Gould]

Dumped toilets. They were houses. See everybody they didn't have no inside toilets at that time. They were all outside. [Albert Chaussart]

You'd wait till somebody went in 'um then run like heck and dump them over. [Louis Varra]

For some reason, on Halloween little kids weren't involved at all. No, the people who were involved with Halloween were ten and over, ... and you were on your own. You went out, went all over the town on Halloween and the next day ... everybody groaned 'cause they had to go outdoors, and all they found were garbage pails turned upside down, refuse scattered all over the yard, hoses cut with knives. Usually some of the worst things would be a wagon that somehow appeared on the top of a roof of one of the churches. All the windows of all the stores were written all over with soap. ... It was legitimate, and it was fair to get even with Mr. Lamps, whom you waited for Halloween to get even with ... because he kept chasing you out of his apple trees and being mean to you all year long ... Parents were lucky, who came out and found their house in tact. [Howard Higman]

We used to have Thanksgiving dinner. The Grange would buy the turkeys, and the ladies would cook 'em. ... The grange paid for the turkeys. Then some dear soul would cook them, and then somebody would furnish the potatoes. Everybody else furnished everything else, and oh yes, we had big turnouts. ... We would have it [before Thanksgiving]. ...

We didn't have a dinner so much at Christmas, but we would have Christmas parties with candies and Christmas desserts and stuff. ... At Christmas time we tried to have our programs. ... Anything the kids could sing or read or something

Christmasy. ... I think we used to have Santa Claus when the kids were little. ... It would be one of the Grange members padded up. [Rosalie Kelsey]

Mr. Boggess at school started many traditions. He had an amazing Christmas program, too. It was the lighting of the Christmas tree. ... They would have a big, big pine tree with four different color sets of lights, and for each different color there were twenty-five little girls dressed up like fairies with white costumes for the white lights, green costumes for the green lights, and red and blue. They had this ceremony with their little wands, and they'd say. ... "We [are] the fairies of the white Christmas tree lights" and ... white lights [would turn on]. Each ... of these [groups of] little girls in the first, second, third, and fourth grades [would do the same until the tree was lighted]. The fifth grade boys would have red and white costumes with a dowel with bells hanging on them and [would sing] *I Heard the Bells on Christmas Eve*. We sang that whole song, and then the whole audience sang. [Pete Franklin]

The only time that I really miss school is at Christmas, because the children's singing was so lovely. ... We always had such a good time at Christmastime. ... I had a little book that I read to them, ... and they loved it. [Jessie Fitzpatrick]

We had a Christmas program. The teacher would begin before Thanksgiving, and we would learn poems to recite and Christmas songs. Sometimes we had plays that we all took part in. Then we drew names, because we had to do this early, and whoseever name you drew you bought a present for. We always had a Christmas tree, and we could make the decorations in school for it. Oh, we used popcorn, the boys would hold the corn popper over the big stove we had in the school, and they'd pop the corn, and the girls would string it. We made chains out of red and green paper, and then we would string cranberries. Every child was supposed to bring a cup of cranberries. ... We had to be very careful with the Christmas tree for two reasons. It might burn. In an old school like that the tree was not too far from the old stove. Then in addition we had real candles on the tree with candle holders. The men were always careful to watch closely that the tree did not catch fire. ... I can still see my father and my uncle and other men standing up by that big stove and watching that tree, all while Santa Claus was handing out the gifts. [Therese Westermeier]

We always had our school program. Santa Claus was there and passed out treats. That hasn't changed much through the years. [Our family] generally all got together and ate all together. We set a real good meal and lots of it. Home-baked bread and everything. [We cut our own tree.] In fact I can remember when I was real little, we didn't have any lights for the tree—I don't know if that's because we were hard up or they didn't make 'em yet—but we put candles on the end of everything, you know, and a certain time we could light it and stand and watch it

115

that it didn't catch anything on fire. That was a glorious moment. Goodness, you couldn't let them burn very long. We had all kinds of sparkling tinsel and a star on top, and maybe we would string popcorn or cranberries. [Ruby Jackson]

I was eleven years old and the superintendent of the mine gave me a doll for Christmas. It was the only toy I got. She had asked mother if she should get me something to wear or get me a doll, and mother told her to get me a doll, because they wasn't goin' to get me any toys. They had to get me what I had to wear. And [mother] wanted me to have the doll. Oh, I loved that doll. I thought that was the biggest doll I ever had. She dressed it so nice. She was sewing on it on Sunday, and I know Mother thought she shouldn't have been. Mother thought you shouldn't do anything on Sundays, and this woman was sewing on the clothes for my doll. It had a sash and a pink skirt; oh it was beautiful. I kept it from 1894 'till 1911. ... Then I had a friend [who] came with a little girl, and I gave it to her. I wished I'd kept it. [Sarah Brillhart]

Stringed popcorn for the tree. A lot of our [gifts]we made ourselves. A lot of our games we made. ... We made our own cards. ... [My sisters] all had dolls. Some of them were homemade. ... Usually the folks got us one present. Something to wear, something to eat, you know, practical gifts. ... My mother done a lot of sewing. My mother was quite a dressmaker. ... She made everybody's clothes. [Samuel Altman]

The neighborhood boys used to go get Christmas trees off the Maxwell property. ... We always had a Christmas tree, and it always stayed up till the end of January. ... We strung popcorn and cranberries and had candles, no lights. ... Practical gifts, mittens and socks and stocking caps, and I usually got a doll. ...

We'd stay up on New Year's Eve to make candy to be fed to callers who were supposed to come on New Year's Day. [Frances Thompson Mabee Waldrop]

I don't think there was a [town of] Ryssby, only the church. It was a Swedish settlement. ... My mother used to tell us about going there to the Swede Christmas tree. ... Grandfather was always very good friends with those people, and they would invite them to the Christmas tree. ... Mama said everything was in Swedish ... and they always had a barrel of apples. Apples were very scarce and hard to come by in those days. ... Everyone who came got an apple. [Amy Sherman Cushman]

When I was a child there was a Swedish church, which eventually was taken over by somebody else. They would not change their ways. They would not speak English. ... So the young people began to drop out of the church. The church literally died of old age, not because of interest, but because the people finally began to die. [Frances Bascom]

We didn't do anything on Sunday except go to church. We three, Margaret, Bill and I couldn't even roller skate on Sunday, because that was too noisy a

Sunday project. We would sit on the front porch and watch the other neighbor kids roller skate. Dad and Mother thought that wasn't proper. You couldn't play cards on Sunday. Mother and Dad belonged to a 500 Club—that was a game they played before bridge—but those cards were put in a drawer and never even brought out on Sunday; it was a no, no. [Elizabeth Graham Demmon]

Louisville had twelve saloons and two churches. You were either protestant or catholic. [Joseph Malcolm]

Speaking of the Congregational Church, it was about the only meeting place ... for a long time. [Frances Thompson Mabee Waldrop]

[My grandmother] was religious but she didn't go to church. She had a little altar in her house. Whatever house she moved to she made this little altar in the corner. It was usually the bedroom. She'd fix it up as an altar. She'd have curtains hanging in the corner. She'd have her saint there and her candle. ... She was very superstitious. She talked about witches. I mean she was real superstitious about witches, witchcraft, stuff like that. I don't think she practiced it but she was "wise" to it. She knew about it. Always cautioning me, my mother, about being careful about meeting certain people. You could tell they were witches because of certain things. ... [My mother] accepted it. Scared the hell out of me, though. I really didn't like it. [Roseann Ortega]

About everybody in the country would go [to church]. ... Before there was ever a church house around there'd be some preacher come in and file on a homestead, and he'd preach at his house. [A] lot of times we'd pull a wagon ten or twelve miles to hear him preach. [Robert Jones]

I think they were Dunkards, ... the church down here in Hygiene. ... They were really German Baptists. ... They weren't supposed to take communion if they had hard feelings between themselves and someone else. [Amy Sherman Cushman]

On Sundays, oh we had to go to church, of course. We went to the Episcopal Church then. I don't remember too much about it except that as I grew older, a teenager I suppose, I always sang in the choir. [Anabel Barr]

Everybody went to church on Sunday ... and they said the reason everybody went was they went to pray that they wouldn't have a drought, they wouldn't be hailed out, grasshoppered out or blizzarded out. [Cecilia "Sallee" Gorce]

We had seven miles to walk to church, but we made it prettinear all the time only just in the wintertime, of course; we didn't then. But we walked to church ... every Sunday. Dad wasn't a church goin' guy but Mother was and she just saw that us youngsters went. I remember carrin' one little youngster on my hip all the time. [Birdie Mather]

I can remember when the road was bad out there. 'Course we didn't have a car. We always had horses. We went to what was our little church; it no longer is there. But most of the time rather than get the horses out, we'd walk to church, which was about two or three miles. ... It was full of a lot of young people at that time. We would congregate somewhere, and all of us would walk to church. That was quite a privilege. I think that we enjoyed ourselves, getting together that way, more than young people do now, but cars are the thing that takes them here and there in a hurry. We'd start to church in the morning. We had Sunday school at ten o'clock. [Irene Smith Lybarger]

Of course, we went to Sunday school, and I remember before we had a car, we walked to the Presbyterian Church and my brother, Bill, who was just a year younger than I, we'd start a little early, because we could go by the courthouse. Dad and Mother didn't know this. But the jail was in the basement of the court-house, and if we walked through the courthouse grounds, we could sit down on the window and talk to the men in the jail. ... They would come to the window with all the bars and gratings and talk to us. ... That was a big thrill. Mother and Dad could never realize why Bill and I always wanted to start out early to walk to Sunday school. ...

We went to Sunday school and stayed through church and oh, boy, those were long. ... That's when they preached longer than now! They'd get through at twelve and then the ministers would go on and on, and oh boy, that was a long day. [Elizabeth Graham Demmon]

[Church] was a big part of the Niwot community. When we were kids, why, the Young People's Christian Endeavor Society was quite a thing in the church. We had a lot of fun there; they'd have parties for the young folks. It was just a good time. Yeah, I didn't go to church much in the daytime, but every night you'd go to Christian Endeavor, and then you'd stay for church. Church was out at nine o'clock. Well, that was the big thing. You'd go there to see if you could find a girl to [walk] home. [Evan Gould]

On Sunday some preacher would volunteer to preach at the school, so every Sunday we would have a different denomination. ... With so many different religions, and each one came to stress his own particular religion, we had every-thing. ... [The Presbyterian] preacher was one of those shouting kind of preachers. Then we had a man come who was of the United Brethren Church, and he weighed about three hundred pounds, ... and he crushed the chair when he sat down on it. He was a great deal of fun for the children but not for the parents. He was the kind that liked to have an evangelist meeting. ... The Mormons didn't come, that was the only one. ... But the preachers were very nice, and they were always invited to a fried chicken dinner. ... But all these different religions left everybody always aloof and not impressed by the religions at all. They didn't lean toward one denomination. ... We were just accustomed to listen to them. ... There was one Catholic church, in a mostly German settlement, ... and a priest would come once a month and hold mass there. There was a little house for the preacher to stay. He would come and stay about five days before they would hold mass on Sunday so everybody could come and go to the church for confession and be ready for holy communion on Sunday. [Cecilia "Sallee" Gorce]

Dr. Lucius Reed ... without doubt was the most spiritually minded man I ever knew. He was wonderful. But he had a very wonderful sense of humor at the same time. I remember him telling me once that he was out in the yard working and a tramp ... came into the yard and said, "Are you the Reverend Mr. Reed?" Reed said, "Yes." [The tramp] said, "Well, the Lord told me if I'd come here you'd give me a pair of shoes." And Mr. Reed said, "Well, the Lord gave you a bum steer, because I only have one pair of shoes, and I've got them on!" ...

The next thing that was started was the rummage sale, which we still have and at which our church makes a great deal of money. And how those women work at that. If you haven't been to one of our rummage sales ... you'd be amazed at number of things that are accumulated there. And by the way, they have some very good clothes that the women of the church buy from each other. [Jessie Fitzpatrick]

Dad was an elder in the Presbyterian Church. Mom was president of the organization called the Golden Circle, which was the women's group that sort of ran the Presbyterian Church. [It was called] the Golden Circle because all of them wore golden wedding rings. ... They were busy. ... They worked hard raising money. [Elizabeth Graham Demmon]

A stereographic view of a teacher about to strike a boy who is across her lap, Erie, 1909. Photo by Ed Tangen. Carnegie Branch Library for Local History, Boulder Historical Society Collection.

CHAPTER NINE

TEACHING THE CHILDREN

The one-room school house is probably one of the most endearing features of the West, especially for those who experienced this form of education. These schools usually began in private homes or in a small building donated by the family having the most children in the area. In order to start a school district, there needed to be at least ten children within the ages of five and twenty-one years. The teachers were usually young, unmarried women, often no more than sixteen years old themselves. It is not hard to imagine the discipline problem presented to these young girls by strapping farm boys in their late teens. Ages varied dramatically within grades. Farm children were needed to work during the fall harvest and spring seeding rather than spend precious hours in school, and the children of hard-rock miners were constrained by the weather in the mountains, which in some cases was so severe that the children were unable to travel to school except in the summer months. These drawbacks made graduating from the eighth grade an uncertain event, especially within a specified time period. One of the most memorable quotes was told by Hugh Smith, "As the fella said, when he graduated from the third grade, he was so excited he couldn't shave!"

In 1837 Massachusetts was the first state to create a board of education whose function was to coordinate the public school system, and in 1852 a law was passed requiring school attendance. By 1918 every state had followed this example. In 1874 taxes were required by law to pay for public high schools. A uniform educational system was evolving in the United States, bringing citizens from all over the country together in their common knowledge and giving them a sense of national unity.

Higher education was also steadily progressing in the 1800s in the U.S. Several colleges were founded by churches and private organizations. In the late 1800s, federal land grants were given to states under the stipulation that they would be sold and the money would be used to create agricultural and technical colleges.

The University of Colorado at Boulder was among these and was one of the main reasons this mining-supply town did not die out as did so many other settlements in like situations. The doors to the University opened to forty-four students in 1877, one year after Colorado became a state. Mary Rippon, the third person to join the faculty was the first woman to teach in a state university in the entire country. By 1882, six men graduated. The university was on its way.

Lower School

My mother always kept my work-clothes hung behind—we had a door here then and that was what was hung behind there. There was my apron that I put on over my school clothes, and I put on my sweater, and then I went to get the chips and gather the eggs and all those little things. [Gertrude Tower]

We were always [with] little white aprons on ... like the book you used to read, *Little Women*, little white pinafore aprons, you know. We wore those to school, with ties at the back and ruffles over there. [Pearle Yocom]

Ordinarily, we would just walk to school. ... We'd be frozen, and the teachers would have to take our shoes off and rub our feet. ... We always had to wear these long underwear with stockings that had to be pulled up, and we wore dresses. You didn't ever wear pants to school in those days, that was just a no, no. You'd wear these big old golashes over your shoes, because it was usually muddy or snowing or something and then when you'd get to school you'd be half frozen, so it would take a half hour to thaw out. [Ara Kossler Yager]

Well, from that place it was quite a ways, but we'd walk up Ninth Ave. We'd go around the corner there, and we'd pick up the Sorenson kids. ... Then we'd go on around west there, and we'd pick up the Davies kids and the Johanson's kids. That was probably two and a half miles about. ... Just pick 'um up on foot; we'd all go together. Went to school just the same [in stormy weather]. We had overshoes, and we just tramped along. My brother was four years older than me, and he wouldn't wait for me. ... But no one thought anything. All the kids walked. We had high overshoes, you know. [Cleo Turner Tallman]

We walked a mile down to school, and we had good school mates. ... We always walked to school. I can remember when the wind was blowing real hard out there, I'd hold Charles Kelsey. When I'd get down there he would take a hold of my hand and keep me from rolling over into the burrow pit or something. Once in a while, if the snow was real deep, they'd hitch up the horses and come along and pick us up. [Mabel Andre Thomas]

Teaching the Children

Oh, it was probably a mile. It depended whether we walked or ran; it took an average of an hour, because we had to go over the Table Mountain there. We didn't seem to mind it. We used to have to take a hoe with us on account of rattlesnakes. We never killed more than a couple, but they would sneak up around the sagebrush that was growing there, and you didn't see them until you were right on them. We always carried a hoe. That was our protection. They used to be pretty plentiful, especially in piles of rock or something of that kind. ...

In the wintertime when it was real cold, my dad would ... always put runners on the sled when there was snow enough. Take us in the sled to school. Or we would pile on horses and ride to school and turn the horses loose. They'd come home. So he'd go get us then in the evenings. We had lots of experience with snow and cold. The Ryssby school had sheds where you could tie the horses if you wanted to, but he always told us to take the bridles off and let them go. They'd come home. ... They knew where their food was. I rode across on a horse with another boy that had his horse. ... It was about two miles to school, and I was just a little tot at that time, six [years old]. [Irene Smith Lybarger]

Oh yeah, I had my own pony and road nine miles to school in the summertime. [Edna Morrato]

Later on there's a milk truck come by there. It come there early so we'd milk the cows, and we'd eat breakfast, and we'd ride to school on the milk truck. ... It went up two or three stops up the south of Lyons, up the South St. Vrain ... two or three stops up the North St. Vrain. ... By the time they got to the schoolhouse to let us out up there it was still more than an hour or two early. So you kind of have to wait around there. [Leonard Loukonen]

I don't remember us ever having to stay home on account of the weather. Sometimes it took a lot of energy to get there, but we generally made it. [Mary Todd Flarty]

We rode in a Dodge touring car to school, and Ted would have to make two trips with kids hangin' all over the sides. 'Course when it got to really colder weather, that's when it had to change to two trips. They were bussing the kids to Nederland. He'd plow the snow up to the dam, radiator boilin', you know, that old Dodge would really be goin' at it. We'd get up to the schoolhouse, and Nederland kids maybe they wouldn't be able to make it to school, but Tungsten kids always got there. His good old Dodge. [Ruby Jackson]

It was summer school. We didn't go in the wintertime. It was in the summertime, because it was too snowy and stuff up there, you know, at that time. It [wasn't] anything like it is now. I remember seein' snow eighteen, twenty feet deep right next to our porch. Snow drifts. Us kids had skis, and we had snow shoes. We had everything that dad could make, and it was all made out of quakin' Aspen. … It's cause it's light, see. It's tough and everything but it's light, and that's what he made our skis out of. [Birdie Mather]

We carried our lunch. Everyone carried their lunch. It was quite a novelty for us when we got to school to all sit in the anteroom … where we hung our coats and things —when it was cold that's where we ate our lunch—and we would trade our lunches around. If we saw something someone else had we would trade off something of ours. We usually took sandwiches, and my mother … would can all this fruit so we always had good lunches. We made homemade bread, and then, of course, mother would fix the meat so that we would have a meat sandwich. We would have a little jar of fruit and most generally donuts or cake. Pie wasn't so easy to carry, but once in a while we would have a treat of that. [Irene Smith Lybarger]

I believe each child brought their own water, didn't they. I think they just brought something like a little lard bucket with a little handle on it. That's all I can remember, no plastic bottles or anything. [Elizabeth Graham Demmon]

The old wooden school, I doubt that there was a drinking fountain on the place. I remember vividly that a tall eighth-grade boy went around every afternoon … with a bucket of water and a dipper. Everybody had a drink of water from the same bucket, same dipper, and we didn't all die of whatever was going around. [Elizabeth Wiest Farrow]

Everybody drank out of the dipper. [Albert Chaussart]

Diphtheria Dipper. [Louis Varra]

You were taught to drink with your lower lip inside the cup so that you didn't get the saliva in. [Evelyn Chaussart]

Didn't even know what it was to have separate cups. They had a bucket sittin' there with a dipper in it, and you'd need to go over there and dip out the dipper and drink, and if there was a little bit left I guess you'd put it back in, I don't know. [Albert Chaussart]

[From] 1873 to date there has been a school there. That is the Gold Hill School. It was two rooms, and they have added an additional two rooms onto it. Coal stove, coal potbelly. Empty the ashes and carry in a bucket of water to stand beside the stove in case it caught fire and carry in coal and wood. I think Ellen did the janitor work. Drinking water, we borrowed it from the neighbor across the street. The latrines were open pit. [Two of them.] [Albert Walter]

Teaching the Children

No [plumbing] in the school. Not at first. They had two outhouses. [Mary Todd Flarty]

We had a little outhouse way up behind the school where you could be excused to go to the outhouse, but rarely did you ask to be. [Ara Kossler Yager]

It had a great big stove, and it had a thing around it, didn't it? In the school. Kind of a metal thing around it so the children would never ... touch the stove. I had to go up before school and build the fire, and I had *never* done anything like that. [Irvin Demmon]

It was one of the real old fashioned round stoves. It probably was a foot and a half across in the middle and tapered down to where the ashes came out into a tray down underneath the stove. Then it tapered on up to the top where it had the device with a couple of little lids in it, and the chimney came out the top, too, and on up through the roof of the building. ...

Yes, we had a furnace we had to stoke with coal, you know. It had an automatic feed, but we'd have to fill that with coal. After school in the evening we would get busy and clean things up. ... We didn't have any electricity in the school. [Charles Snively]

Wood was kept out there and the coal was kept out there [in the ante-room]. ... The miners took care of [hauling coal to the school] but the kids took care of the stove. [Louis Varra]

The poor teacher had to build the fire and keep it going, put logs in it all during the school day. We did have to wash blackboards and sweep the room sometimes. [Ara Kossler Yager]

The children used to clean the boards, of course, and dust the room. ... Two classes to a room; four classrooms in the building. [Elizabeth Wiest Farrow]

I didn't start school until about seven. Mrs. Tyrer give us music lessons if we'd clean the school and bring in the coal and the wood and stuff— Mrs. Tyrer didn't like to clean very good. She was so sweet though. Anyway, we cleaned the school house. [Dorothy Burch Walker]

Amy's husband, they grew up just south of here. ... He says [to my oldest brother], "Hey Phil, get this piece of waste paper." There's a shot gun shell in it. He says, "Throw that in the stove for me." My brother, being a little guy, he walks up and throws that in the stove. Pretty soon—the stove set kind of in the middle [of the room] towards the front, and then it had a pipe kind of from here to that door—pretty soon ... BANG and the door flew open and all that pipe fell down! The teacher, she says, "Phil, what did you do?" He didn't know what happened! [Jacob Schlagel]

He was so darn ornery; he wasn't afraid. The kids used to go up where the bell was, and oh, quite of few of them would crawl around and set up on top there—just orneriness. [Beth Dodd]

It was high. Well, her uncle, Dave Conilogue, he crawled up the face of that thing one time. The teacher was out there about had a fit. [Evan Gould]

I remember one time, wasn't it you and I who played hooky? When we got to school we both got our hineys paddled, and when we got home we got them paddled again. [Albert Chaussart]

What do you mean paddled? I got a beatin'. My dad didn't spare the rod. [Louis Varra]

I think that was the last time I played hooky. [If you talked back to the teacher] you got a whoopin'. That's the way it oughta be now. [Albert Chaussart]

In those days when you got in trouble in school you knew you'd get in trouble at home. [Cleo Turner Tallman]

You got in a lot worse trouble at home. [Glenn Tallman]

Kids didn't do like they do nowadays. They knew when they went home they'd catch it, too. [Cleo Turner Tallman]

They were like every other pioneer that came here. They were very strong people, very religious. They had to be in order to survive. They depended upon one another. They disciplined their children. I always get the biggest kick out of Bill's dad talkin' about his mother. She never ever spanked him or anything but if they ever did anything wrong she'd go and grab 'em by the ear and twist 'em and lead 'em all the way home. By the time they got home they had had punishment enough. [Blanche Moon]

The principal, well the one I remember the best, was a great, big, fat lady, and boy, when she'd get mad, red spots would raise up on her neck. About the next thing she'd say was, "I'm going to cut your tongue out and hang it on the clothesline to dry." Boy, I think all us kids believed that, too. And yet she was a good old soul. She was a good teacher. [Evan Gould]

The old man Elks used a rubber hose on me. In grade school old man Elks beat me, because I was a mean kid. Do you remember Mr. Elks? Oh, he was a mean guy. [Louis Varra]

They'd take a ruler. [Louis Varra]

Across your knuckles. Mrs. Spicer, god she used to use a rubber hose on me. [Albert Chaussart]

Elks used rubber hoses. You'd bend over a desk, and they'd let you have it. Today you can't touch a kid even if they need it, but in the old days they didn't have any pity. They beat you. [Louis Varra]

TEACHING THE CHILDREN

We used to take Spicer's rubber hose and throw it in the furnace. I remember her so well, because she used that rubber hose on me. [Albert Chaussart]

Well they had some pretty good willow switches down there and they weren't afraid to use them, and you had a lot of respect for them, too. We never had much of a problem with discipline. Gosh, most of those teachers, when they spoke, why, you listened. [Glenn Tallman]

Her name was Ethel August, the teacher that we liked so well. She was pretty young, in fact she was more like one of us kids. She would get out and play with us and in fact sometimes during recess the morning recess might run clear over till noon. We'd have our lunch and go to school in the afternoon. [John Jackson]

Biggest school we had was thirty-four kids in eight grades. Well, the one that I loved was Miss August. I even got up a petition to run around and get every kid to sign it and give it to the school board to get her back the second year. Why she was good, but oh God, she could swat hard though. Sometimes it was just her hand, sometimes it was a ruler, and then once in awhile it would be a pretty good-sized stick. It depends on what you was, but her main thing was write them times tables so many times. [Ralph Yates]

Miss Lovelace taught us art. I will never forget those art lessons! If they started in the morning art would go on all day until you drew that picture right. ... You couldn't be creative or Miss Lovelace jerked your paper, and you had to start all over again ... So you see, we shaped up fast in art class. I was always real good and tried to please my teachers. Now my brother, Bill, ... he was a nice kid, but he was kind of a pest, bad boy. He was always in trouble. Miss Lovelace would shake Bill up so hard. Shook him by the shoulders. Oh, she shook the big boys, and she'd shake so hard it would shake the buttons off his shirt! Mother quite often had to sew Bill's buttons on again. You can't touch a child now. I don't know. It didn't shape him up too much. He was a good student, and he never did anything mean, he was just in trouble. [Elizabeth Graham Demmon]

Oh, there was a little [discipline problem], not too much. ... [The teachers] would either board at one of the boarding houses. There was two boarding houses. ... Generally the two teachers would go together and rent a house. [Mary Todd Flarty]

Usually there was a little house around that the teacher rented. I remember they had two houses over there. One of them was across the creek and the oldest boys especially, would make sure that she would have wood or coal or whatever, you know, for her night, and most of them had to carry water from the town spring, town pump or whatever they might have. These boys would usually take care of that part of it for the school teacher. And she appreciated it. They were comfortable. [Ara Kossler Yager]

'Course as I say, the teacher boarded with us and lived upstairs. [Hazel Faivre]

[The teachers] were always boarded by the family that had the most students in the school. [Ara Kossler Yager]

All these teachers wore black dresses, and the dresses came down to their ankles, oh maybe a little above. They all wore very sensible shoes with Cuban heels. Nice square oxfords. [Elizabeth Graham Demmon]

Oh yes, it was a cardinal sin if you got married. If you got married you lost your job right away. An unmarried woman was employed. I think we didn't think much about it. It was so and that was that. Of course, it was very silly. [Jessie Fitzpatrick]

As a matter of fact there were two opinions [for women], you could be a nurse or you could be a teacher. ... I don't really know what else girls did. They worked in shops, they got married, but most of my friends who went on to University the same time I did went on to teaching. [Elizabeth Wiest Farrow]

I got along pretty well with my students. I walked about a half a mile up to the schoolhouse. Had to start the fire. Now, here I was. I'd never been away from home. And it was rough. We had a bucket with water and a dipper. The kids all brought their own lunch, and I had my lunch. During the noon hour we played games. We sat outside and ate our lunches, and then we'd play something. There were only six of us, five students and me, and we played pom-pom-pullaway; we played baseball in the school yard. Then when it was cold we had to eat in the school. They had a big round stove in the corner and the desks were those kind we had at Mapleton School where there's a desk connected to another one. The seat in front of you is connected to the desk. Up there at Magnolia they didn't have very good supplies, and there were a couple of double desks. But we got along all right. I taught reading. The kids were good readers, and I'd bring a lot of books from the library and from home on the weekend, and they'd read. [Elizabeth Graham Demmon]

[My father] went to school up here [through the eighth grade] in a little school, and at that time there were probably twenty or thirty children in the school because of all the homesteaders as opposed to when I grew up we had just our own family. We went through the ninth grade up here in our little school. The most we ever had in it was probably six at one time, just our Kossler family and before, ... some of the Walkers. ... [The school] was half way in between the two ranches. The teachers were hired by the school board up here. The teachers had to teach all these grades in one room with having to stoke the fire in the middle of the room as well as bring your own lunch and bring your own water to drink. [Ara Kossler Yager]

I had to have certain credentials, but it seemed when I started out I had seventeen [students]. I got seventy-five dollars a month for [seventeen kids and eight grades]. ... I rode a horse to the school. ... It took something to be sure the fourth grade boy got his spelling and the third grade boy got his arithmetic test, and then you'd have this girl in the geography class. What I mean is you didn't lose much time. [Emma McCrone]

Yes indeed. There was no secretary and there was nobody to help you when you were teaching in those days. Even in 1908 when I started, there wasn't any help. You taught your grade. You were principal, and you did all the odd jobs as well as taking care of your own things for practically no salary. My magnificent salary when I started to teach was fifty dollars a month! If you were satisfactory, you were raised to sixty-five at the end of three months. ... You taught for the love of teaching in those days. [Jessie Fitzpatrick]

Miss Eggleston, I remember, she was a nice teacher. We had one that wasn't. That's when we made up that rhyme ... what was it?

Oh Lord of love
Look down from above
Upon us poor scholars
For we hired a fool
To teach our school
And paid her thirty dollars.

But we didn't say that about Miss Eggleston, we all loved her. She was nice, it was just a different attitude. [Maude Moomaw Beasely]

Mr. Cordes. He was an older man, quite heavy set. He came from the east somewhere, and he was a very nice teacher. But he'd sit on the desk and teach us. We all come up to recite. We would come up by classes. The teacher would say, "First class come up." They'd sit on these long seats in front and recite their lesson. Then they'd go back to their seats and the second grade would come up. He had all eight grades if [there were enough students]. ... But he had a bad habit of spitting on the floor, and then he'd take his shoe and rub it in. We had the, you know, the boards, the plain board floor. Oh, we didn't like that a bit, and we told our parents about it and the board got after him and made him quit. [Maude Moomaw Beasley]

Basically she catered to the younger ones first. ... Each one got individual attention. ... A lot of the older ones would have to answer questions, and they'd do it on the blackboard. ... It was just like having your own tutor. [Ara Kossler Yager]

When kids recited they had a big old bench up there in the front, and they'd all go up there to recite. They had all the eight grades there, I know, and [the little ones] sat off to the side. But I know that's how I learned to read by listening to some of the others, you know, go up there in the front and read and all. She'd have things on the board, and I can remember that's how I learned to read was by listening to those other kids. [Cleo Turner Tallman]

Usually during the afternoon recess the teacher read to us, and I think that's what inspired all of us to read. [Ara Kossler Yager]

The seats were graduated the smaller ones in front, and then it got a little larger. ... The first grader sat here, and they came up to recite. The eighth graders would [also] recite. ... Then we moved back the next year. Then we heard those lessons all over again, and we moved back again and heard them all over again for eight years. ... Geography and diagraming ... history ... and writing and spelling. Reading with very primitive books, you know and the same books year after year. ... We had no reference books whatsoever. ... You can't imagine what a change it was to go from the eighth grade here ... into a big school like in Boulder at the high school, which was then the State Preparatory School. We were completely lost and our social life was practically nil. [Hazel Faivre]

The teacher had a regular desk. ... Of course [the school] had the old desks, the regular desks, and they had the double desks. They didn't have just a single, they had some single and some double. Maybe most of them were double, and so two [students] had to sit together. You know how the desks are like. They have the ink wells on top and the place for pencils. They had slates. I was thinking the other day about how I have some slate pencils, but I don't have any of the old slates. We used those still down in the Montgomery schoolhouse. They were bound with cloth ... and some of them had double slates, two slates made together. You could fold them in. We used those, and we had a wet cloth or we'd go and wash them off. The teacher would let us wash them off. We didn't have paper. We had a blackboard, but we did our own figuring and writing on our slates. I still have a little slate pencil; they were tiny, about this long. Instead of using chalk, we used slate pencils, regular slate pencils. They didn't scratch; if you watched out they didn't scratch. Then we'd have a wet cloth and just wipe it off. Those slates, I wish I'd a kept one of those. Oh, we had lots of fun with our slates. [Maude Moomaw Beasley]

Teaching the Children

It had the desks in it that folded down, and there would be at least two children that sat in one seat. The desk tops had the holes for the ink wells. [Jacob Schlagel]

All those school buildings were probably a building maybe twenty foot wide and maybe twenty-five foot long, and they had these great big wood/coal burning stoves in there. For light they had large kerosene lights. Some of them hung down from the ceiling and some of them kind of set on the shelves out from the wall. ...

The second grade I remember, because up at the front of the building on each side they had a little stage affair thing, and on each side of the stage they had bookcases in there with glass doors on them. Inside of these was the school books that we used. There were books in there that we used from the first grade clear through to the eighth. ... At the end of the year they were put back in the book case. Before school would start at the beginning of the year the school board would hire the teacher. Usually she would come and would look over the library and make sure there was the right books there to teach the classes that she was going to have. Usually, she would have one or two in about every one of those grades. [John Jackson]

The fifth grade ... was when we started sewing. From the fifth through the eighth grade we were taught sewing, and the boys went to manual training and learned woodworking. ... The girls in the eighth grade all made their own graduation dresses. [Marguerite Sherman]

There was four [rooms], and then during the tungsten boom they built an extra room on. ... At first it was just the first eight grades, and then ... they put in two years of high school and finally they got four years of high school. But then only from three to six was all they graduated out of high school; that was the number of the pupils they would graduate. They could have all four grades of high school in one room, because there was just a few pupils in each grade. ... We were in a study hall, and then when we'd go to recite we'd go to a room where there wasn't a lot of pupils. ... I graduated about '28 or '29 I think. [Mary Todd Flarty]

Potato Hill School was a small frame house, probably not much larger than my living room and dining room together. Maybe a little larger and then the outhouse was out back a little ways. They had cistern water. A lady by the name of Berryman taught school there. A one-room school with about twenty children. [Irene Smith Lybarger]

The girls and boys were divided. We went into school in separate lines. And a great punishment was to have you stand in a corner if you misspelled a word or something like that. ... Miss Lichtenwalter, Viola Lichtenwalter [was the principal], and she bragged that she outlasted the plumbing in the school! [Frances Thompson Mabee Waldrop]

Sometimes when the boys and girls would get mad at each other, the teachers would let the girls play on the Arapahoe side [of the school] and the boys play on the other side. Then when they could behave like little ladies and little gentlemen, then they could play together again. Sometimes they would have awful fights. ... We had one swing and some of the fathers made that one. But we had lots of games we could play: hide and seek, run sheep run, duck on the rock. [Therese Westermeier]

We jumped rope and we played hop scotch and baseball. ... And we had swings ... fastened to the limb of a tree. [Mary Todd Flarty]

We didn't play much ball. Just tag. We didn't have a playground. We played out on the road or up on the hills. Right out here was the road. Over here was the coal shed. Yeah, I think the girls was tougher than the boys! [Dorothy Burch Walker]

No, we didn't have those things. No. We used to play Anti-I-Over where you throw the ball over the roof. Kids was on that side and one on this side, and if you caught the ball you could come around and tag somebody. No there wasn't much. We used to play tag, pom-pom-pullaway. [Earl Logan]

Well, we didn't have any place to hide, that's for sure. So we usually played pullaway, and we played baseball. That was about the size of our games. 'Course we'd all get together, the girls on one side and the boys on the other, and we'd pull to see who was the strongest. We called it pullaway. And we played a lot of baseball; girls and boys all played. But it was just a little school that set on the corner. At that time we thought it was a real school house. They had a bell. They rang the bell for us to come in and out. I can't say that we were separated from one another. There were just so few of us that we all played together. [Irene Smith Lybarger]

But some of those kids were big, my goodness they were big ... Some of the bigger kids threatened the teachers, and one of the teachers quit soon after she came. Some of those big kids were so ornery she had a nervous breakdown and quit, but that was before I ever went there. [Cleo Turner Tallman]

Oh, some of those kids were eighteen years old and still in school. [Glenn Tallman]

Eighteen or twenty, and they were big farm kids, you know, and I guess they were kind of ornery at times. [Cleo Turner Tallman]

TEACHING THE CHILDREN

Those teachers, I don't know how they did it. They had some kids in class those days—you see the farmers would keep the kids out to work in the summer. Well, some of them got to be twenty-one years old before they got out of the eighth grade. And them big kids, you know, would cause the teachers a lot of problems. But they had to pass. They'd come back, you see, and if they didn't make the grade they'd have to take it over. That's how they'd become so old before they graduated. ... [The teachers] taught 'em. They knew how to handle 'em and they knew how to use a stick, too. You got it once in a while. [Edmund Darby]

I went to University Hill School. As long as I could stay. I was in eighth grade. I remember I come from a farm see, and the kids where I come from ... were bigger 'cause they didn't go to school like they did here. You'd husk corn late in the fall and then start [school] after that. Then early in the spring you'd quit to help plant. And a lot of times we didn't have a teacher [all the time]. After that we come here to Boulder, and the kids would only come up to my knees! [Hugh Smith]

I graduated from the eighth grade, and that was it. [Birdie Mather]

In Indiana I got to go to the first grade, and then I missed [school], because mother was havin' babies all the time it seemed like, and every time she had a kid I stayed home. I sat in on the eighth grade up here and got my diploma by just setting in on the class, because I wasn't really supposed to be goin' to school there. That was the only education I had, was first grade and eighth grade, but I'm sure good at changin' diapers! [Delores S. "Dee" Bailey]

We went to school to try to learn and that was it [no extracurricular activities]. I went partly through the tenth [grade]. I got smarter than the teachers. [Louis Varra]

I finished the tenth grade. I tell you I quit school, because I thought I was smarter than the teachers, too, then I went to work in the mine, went to work in the coal mine then. [Albert Chaussart]

I thought [the schools] were good, 'cause I was raised in an itty bitty town and never went to school much. But I thought these schools was just great. ... They learned pretty good, yes. [Mrs. J.A. Deavenport]

I'd run and I'd whistle, every step of the way [to school]. It was much better than home 'cause at home I had to work. [Louis Varra]

We were called to class by the bell. And when we'd go out to recess after the fifteen minutes was up the bell would ring, and we would go back to class. [Marguerite Sherman]

133

There was a big bell in the tower with a big old rope hanging down from it. You visualize the little friars ringing the church bell and going up and down, well, we used to ring the school bell the same way. [Albert Walter]

Well, that was a cold day. Charles [Kelsey] and Ralph [Bixler] had gone out to go down to the outhouse, and they noticed all this smoke coming out of the eaves of the schoolhouse. We were inside and didn't know anything about it, you know. So they came in and told the teacher. Miss Jordan got us out. They did ring the school bell like mad. The farmers all came down as fast as they could. They took us all over to the grange hall. There were eight grades in that little school room. They had one of those great big potbellied stoves, and I think there was just too much heat in the attic through the pipe. We then went to school in the grange hall. There must have been thirty to thirty-five students in the school. [Mabel Andre Thomas]

Then the third grade was Miss Armstrong. ... She was kind of a nervous wreck as I remember. It was during the war, the First World War, and every morning when we came in we said to a big picture, "Good morning, President Wilson." When we left at night we stood up in our rows and said, "Good evening, President Wilson" and lined up and walked out of school. I was in the third grade when the war ended. The schools had been closed for two or three weeks because of the flu epidemic, and we were to go back on that day, which was probably the 11th of November. All the bells in Boulder rang, the Methodist Church, the Mapleton School bell, all of them. We couldn't imagine. The war was over! [Elizabeth Graham Demmon]

Higher Education

High School

I graduated in 1919 [from State Preparatory School] and the high school had both boys' and girls' stairs in those days. We were separated. We were not allowed to mingle, except in the halls between classes. We had chapel every morning in the auditorium, at least two hymns and a reading from the Bible at the State Preparatory School. ...

When we had rallies, which was often in the fall at least, people would gather on the third floor and the head boy would stand on one of the radiators and lead the cheers and the whole building swayed a little while this was going on so after a while they gave it up. [Frances Thompson Mabee Waldrop]

Flag Rush was a contest between the *onies* and the *toots*, the first year and the second year of Prep School. ... The idea was, there were three flags on a stick probably two feet long. ... The lower classmen were to put those three flags up on top of flagstaff. If you won, you were almost upper classmen. But if you lost then you couldn't do certain things for a month or so. [Samuel Altman]

They would compete with one another ... to see who got a flag up to the top of Flagstaff first. And no holes barred. If you ran into one of the opposite class, why you detained him as long as you could. And then there were false flags and there were true flags. ... My husband was one of the flag carriers when he was in high school, and he went all the way around the back of Flagstaff to get up to the top with his flag. [Cecilia "Sallee" Gorce]

The girls did not participate. We were supposed to be more ladylike. About the only athletics that we participated in was volleyball. We didn't even have at that time a basketball team. [Lois Huston Baum]

We had sororities and fraternities in high school. They were wise enough to realize that being small humans, we were going to form cliques so they let us call them sororities and fraternities. We did stress scholarship, and you were invited, you would "bid" to become a member of one or the other of the organizations. ... We were known by initials, for the girls there was the KTD, the LDCs, and the MGAs, and I can only remember one name of the fraternities and that was the DKs. We met once a month. We had dues that I think were a dollar a month. And then we had two big dances a year. One was at Christmas time and the other was in the spring just before school was out. [Lois Huston Baum]

Boulder High School was a good high school. The classes were small; the teachers were good, and you felt like when you got out of Boulder High School you had something you could really be proud of. That's in the classes. Outside of the classes as far as recreation was concerned [if you were Negro] you had no part whatsoever. You were *persona non grata*. [Ruth Flowers]

University of Colorado at Boulder

This was a bleak, barren place. No trees. ... My great grandfather was too smart to get into the gold rush. He hauled produce up to the miners. ... My great grandfather was the only one with any profit. ... In fact I got into the University without tuition or fees, because he gave land to the university and gave money and bribed a key legislator. They were more open in those days. He said to the legislator, "You get the university up here, and you come up to my corral, and you can take your pick of any horse in the corral." They were rough and ready in those days and the legislator, after it was decided, jumped up and said, "By god, I've got a horse!" ... Boulder wanted a railroad and a university, and that was all they wanted. [Robin Arnett]

In January, 1872, a number of Boulder people gave the land on which the university now stands. ... The first building erected on the campus, and the only building for a number of years, was Old Main. ... It contained classrooms, living quarters for the students and also living quarters for the president and his family. ... The first graduating class of the University consisted of six men. [Sanford Gladden]

The university sort of sat up on the hillside all by itself. [Frances R. Bascom]

The university was just getting started. There was Old Main, the president's home, the civil engineering building and the chapel. They had a beautiful chapel. The tuition was forty dollars a quarter, three quarters for one hundred and twenty dollars, which was very reasonable. ... There was no place to live except rooming and boarding and private homes. [Marguerite Ensz]

[The head of student housing at the university] was trying to get housing for all these kids coming back, you know. ... .This was just a little thirteen room hotel [called The James Hotel]. ... She called up one time ... and talked to my dad, and she said, "How many rooms have you got in that hotel?" He said, "Oh, we've got a lot of room down here." She said, "Well, I've got about thirty-five young men down there," and he said, "Oh well, we've got them all, ... they're here. ... They're livin' in the basement, and they're all over." He gave them all permanent addresses, so they could register for the University. And that's how they got in. ... Down in the middle of the block there was a woman who had a chicken coop. ... So [the students] ... took that chicken house, and they took all the stuff out of it. My dad helped them, and they painted it. ... They used the bathrooms and every facility at my mother's place. We bedded all those kids down, and they were the best kids you ever saw. [Edna Morrato]

No black student at the University ... could ... live in the dormitories; that was out. [Ruth Flowers]

My feeling always was that [fraternities and sororities] played a very important role on the university campus. They were groups, you know, that could take action. They didn't always take the action we liked, but nevertheless, I think they were a very positive force on campus. ... Students have their interests in addition to studies. [Jacob Van Ek]

University days were fun. I was a member of Pi Phi. ... We didn't have any hazing, but I can well remember as a pledge I had to help scrub the front porch with a tooth brush. That was a real job. [Louise McAllister]

TEACHING THE CHILDREN

There were all kinds of functions [during rush week]. They'd go from one sorority house to another, you know, 'bout like they do now. They'd have teas and different little functions. ... It was all small. ... So much more intimate. ... There were no cars there at that time, so we walked everywhere. People just didn't have them then. Kids didn't have cars. ... Very few of their parents did, even. ... We just walked every place. Up in the mountains for beefsteak fries, and when we had our formal dances, each of us had our slipper bag to match our evening wrap. We put our dancing slippers in that, and we wore our regular shoes down to wherever we were going. Once or twice, I think, we went on the streetcar or something, but anyway, when we got off the streetcar we always had to walk a distance so we had our slipper bags. The Boulderado [Hotel] was very new, then. It had just been completed and so we had many of our formals down there. It was really something. ... [We had an orchestra] and our chaperons. ... One year Mother was up at that time, and they asked her also to be a chaperon. ... Oh, that pleased Mother so. She enjoyed that so much. And I can remember how pretty she looked. ...

They called it *fussing* then. ... Dating was called fussing. It was called fussing. "Who are you fussing tonight?" ...

Then they had Dandelion Day which was fun. They'd mark off little squares with string, and there would be so many for each plot to dig dandelions. That was more fun. ... That was part of their curriculum. ... We always had Dandelion Day. We were assigned—and it was so much fun. ... There were about eight [people per square]. ... Usually it was a mixture of boys and girls. [Alma Leatherman Husted]

It was a beautiful time at the university, a lovely time. It wasn't too big. The entire student body met every Tuesday morning at eleven o'clock for chapel and sat in Macky; the whole student body. ... They had some splendid teachers, friendly. [Elizabeth Wiest Farrow]

I worked on Macky Auditorium around 1917 or '18. The building was all erected. What I helped them do was hang the light fixtures in the auditorium there, which were pulled up from below, up into the ceiling and tied. That procedure had to be repeated whenever a lamp burned out. [Lyndon Switzer]

The problem with this town is that the university has dominated [it] for so many years. In the early years, that's all there was in town was the University of Colorado. But by reason of its location here, and at that time consumptives were recommended to come out to this high, dry climate, so the

University of Colorado has terrific faculty people, because [so many of the professors] had tuberculosis. [JH Kingdom]

I remember the first faculty meeting I attended in the fall of 1924 ... the [chairman of the] Biology Department, got up and he said, "Now this fall we have twenty-five hundred students. That makes us a large university, and so we must begin to act like a large university." [Jacob Van Ek]

The University at the same time [around 1920] was a very fine university. ... Classes were small except for psychology and American government. The classes were about twenty-five to thirty, and they were taught by professors—the professors themselves and the heads of the departments. There were no TAs [Teaching Assistants]. Consequently the information that you got you felt was valid information, and once you graduated from CU, you knew that you could stand up against any graduate from any other school. That is one of the benefits of a rather small college. [Ruth Flowers]

Classes were small. I knew all the kids [that I taught] in my class. I could meet them downtown and say, "Hi, Bill, Hi Mary." ... When classes were small, students could stay around, and you could talk about things. I always enjoyed that sort of thing. ... We grew slowly and steadily until the war [World War II]. Then, after the war, there was a big jump in the population of the town and on campus, too. ... We had to get more appropriation from the state, to get some more teachers. But there was a nice spirit at the university, a wonderful spirit. ... Everybody just worked and sacrificed to make the university good. During the Depression, if somebody died or retired, we'd just take up the extra work, the extra slack. We'd take an extra class, not expecting extra pay, to make things go. [John B. Schoolland]

About fifteen hundred at the most, and it stayed fairly small for a long time. There were only about three thousand students, I think, when World War II began. I think during the war it got up to about four thousand students, most of whom were navy personnel here in a radio school, a cooks and bakers school, and a language school. [Clifford Houston]

Tuition was only sixty-six dollars a year, and there were no extra fees. [Louise McAllister]

There was one called Greenman's. A man named Greenman ... was a great benefactor for students to the extent that he was quite willing to lend a student money for his tuition if need be. As long as people paid him back, he went right on loaning money to students. [Clifford Houston]

TEACHING THE CHILDREN

There was the Greenman's Drugstore on the Hill. ... Greenman's was the hangout, and we used to say you were nobody if you weren't seen in Greenman's Drugstore at nine o'clock in the evening having an ice cream soda. ... All the [University] students knew and loved [Mr. Greenman] and would come back years later. He always remembered everybody's name. He cashed our checks. ... That was the hangout and for years we bought all of our books there; we bought our drugs there; we did everything at Greenman's, you know. But he was just a great guy and everybody loved him. And he had a phenomenal memory. [M. Helen Carpenter]

The inside of Dr. Lafayette Z. Coman's office, Boulder, ca. 1890.
Carnegie Branch Library for Local History, Boulder Historical Society Collection.

CHAPTER TEN

SURVIVING DISEASES
AND THE ELEMENTS

Fighting outside forces such as disease and the natural elements required more individual time, energy, and ingenuity in the 1800s than it does today. Vaccination research, beginning in 1796 with Edward Jenner's preventive smallpox vaccine, gave hope to people suffering from illnesses that formerly were fatal. The germ causing tuberculosis (TB), a highly contagious disease, was not identified until 1882 and effective treatments were not discovered until the late 1940s. In the meantime, patients had to find their own remedies.

One factor that doctors believed was important to tuberculosis and asthma sufferers was the weather. Doctors hypothesized that a dry climate could have a salutary effect on tuberculosis, also known as consumption. Many who personally battled with the tubercle bacillus were convinced that their cure was a result of moving to the 5,420-foot altitude of Boulder, sleeping in screened porches all year long and breathing in as much clear air as possible. In fact the Seventh Day Adventists built a sanitarium at the foothills of Boulder in 1895, because they were sure this was the perfect climate for those with consumption. Although medically this is not the cure for tuberculosis, people from all walks of life came either for themselves or for family members, and many were convinced that they lived longer and healthier lives because of the climate.

One of the diseases that the climate could not help prevent or ease was the Spanish flu of 1918. This epidemic, which lasted into 1919, killed more than twenty million people around the world. By the time Boulder tallied five hundred eighty-eight cases, the doctor in town enforced a quarantine on the citizens. Nederland, with its population of six hundred, lost forty-one residents to the disease. Almost everyone lost a friend or family member at this time.

Fresh air was just one of the many so-called household remedies that were passed down from generation to generation. Psychologically, and in some cases physically, these remedies were beneficial, and those that were not were left by the wayside. Many seemed to hold to the tradition of "If it tastes awful it must be good for you." Drinking kerosene is a case in point! Kerosene is a refined coal oil and is commonly used for fuel to run tractors and farm machinery as well as for artificial lighting. It is a poison. Yet several people mentioned kerosene as a cure, explaining that they poured a few drops on a spoonful of sugar. Even this small amount must have packed quite a punch.

The more palatable remedy of fresh air and sunshine was probably a better approach to regaining health. And Boulder County has plenty of that, at least according to today's Chamber of Commerce, which boasts roughly three hundred sixty days a year of sun. But, of course, the weather is not always ideal. There are the usual snow and wind storms found at high altitudes, and every once in awhile nature takes over with its awesome power. For example the memorable snowstorm of 1913, where residents were forced to tunnel out of their homes in order to feed their animals in the barns. There are frequent, unforgettable winds in the mountain areas that can easily reach over one hundred miles an hour, and there are the Chinook winds (named after the Chinook Indians) that blow warm, dry air from the Rockies to the plains, melting the winter and spring snows with remarkable speed. These winds can result in flooding, such as the big flood of May, 1894. Sixty hours of rain and a Chinook, which quickly melted an abnormally large winter snowfall, caused a flood that washed out trees, roads, bridges, and buildings. Although the devastation was extensive, there was not a single death recorded. As with the many other trials challenging them, the people endured the discomforts and continued on with their lives.

Illnesses

I remember when I was in the fourth grade I got lice. The reason I got lice is because people wasn't as clean as they are today. We didn't think anything of takin' a bath only once a week. Sometimes if the weather was too cold, and you couldn't keep the kitchen warm enough, you didn't take a bath that quick, because it was just difficult. Can you imagine heatin' all the water that you want on top of the stove, pouring it in to a round laundry tub and then you standing in front of the stove and bathe yourselves just by reachin'? You couldn't sit down in the tub unless you were pretty small. That was the sanitation that we had, and there wasn't any wonder why we had epidemics. I think I was in the fifth grade when we had an epidemic of smallpox and that was just when the vaccination started. If you can imagine a town as divided over a vaccination as [it is today over Vietnam]. ... Then we had diphtheria, too. I can remember one time of having a celebration in Lafayette when we posted guards at all the entrances to Lafayette so the people of Louisville couldn't come in, because the Louisville people had an epidemic of smallpox. Several times Louisville did the same thing with us. [Frank Miller]

Six boys and a girl. ... Frank died when he was a young boy, and their daughter, May, she died when she was twenty-one of diphtheria. [Ralph Miller]

We had smallpox. I and my brother had smallpox. The quarantine officer came out, and I had seven spots on me. My brother was down at the field working with Dad, but we had to be quarantined. My mother was sick. They were out of their heads with fever. My mother's fingernails were even red underneath where the smallpox were breaking out. They were real sick. She was out of her head [because of a] high fever. [Mabel Andre Thomas]

When I was six or eight, I had scarlet fever. I got it the first of May, and my mother and brother got it. My sister, who was the delicate one of the family, didn't. But my father couldn't come home from the first of May until the first of July, because we would go down one after the other. There was a pest sign on the house. Nobody could come into the house, and nobody could leave. Kind-hearted people brought us our groceries and Dad, when he was in town, did the same thing. You were definitely isolated. [Elizabeth Wiest Farrow]

We came here in 1920. ... [My mother's] problem was asthma. She had a severe case of asthma. She had had asthma since the time she was twelve years old. The medical community felt that she would be better in a dryer climate. And she was up to a point, but it certainly didn't bring about a cure. [Lois Huston Baum]

My father came out here in I believe 1906. The family moved out here for the benefit of his father who was an asthmatic. They came here from Marion, Indiana. [D. M. "Dock" Teegarden]

My grandfather Sellers came because he had stomach trouble and asthma, and they thought maybe this altitude would help him. He came out and became a miner. He lived to be ninety-three. [Ruby Roney]

George P. Darby. ... He come out here with throat and lung trouble. Lots of 'em used to do that. And he got well. He only weighed a hundred and twenty-four pounds when he come out here and he got to weighin' about three hundred, three-twenty. When he died he weighed two-sixty. He was eighty-two. [Edmund Darby]

There are four of us living now. Most of my brothers and sisters passed away before they were eight or nine years old. Some of them, three or four. At that time I heard my mother talk a lot about diphtheria and stuff like that. Of course, a lot of people had bad lungs, too. My dad had asthma, you know, pretty bad from working in the coal mines. He was only about fifty-six when he died. [Helen Warembourg]

During the early days they had two epidemics of diphtheria, and there's three children buried side by side. ... Two of them are daughters of my uncle Barnum's two children; one was ten and one was twelve. They died about a week apart, and then the little Burch girl died. Later the Richards lost three children. ... There was no cure. My Aunt May used to stay with the Dodd children, and they just choked to death. It was so sad. ... It was hard on the community, obviously. [Inez Dodd Johnson]

It was a very hard time to come [in 1893]. Things were very bad. There was a panic on. My father couldn't get work. It was very hard. We all took typhoid fever after we got here. My little brothers died in just a week of each other; four and eight years old. They had never been ill a day in their lives. My mother was down real low. We didn't think she'd live, but she did. I was very bad, too, but the little boys died. We lived with my aunt out in Lafayette. It was so crowded there, and they didn't have the care that they should have had. It nearly killed my father; he couldn't get over it. There was no hospital then. We could have got [typhoid fever] on the ship. [Sarah Brillhart]

But this same year, 1914, I got typhoid fever, because we couldn't get to the spring at school, so we were drinking the water that was running down under the snow. I didn't get to go to school any more that year. That was in February. [Gertrude Tower]

Tuberculosis

The man across the street came from Nova Scotia. He was dying of TB and the doctors said he wasn't going to live very long. So he built this little frame house and lived there alone for a number of years. Then he got better and married and had two daughters and eventually built the whole house. A lot of people with TB came out here. [Marguerite Ensz]

We had a nice frame house, but in those days, because of [Mother's] tuberculosis, they made the whole family live in tents [at night] outdoors. That was the way to cure it. Live outdoors. I'll tell ya, some of those winters were pretty cold. If I hadn't had my little dog keepin' my feet warm, I would of froze. Dad and I were in one tent and mother right next door in the other. We lived there until Mother died in 1911. ... In the daytime we could get back to the old black stove to keep warm. [John Valentine]

My grandfather came to Colorado in 1905, the purpose being that my grandmother, Clara Burr Valentine had TB. ... Colorado, of course, was the place where many people came to recover from TB—from any respiratory disease. [Jane Valentine Barker]

The reason they came to Boulder, his brother, I think, had tuberculosis and years ago Colorado was where they came if they suffered from that. It's supposed to be a healthy climate. [Mary Lou Miles]

We came to Colorado for my mother's health. They just said that mother had spots on her lung, and it was going to turn into TB. [The doctors said we had] better get her into a dry climate so we come to Colorado. That was in 1902. [Ruth Davies]

I think Mr. McCoy came to Boulder because he had tuberculosis, and that is why a lot of people came to Boulder, because it was the perfect climate. As a child I remember so many people had tuberculosis, but they were getting over it with this nice, pure air that Boulder had. [Elizabeth Graham Demmon]

Grandfather came because he had a daughter sixteen with TB. And she got it. It was real deadly in those days. ... We were two when she died. They had to build a glassed-in bedroom for us so we wouldn't get it. We never did. But my mother died when we were four months of age. [Prudence Benway]

I can remember my mother worrying because these tubercular people would come down the street expectorating all the way, and she worried a good deal about that. [Jessie Fitzpatrick]

My grandfather came from Granville, Ohio. He was born in 1853. He had tuberculosis and was not expected to live. He came out here immediately after graduation from Columbia Law School ... The University [of Colorado] in its early days had a very distinguished faculty, because a great many of [the professors] either came for their own health, in other words tuberculosis, or because someone in their family needed to be out here. Therefore, [CU] got men of a caliber who didn't turn up later, quite often because they had to be here. The Battle Creek Sanitarium, now the Boulder Memorial, was founded originally for a sanitarium for those with TB. [Charlotte Seymour]

Spanish Influenza of 1918

I was in the drugstore [business] when we had the first flu epidemic in 1918. Luckily, I only had a touch of flu for one day. But, oh my, people were dying just right and left. ... I remember our milkman was a great big, husky, well-built man that you'd think would never get sick. Well, he took that flu and died in just a day or two. [Grovenor Ketterman]

My father died in 1918 in the Spanish Flu [epidemic]. A lot of people passed away with that. [Hugh Smith]

We didn't call it the Spanish Flu, we just called it the flu. Well, yes, it was awful. The nunnery sisters were nurses at the sanitarium, and one of them would go from house to house taking care of people. ... It was pretty bad. ... Not one of us ever caught it. ... It was nationwide, it wasn't just here. ... It spread like wildfire all over town. A lot of people had it and a lot of them died. ... That was the worst epidemic we ever had in Boulder. [Marguerite Sherman]

My brother died from the flu. He lived in Hygiene. He hadn't been married very long. I don't know. It seemed like [it was] the young people, the strongest people that it took. I had it, and my dad had it. My mother nursed half the town of Hygiene. She never did get it. It was awful. [Wanda Burch Armstead]

We had a neighbor. She knew that we had the flu, and she wouldn't come near [us]. She wasn't going to get it, and she and her son—her son was a grown man—they wouldn't come near us. When her son got the flu, my mother wouldn't go up there. My dad about died. He said, "You should go up and see her." Mother said, "I have three sick little girls, and she didn't come to see me." I think I would have gone up to see her though and to help her. However, her son lived. [Annie Bailey]

My father, it was the first time he was ever sick in his life, and my sister, Margaret, had the flu very badly. We had a nurse all that time; they got well. I think the hospitals were full. ... But Mother and Bill and I didn't get the flu. It was a frightening thing because there wasn't anything you could do about it. [Elizabeth Graham Demmon]

It seemed to me like everybody was sick. ... It wasn't anything unusual to take as many as three dead people out of the hospital today and put in five or six more people. They didn't know how to fight this epidemic. It just hit this community terrific. Out best friends, we would take 'em in. They would just be so sick. I don't know what kept me from having it. ... I think I probably took twenty-five maybe fifty ... people into that hospital myself, helped the nurses get 'em in bed, furnish the milk for 'em. Then maybe the next morning, why—it was very sudden. Sometimes they would live two days, sometimes three, sometimes they would come out, but it was the worst epidemic that ... you can imagine. [Frank Miller]

We were living out here by a mine. We all had the flu. I had an uncle that died of the flu. That was terrible. My sister, she nearly died. ... There used to be an old hotel ... and they converted that to a hospital. ... Everybody was dying. Nearly every household would have a death or two. It was terrible. You can't imagine what it was. We were lucky, that in our immediate family, we didn't lose anybody. We nearly lost my sister. They brought her here to the hospital, and they packed her head in ice, she was so hot. Otherwise she would have had brain damage. [Annie Bailey]

You were so weak for so long afterwards, that's why we couldn't go back to school that year. A fever of one hundred and five or so, you'd have that for maybe a day or so. And you were just so weak that you didn't feel like living. It was terrible. ... There were certainly plenty of people who had it. [Charles Snively]

It was tragic. Everybody that could was out here digging graves up here in the graveyard. This tungsten miner; he had had it. He got up [out of bed] ... and was digging a grave one day and says, "Well, tomorrow you'll be digging mine." And he died. He shouldn't have been up. [Annie Bailey]

There was a big camp [for the soldiers of WWI]. ... That was a big, big army camp and when the influenza struck, the men just died. It was terrible. When Dad would come home, I remember him telling Mother how many soldiers had died. They had to bring the bodies in the caskets down to the station and put all those caskets on the train to send them to [their] homes. [Elizabeth Graham Demmon]

There wasn't much treatment. There was a doctor that would go around and prescribe medicine. I was too little to know what it was. [Annie Bailey]

None of us had flu, I'm happy to say, but I do know there were deaths all over the place. ... Schools, of course, were closed, churches, theaters, the whole bit. ... Doctor Jones ... never lost a patient. He treated his with whiskey, hot toddies, and brought them through. It was a very serious thing. [Elizabeth Wiest Farrow]

Remember there was no communications in this part of the country. Only by word of mouth and by riding to neighbors. They took care of their dead people, they took care of their sickness. We had some of the craziest remedies you can imagine. [Frank Miller]

Home Remedies

During the flu epidemic ... Dad had an idea. Somebody told him if we wore a little thing called asafetida around our necks that might help us with this flu, see. That was kind of a mystery flu, and we wore it; it smelled terrible. There was somethin' in there, and it was wrapped up just like a little, tiny package. You wore it on a little string around your neck. [Elizabeth Graham Demmon]

[Mother] took care of us here [when we got sick]. One of the things that they used to breath in was ... asafetida ... terrible, stinkin' stuff and if you wore it around your neck, you warded off these diseases. ... It was kind of like a clove. [Hazel Faivre]

I do remember the flu epidemic of World War I when so many of them died. ... Mom had quite a treatment. My dad always said that it was her treatment that she used on him that saved him, and she probably used it on herself. But I think all it was was hot cloths rung out of hot water with turpentine in it and [these cloths were] laid on their chest. I know she used it a lot. When I was a little older I could still remember the smell of turpentine. It must have been really penetrating or something, because it really did the trick. [Ruby Jackson]

I had nine sisters, and one boy. There were two of us but my brother, he died in 1940. Eleven altogether. We lost four sisters in Denver, diphtheria and scarlet fever—lost four of them. 'Course that was 'fore my time. Well, you know, those smallpox and scarlet fever, diphtheria and stuff like that. My god they didn't have no antibiotics; they didn't have nothin' for 'em, see. And you know, you just took chances, that was all. You lucky you come out of it. ... That's the fact. Today you don't realize. My mother cured more people with pneumonia with pancakes and turpentine and lard. She'd fry pancakes. Just water and flour. She'd fry 'em and put a rag on the chest here and put the pancake on there that's dipped in turpentine and lard. Put it on there and cover it over. She cured more pneumonia cases ... I never seen a doctor until I was nineteen years old. And a horse fell on me then! [Charles Perkins]

My mother used kerosene and sugar a bit. Kerosene was a real clear liquid, it was not what they have now [which] is some other kind of stuff. It isn't good kerosene. She'd put a teaspoon of sugar and put kerosene on it—several drops of it—and give it to us. We'd swallow it, and, oh, it would bring us out of it all right, but it was pretty bad. [Ena Jenner Bolton]

'Course they told about the kids at that altitude, you know, their throat would swell, and they lost a lot of young kids. This story—I don't know whether it's true or not. They told about an old fellow sellin' brass lamp burners and wicks, you know, for coal oil lights. He said, "If you get me some pure lard and black gun powder, I'll cure everyone that isn't too far gone." So he made a big swab, and he swabbed their throat with that. He did help a lot of them, they claim. It may be just a story, but it was told for the truth. [Hugh Smith]

I can't remember anybody ever getting sick. We'd get colds or something like that but, you know, the medicines they treated you with those days, you didn't dare get sick! ... I remember my mom had some kind of a bottle about six inches tall and a little, thin like a vanilla bottle, but it was some kind of cough medicine. It was the terriblist tasting stuff—oh boy! It was awful, it sure was. [John Jackson]

A woman taking care of her children was more or less thrown on her own, because you didn't call for a doctor at the drop of a hat. ... I remember,

Doctor Cattermole said (I think my brother at one time when he was quite small had pneumonia) and [Doctor Cattermole] accredited mother with having saved [my brother's] life by giving him catnip tea. ... It suppressed fever, I think. ... Kerosene [was] usually administered on sugar. Some people could take it more or less straight, I guess, but Mother used to put it on a dish of sugar. You could take it a little at a time. ... Then there was grease of all kinds: goose grease, mustard plasters. My dad had an unbelievable remedy. It was hyposulphite of soda. Now that, they tell me, was used in photographic development, and wherever he got the idea that it was a laxative, I don't know, but let me tell you it was! Castor oil was also extremely common, and you certainly didn't mention any slight illness, because the immediate response was, "Well, give a dose of castor oil." ... They made their own cures as far as they were able. [Elizabeth Wiest Farrow]

Well, of course, if we had a bad cold there was mustard plaster, and we had them several different times. ... We still use them. Allen and I were sick this winter, and we had to use mustard plasters: ... flour and ... dry mustard. Mix them up together, and then put warm water in it to make a paste. My mother used to put it on a rag. Then put another rag over the top, and then put it on your chest. ... Put the mustard on there and another paper towel over it and lay them on your chest till you get red under there, not to burn you but just till you're good and red, and then you either grease yourself with camphorated oil ... or somethin' like that. ... It really brings you out of pneumonia and all sorts of things. [Ena Jenner Bolton]

We always used a lot of greasing and that sort of thing, castor oil and all that. We didn't have Vicks then, but we had mustard oil and all those nice little burny things. 'Course years ago they always used mustard plasters, but this [mustard oil] was supposed to take the place of mustard plasters. It was real hot, and that is what they greased your chest and throat with to take away the hurt. [Gertrude Tower]

We took castor oil, though. I do remember that. And we used turpentine if you had a cold. You put turpentine and lard on your throat. I think it helped. I think turpentine may be used in some forms yet. [Edith Parker]

I remember castor oil. I hated it. Dad and Mom always put orange juice on top, and for years I couldn't eat orange juice, because I thought it tasted like castor oil. Sometimes Bill and I, my brother, had to take castor oil just 'cause we were bad, because they thought we were getting sick. So Bill and I didn't act bad very often. [Elizabeth Graham Demmon]

I can't remember having a doctor at our house very often. The only time I can remember having a doctor [come out] as far as I, myself, was concerned was when I had typhoid fever. We had a doctor then 'cause I was in bed about a month. And my dad had the measles; the doctor came then. Then Marion broke her arm, and we had to have that set. But I really can't recall the doctor being at our house very often. We weren't sick that much. [Edith Parker]

He said, "Put raw potato on this burn, raw potato to take the fire out." So my mother did, and we walked to the doctor, ... and he said, "You couldn't have done anything better than to put raw potato on that burn." [Della Friedman]

They were not specialists then, they were all family doctors, and they'd make house calls and all that sort of thing. [Anable Barr]

There was one doctor in Boulder, and the funny part of it was, he was never considered too much of a doctor. He didn't have too much of a reputation, but he hit upon the idea of people keeping a small box of Arm and Hammer Soda on the table and taking a tablespoon full of soda and water. He had better luck with his patients using Arm and Hammer Soda than any of the other doctors. [Grovenor Ketterman]

If you had a sore throat you took your sock off and you put the foot of it around your neck. That was supposed to help your sore throat. ...

So anyway, one of my children would come in. They would have a sore throat, and I'd give them a hot cup of tea. They'd come in with a stomach ache, I gave them a hot cup of tea. And if they fell off a horse and got hurt, why, I gave them a hot cup of tea and laid them down to rest. So anyway, my youngest son had a bad cartilage in his knee and had to go into the hospital for surgery ... and [a friend] asked my dad how my son was coming along. My dad said, "Well, he's still in the hospital, and I don't know just when he is going to come out." She said, "Oh my, it's a shame Gertrude couldn't have cured that with tea!" It was just plain old tea. [Gertrude Tower]

Some of the juniper berries was good for fever. ... Willow bark was food for the fever. She taught Mamma how to boil it down. ... It seems to me we had a gallon o' coal oil and a pound o' lard and a bottle o' camphorated oil, and it always set mixed together on the back of the stove and of course, the soot would get in it. When you got a cold, every kid in school I think—I don't know how we ever stood each other—but everybody had that rubbed on their chest. Soot and all would be rubbed in. That's how they would conquer the colds. ... It worked. Smelt to high heaven, but it worked. ... I think we killed the germs in the whole school with that. [Delores S. "Dee" Bailey]

Surviving Diseases and the Elements

I used to get the earache every spring, and my folks sent to Chicago for a box of—oh, they'd get teas, medicines, liniment, also food: dried fish and smoked fish. Stuff like that. They'd buy a box of stuff every year. And they had earache medicines. It said on it *Walrus Oil*. I don't know. But anyhow I used that in my ears, and I never had the earaches since. The one Hartman boy, he had an earache every spring, too. I took the medicine over to him, and it stopped his earaches, too. [Elbert "Al" Specht]

Well, I was probably about ten or twelve years old. The one [medicine man] I remember the best stayed maybe three or four or five days, nights, evenings. ... They were sellin' stuff that was s'posed to cure pain and snakebite and things like this. He had a fella [who] would get up and shout and wave and holler. One of the acts he went through, he would take a bottle, take his shoe off and put his foot up on a stool and hit hisself on the foot with this bottle just as hard as he could. You could hear it all over the lot. Then he'd immediately open this bottle, you know, and rub this medicine on it. Stand up and show his foot to everybody that it never had a bruise on it. He also had a rattlesnake that he'd let bite him. He'd get it right behind the head and hold it. Everybody could hear it rattle. He'd let it bite him, and he'd pour this medicine on and go on talking just like nothing ever happened. But the thing I think I remember the most was the way they sold this. They had three or four fellas—young fellas—two of 'em were black, and two of a 'em were white. They would run out into the audience with one bottle at a time. The stuff was sellin' for one dollar a bottle, and every time they sold a bottle they'd start "All sold out, Doctor" and run back to the stage and get another bottle. They put on quite an act. They really put on a show selling the stuff. ...

'Course nobody in our family that I know of ever bought any of it. But I don't know whether it was any good. Whether it was water or what was in it, but he had a real good act. The snake had probably bit him so many times it probably didn't even have teeth. It was fun. It was something to do and everybody'd go up to the medicine show. [Charles Waneka]

When we'd get a real bad cold my dad would make us a hot toddy, or we used mentholatum and a mustard plaster. For smallpox we didn't take anything as I recall. [Mabel Andre Thomas]

I remember in those days diphtheria and scarlet fever and smallpox were terrible. When they'd have those scares, they'd put this powdered chlorine in the toilets, and that smell I always associated with the time I was up there. It kind of reminded me of death. [Irvin Demmon]

I remember the people that lived there. ... The woman was pregnant, and I remember we went to visit her one day, my mother, my grandmother and I. She was in labor, and my grandmother delivered the baby, but the baby was dead. I can remember helping wash dishes and clean and stuff, because they were very, very poor. Worse off than we were, and I thought, "What poor people. They don't have anything." I know that they were living there for a very short time probably to work beets or whatever. The baby was born dead or died shortly after birth. ... My grandmother took care of everything. ... They put the baby in a little box. [Roseann Ortega]

I had a doctor when my two youngsters were born, and I also had what was called a midwife. She was a neighbor woman, and that's all that she did. I also had a hired girl that took care of the washing and so on. Of course, after the baby was born the midwife stayed and took care of the baby and took care of me. ... Anywhere from ten days to two weeks was what they were asked to stay in bed then. That was what was considered you should stay in bed. Most of the [babies] were breast-fed. ... When I was a youngster ... every family in the neighborhood— I think the least would be three or four children from that up to ten [children]. [Nell N. Jones]

Before, [girls] didn't go around telling everybody they were pregnant, that's for sure. When people found out that was all right, but [girls] didn't make any fuss about it. They just didn't do it. They thought it was soon enough when it showed. And there were clothes that were more or less proper. ... I didn't stay in [during pregnancy], but I didn't announce it. I didn't even tell my mother for a long time. I thought there was time enough for them to worry about it. [Edith Parker]

Hospitals

In fact, when I had my adenoids taken out, it was on the kitchen table at home. [Dorothy Allen Greene]

I had to have my tonsils removed when I was about five or six, and where did I have them removed? I was on the dining-room table in our dining room, and this doctor from Kansas City came, and our local doctor was there and my father. [Mabel Edmondson]

I remember my mother, who had a great interest in medical things, used to watch the operations [tonsillectomies] as her children had their throats slashed open. She really wanted to be a doctor, but she had to settle to be a physical education teacher, because the medical education was so difficult for women in those days. [Franklin Folsom]

And I remember Mrs. Hartman used to ride horseback. In the middle of the night she'd get a call that someone was about to be delivered, and she would get on her horse and go deliver that baby, because there were no doctors. So you see the women around here were pretty sturdy, and they were always ready to help. ...

The first hospital I can remember was down across the railroad tracks. A very dear woman, Anna Fender, she had this little hospital and later on she bought a big house, the old Gilbert house. She made a hospital out of it. That's right where part of the parking spot is for the courthouse. She was such a wonderful person, and during the flu and everything like that she never gave up. We just loved Anna Fender. The first I can remember was in 1909. [Mabel Edmondson]

Boulder County Hospital was originally called the Boulder County Poor Farm. If you had to go to the poor farm, that was bad news for the ego. ... They didn't have nursing homes or rest homes. ... They were single people, whose spouses died, and they weren't able to manage at home any more. ... You'd go by, and you could see all those old troops in front of the Poor Farm. ... That was clear out in the country. [Dorothy Woodbury]

It was a hospital, but you came to get the good Boulder air, and they believed in a lot of hot packs and things like that. And it was a nice place to come and spend your summer. You didn't have to be sick like you are now to be in a hospital, you could just come, and if you weren't feeling well you could come. ... It was a nice place if you lived in Texas or Chicago to spend a nice cool summer, and you probably had to come with a little tendency for tuberculosis or something, but you could stay as long as you wanted. [Elizabeth Graham Demmon]

The Chautauqua was full of those wooden-bottomed, canvas-topped tents where people stayed. Many of them did come indeed for their health. The sanitarium was so called, because it did take many of these people largely from Texas, but there were sanitariums all around. ... The yard was dotted with these little cottages where people stayed. Cold air, fresh air, was supposed to be the cure. ... Mom said she went up there [sometimes] and a woman had a little boy, ... and the child's diaper would be frozen. So they believed in cold air. ... It's supposed to be a very healthy climate. [Elizabeth Wiest Farrow]

Natural Hazards

Snow and Wind

The snow of 1913, April 1913, everything stopped. People sort of beat a path, which dropped maybe a foot below the top of the drifts, which were four or five feet high. There has never been one since like that. Everything was tied up, of course. [Frances Thompson Mabee Waldrop]

I was five years old. ... I can remember getting up in the morning and the house was dark. I couldn't figure that out. ... The snow was piled up against the windows. You couldn't see out. ... Oh, my, that snow was a long time in going away. [Amy Sherman Cushman]

I can remember walking on the sidewalk with the snow equal to my height [about six years old]. That was a real big one! [Ruby Roney]

I do remember the 1913 snowstorm and my dad having to go out the transom over the door. ... He went out, and he shoveled snow to get to the wood shed so we could get some fuel, see. I was a little kid. I wasn't very big and thirteen foot was a lot of snow. [Roy Fling]

Yes, we lived there at that big blizzard, and I can remember those drifts. We couldn't even see the fences. No, we didn't get to school or anywhere. We didn't get anywhere. [Cleo Turner Tallman]

I was four, and I can very plainly remember that my dad and brother had dug out a path, and all you could see was snow. That's all. ... I can remember that snowstorm just as plain as can be. Walking around that house following Dad and my older brother Jim, he was eight years older than I was, and I can remember all in the world I could see was solid white. Oh, that was some blizzard. ... There was this old guy down there south of Hygiene; it took him, what did he tell us, seven hours to get home, four or five blocks, ... seven hours. ... Just crawl on that snow, crawl on, crawl on. ... Oh, that was some storm. [Glenn Tallman]

We were there the year of the big snow, and we were snowed in. One of my cousins who lived up the road, he finally got down to us. ... He came and shoveled us out. We had to get to the toilet. So he did that and brought us coal and kinda looked after us until they got the roads cleared and everything. [Wanda Burch Armstead]

It took my father and my uncle five days to get to Hygiene, which was three miles away. They were working with horses. One team we had, whenever they'd get tired they would just lay down and wallow in the snow, and then they could move a little faster when they got up again. That's how they got to Hygiene to get the groceries. ... How do you clear five feet of snow from the road?. ... My father made an A with a couple of big boards—I imagine one-by-twelves or two-by-twelves ... and made it in a V shape and hitched the horses to that and shoveled the rest of it. That was the only way they could get through. They had four horses working, so it was a lot of work. [Irene Smith Lybarger]

I can also remember the big snow storms that we used to have from 1913 to the latter '20s. The Miller boys ... used to come up the highway with a snowaway trying to break a lane in the highway. They would have eighteen to twenty horses. In some places the snow was up to the horses' stomach. They would be jumping trying to get the snowaway up the highway. Other people who had to get to town had to make themselves some snowshoes out of boards and straps across the ankles. [John James]

'Thirteen, that's when we hit the big snow. Five feet in January. We stayed down here, and I remember that teacher wouldn't let no kids go home, and Dad Crane got there, I don't remember, it was along in the middle of the night. [With] four horses, a sled. Took the kids all home with him. Let the folks worry that night, and then the next day he started deliverin' 'em. 'Course I don't think the folks worried about the kids then like they do now. What the heck—lost a few of the old, make a few more! [Ernie Ross]

We had a Shetland pony, and my sister and I drove out to school. ... Long about the middle of the month, it was about two weeks before Christmas, it started snowing ... and kept on snowing. When they let school out, there was about three foot of snow so we started out with the pony. I knew she would never make it clear up to our place, so I says, "We will just stop at Grandpa's house and put the pony in there." And that's what we did. We was there for two weeks 'fore we ever got home. Ended up with four foot of snow. My parents were just greatly worried, you know, and Dad says, "They'll stop at Granddad's; you just be sure." Well, the next morning he manufactured a couple of skis out of a couple of boards, and he skied down to Niwot and there we were in Granddad's house. Never got home for over two weeks. [Allen Bolton]

In 1913, we had a real heavy snow. The fences were all covered. And my dad made us some skis so my brother and my older sister and I had skis. We took the other children on the back of [our skis] ... so we had to ... be in step in order to go to school on skis. It was quite a thing. We went a mile across the field, because everything was frozen so we took a shortcut across the field, we didn't have to go on the road. But it was quite a thing to get the little ones to step when we did. It was mostly short steps and sliding. They enjoyed it, that was for sure. We didn't know what a ski pole was, we just used a stick. My father made the skis out of one-by-fours, and then he put a piece of metal onto the front of them so we wouldn't be sticking them into the snow all the time. He shaped [the metal] so that it was turned up. [Irene Smith Lybarger]

The big blizzard of 1913. Mother went to school there. The older brother cut up an old barrel, took a barrel apart, and they used those [boards] for skis.

They'd put those barrel staves on their feet, and then they'd just walk across the fences and everything else going to school. [Howard Morton]

Lot of snow. I remember when Mrs. Tyrer was teachin' we had a big storm that winter. I wanted to go to school, because she had somethin goin' ... [and] I was puttin' a lot of effort into [school]. ... I didn't want to miss school, 'cause I'd be absent, you know, and somebody'd get ahead of me. So there was three days we couldn't go. So finally my dad took me the third day, but nobody came to school those three days, so I didn't miss anything. Nobody came. It was deep snow. [Earl Logan]

One person asked me, she said, "Well Ray, does the wind blow up here in Wallstreet?" You see, they were flatlanders. ... They were curious. And she asked the question, "Does the wind blow up here in Wallstreet?" Well, anybody around here knows what the wind is like. ... Does the wind blow in Wallstreet? I didn't laugh at her, you know, but in all seriousness - "Does the wind blow up here in Wallstreet?" And I says, "Does the wind blow up here in Wallstreet?" I says, "Well, I've seen a hen with its tail to the wind lay the same egg five times!!" That answered the question! [Raymond Friese]

I remember the wind blowing. You ran from tree to tree as you were coming home from school to hang on. Being pretty small, the wind blew me pretty badly. ... The trees all had their branches on the east side. No branches grew on the west side. The wind was born in Caribou. [Ruby Roney]

You might not believe this but this is a true story. There was a bunch of us working at the Comstock Mine at Caribou. That's right up on top of the mountain, and the wind blows awful hard there. ... We stayed up at the mine durin' the week and on the weekend we would come down. Durin' the evening we didn't have much to do so one of the fellas built a little windmill. We had a big square table that we used to eat on—we had to do our own cookin' there—and we fastened it to the corner of the table, and that windmill never stopped turnin' for six months just from the wind that blew through the keyhole. [Russell Flarty]

I remember one night the wind blew out the windows on the west side of the dining room. [It] blew the books and bookends off the library table and went through and blew through the living room and the dining room and blew out the east windows on the east side. ... We had some really severe winds. [Marian Cook March]

I remember one time while they were building [our house], they had built a little frame building—it was probably like a garage now—that we lived in while they were building the house, and we had just moved into the big house when one of our nice Boulder wind storms came up and took that little frame house and knocked it down to kindling wood. Took it out over the open field. [Rosena Hall]

We had a bad windstorm. It blew the freight cars off the track at Marshall. It must have been around 1912 or sooner. I was out at the coal mine to get a load of coal that day the wind hit. They had a little mine there in Marshall that had a mule there that pulled the coal out the tunnel of the mine … and the wind got blowin' so hard they couldn't pull their cars up, you know. And I was waitin' my turn. … Finally I decided I'd just go home. Wind wasn't goin' quit. Oh it was blowin'. … I took the seat and put it down in the bottom of the floor of the wagon. Tied the lines around the dashboard knob and sit down on the floor of the wagon myself. Turned the horses loose 'cause they were an old team, could depend on them. At the foot of Shanahan Hill the road was kind of up graded there a bit, and the wind just blew the wagon around. Pulled the wagon and horses off down the side of the road. Didn't blow us over or anything. Then it come up again. … Just before I pulled in the yard the wind quit. Just like that. Just stopped. I had a bicycle. I jumped on my bicycle, and there were several telephone poles down [on] the [street]. They had braces against the telephone poles. I rode down Shanahan Hill. I counted seventeen poles blowin' down in spite of the braces, and the wires were blown off the fences. Just pulled the staples out. Boy, that was the worst windstorm I have ever seen. [Elbert "Al" Specht]

Fire and Floods

At Caribou, the first time [the town] burnt, the wind was a hundred miles an hour and my mother was livin' at New Cardinal, that's a little town—it's gone now—right below about a mile or half a mile from Caribou. They were dynamitin' a building out to leave a gap to try to stop the fire from comin' on down, and she said burnin' planks sailed right over their house. [Hugh Smith]

In the very early days, the fighting of fires in Boulder was accomplished by a bucket brigade. A line of people would form from the nearest water supply to the fire. … This was a very inefficient way to fight a fire. … By 1875, the town of Boulder had built its first water system with fireplugs scattered over the community. Now it was possible to use fire hoses rather than to employ a bucket brigade to fight fires. [Sandford Gladden]

I remember these two horses … from the fire department. In those days the harness was hung overhead and the horses—the bell would ring, you know, and the horses would go in there. The harness would drop down and the firemen, all they would have to do is buckle the harness and go, you see. These horses would do that at the ring of the bell, you see. ... There's no way of stoppin' them; they was goin' to that fire. [Roy Fling]

In our hotel—when we was [living] in the hotel—we had lamps. ... We got gas later. ... I can remember us kids was all crowded into one room, and my sister slept in that room with a girl that helped us. The girl ... was late goin' to bed. She had a candle in the room. There was no lamp in there. She forgot to blow out the candle, and the candle burned down, you know, and set the things on the table on fire. It wasn't bad, but the smoke woke her up. I remember my dad runnin' down and gettin' water and puttin' out the fire. [Ina Gerry Wild]

I don't know whether [the courthouse fire was because of] poor wiring or what, but I don't recall what had set it afire. I think they had plenty of time to get out. ... I was in junior high up here, and when school was out we looked down and saw this smoke coming up. So we ran down. ... It would have been around '29. So we kids all ran down, and I remember they were telling us to throw rocks at the windows. They were telling us to break the windows to get the water in or something. But I remember thinking, "Imagine, we're throwing rocks at the courthouse and breaking the windows, and it's okay." You see we were law-abiding kids in those days. Yes, that fire I remember! [The Boulder County Courthouse fire was on February 9, 1932] [M. Helen Carpenter]

We were in school when the ... courthouse burned, and that afternoon when school was out several mothers drove us over. We stood right across the street ... and watched this building burn. It burned until the point where they had to tear it down. They said it started up in the clock tower somehow. They had no real precautions in those days for fire and a lot of the Boulder city and county records were burned. They weren't in vaults or anything. They learned their lessons that way. I know there was a tremendous amount of smoke. ... Oh yes, there were ten thousand people down there watching that thing burn. It burned away until the night when they finally put it out. [Pete Franklin]

In 1919 we had one of the worst floods in this part of the country that I have ever seen. ... [Coal Creek and Rock Creek] converged down there. It washed out seven or eight houses. ... It lasted for about three days or three days and a half. We didn't get our cows across the crick from over on the [other] side. ... You couldn't come from Boulder east. ... My son happened to be born during that storm, and the doctor had to come from Boulder to deliver him. We couldn't get to the hospital—in fact you didn't go to the hospital for those kinds of things in those days—but the doctor had to go through Niwot [and] come across Boulder Crick over here in order to get to Lafayette. ... I've seen two floods like that in my time, and I hope I never see another. [Frank Miller]

The whole thing was flooded by the depot, but I don't remember the year. But where the town house apartments were, the whole basement was flooded. See it came right down Walnut Street. The Chamber of Commerce building used to be there, and that all flooded and came down Boulder Canyon. We had water in the town house, and we had to bail water out and everything. The water came down Pearl Street and all through there. There was a lot of open space where it spread out. It went by Central Park. [Edna Morrato]

We used to go swimmin' down in Boulder Crick—Twenty-eighth and Arapahoe. ... Talk about floods in Boulder, we had a bridge there, 'course the bridges was all wooden in them days. I saw the wooden bridge wash out two times in floods on Twenty-eighth Street, and then they put in a steel bridge, twelve-inch girders goin' across the length of the bridge—twelve-inch I-beams—and the flood washed that out. It just twisted them into knots, the steel girders, that's how powerful the water was. [Elbert "Al" Specht]

A hobo jungle north of Boulder during the Depression, ca. 1930. Photo by Ed Tangen.
Carnegie Branch Library for Local History, Boulder Historical Society Collection.

CHAPTER ELEVEN
COPING WITH THE TIMES

As powerful as the weather was, it could not cause as great an impact on people's lives as did Prohibition (1920–1933) and the Great Depression of 1929. After years of fighting, temperance groups finally persuaded the United States government to enact a law prohibiting the manufacture, transport and sale of alcoholic beverages, a law that remained on the books for thirteen years. Although prohibitionists argued that alcohol had a debilitating effect on the human mind, it was not until they claimed that it was unpatriotic to use grain to make liquor during World War I that the government approved the Eighteenth Amendment to the Constitution in 1917, and three-quarters of the states approved it by 1919. Shortly after the war ended, the law took effect. But no sooner had the measure passed than citizens felt it took away one of their individual rights and immediately began making bootleg liquor, a very dangerous drink made with industrial alcohol. Underground gangs began acquiring and selling huge amounts of liquor. Speakeasies, or illegal bars, began to sell the homemade brew, and the very fact that liquor was against the law, drew people to these bars. Women, who previously were not known to have drunk much alcohol, began joining their spouses with gusto. Prohibition seemed to cause more harm than good, and when the Great Depression of 1929 began, it was argued that if liquor could be sold again, it could be taxed, thus bringing in a large revenue for the government. In 1933, the Twenty-first Amendment was passed, repealing the Eighteenth Amendment and ending Prohibition.

Prohibition changed lives; the Great Depression changed lives. In October, 1929 stockholders suffered huge losses, sending Wall Street into a crash that was felt around the world. Investors lost everything overnight, and many businesses and banks closed, putting millions of Americans out of work. The government stepped in with various programs to provide jobs for those unemployed and charity for the poor, thus escalating government's influence on the national economy. Franklin D.

Roosevelt encouraged Congress to establish the Civilian Conservation Corps (CCC) in 1933 in order to create employment in conservation projects. The National Recovery Administration (NRA) established fair-practice laws for businesses. The Public Works Administration (PWA) gave jobs to those who could build bridges, dams and schools. The Works Progress Administration (WPA) created jobs for men constructing highways and other public projects (1935). And, finally, in 1935 the Social Security Act was passed providing money for the unemployed and the retired.

Not all people suffered equally during the Great Depression, however. Those who could keep their jobs and those on small farms who grew most of their own food, found prices actually lower than in the 1920s. They found a willingness among neighbors and friends to help each other that surpassed earlier ties. There was a pulling together, a closeness never before felt.

Prohibition

When Boulder was in its early days, there was Prohibition. ... My grand-mother was always very much against any form of alcohol except beer, because she had seen and helped families of men who had come in and spent all their money on liquor. I think a great many of the pioneer women were like that. [Charlotte Seymour]

My father ... was active in support of Prohibition. He saw the damage that liquor had done in Boulder. We were so close to the mining areas and saw what devastation alcohol had worked. They didn't have any understanding of what the causes of alcoholism was at that time. They thought the best thing to do was to put alcohol out of existence, but of course, it didn't work. [Franklin Folsom]

During the Prohibition days under the Volstead Act the possession of alcoholic beverage was a felony—a felony, one year in the penitentiary! And you were scared to death you'd be caught. So when we went to Louisville to get some booze, we'd get it in a gallon jug and let a guy sit in front and take the floorboards out, so if we got stopped, or anything, the guy would hit this thing with the hammer, and it would all go down on the concrete, on the road. And then you got a fine for breaking glass on the highway instead of a felony. So that's the crazy—ah, it was a lousy period, a lousy period ... terrible. Everybody drank just like they do today, but they ran them underground. It was a lousy period. It proved to be unsatisfactory. You can see it built up the mobs, it was the beginning of organized crime in the country. Only thing comparable today is the drug traffic. [J. H. Kingdom]

There was a lot of bootleggers then [during Prohibition], and they would come in from Louisville. They were tough. They were *Eye-talians*, and they'd beat us poor boobs up and take our girlfriends. They had nice, fancy cars, and we had nothin'. ... Model A ... or Model Ts, all fixed up. [Hugh Smith]

Those [coal miner] fellas were not what you call big bootleggers. They had a small still, and they just—to augment their income [during the summer when they didn't work] till they could work in the mines. That was all. It was during Depression days, things were hard, they had families. ... I think mining camps have always been known for hard drinking. [Joseph Malcolm]

Prohibition, yeah. Had Prohibition all right. They had liquor everyplace. I used to hire a truck in the 1920s in the Black Diamond Mine ... and I was haulin' coal in to Boulder and after a couple of years, why, the two guys who had the contract to deliver the coal quit. ... The coal business had changed. They were startin' to ship in coal by railroad from bigger mines. Quinlan, he liked his liquor pretty well. One night he come by the house. It was snowin' to beat the dickens, and says he got a car over at ... the corner of Baseline and Thirty-first. So I went over and pulled them out. After I pulled them out they put a gallon jug in the truck. He says, "Here, take this for your troubles." A gallon of moonshine. They'd been out to Louisville and was bringin' in some moonshine to friends in town. The guy with him was ... an agent. He was helpin' with the liquor! Great old days! ... I kept that gallon for years. I gave it away, I never drank it. [Elbert "Al" Specht]

[My father] made whiskey and hauled it to the coal miners and traded it. See back in ... the Depression time, people didn't buy and sell so much, they traded things. Everything was on a barter system. [Jack Rowley]

Some people captured a still up by Allenspark ... in 1933, and the sheriff called on me if I'd go up and haul it down. Called up one night about midnight. So I says, "Okay." So I goes up there. ... They said to go on ahead, they would come up behind me and get there about the time I did. When I left Boulder I noticed a car pass me, and before I got to Lyons the car passed me again. It was no traffic in them days at that time of night, you know. Appeared to be the same car. I didn't pay too much attention to it until I got up above Lyons. I noticed the car parked up a side road. Why I happened to glance there, I don't know but I did. Down the road awhile ... further, the car passed me again. It seemed to be the same car. ... It passed me three more times. It passed me just after I turned into the gates of this ranch. I had to get out and open the gate, wire gate. After I opened the gate here this car come by me again. Well, I got to thinkin' that's sure funny. I drove down into the ranch. I got down there and was sittin' in the truck waitin'. Turned on the radio. Had to wait about an hour. Nobody showed up so I thought, "Well heck, might as well look around to see what they've got to haul back." So I got out of the truck. Somethin' jumped on my back— a great, big, ol' German shepherd dog. He was tickled pink to see somebody, but it scared me. It was dark, so we got friendly, and I went in and found the still. Whole bunch of kegs and barrels and pretty soon here they come, you know. And they loaded up the still; the biggest still they ever found, I guess. There's a picture of it in the courthouse yet—at least they had a picture there for years. … But anyhow, comin' down, Bill Kight, he rode with me, he was deputy. He liked his liquor pretty well so he was feelin' pretty good. He had a bottle of that moonshine. He wanted to test it out to see how good it was. They left a gallon under the backseat. They stuck it in there for me. We had around, it seems to me, five or six hundred gallons of liquor on that truck. It was a big still. But comin' back anyhow, the same car passed me different times. I was beginnin' to get a bad feel about it thinkin' I was goin' to be hijacked. So when I left Lyons, I figured if they was goin' to try somethin' there was one spot between Boulder and Lyons where they'd try it on account of the roads, you know. Try to run me in the ditch or somethin.' When I got close to that, they come to pass me again. I never let 'em by. I'd just pull out. They followed me into town, and that's what I heard afterwards. That's what they was goin' to do. They was goin' to hijack the truck. [Elbert "Al" Specht]

I happened to be on the city council. I made a few raids with the different officers. We would make a raid, break up the gang, and then the next week they'd set up someplace else. They did make their own home brew, their own liquor and sold it as bootleg. We went through quite a spell here in 1922 or '23. [Frank Miller]

Boulder had a lot more bootlegging than [they'd admit to]. … They all had stills. Marshall was one of the main places. … Tommy … was goin' to high school, and he had a great big bank account. His mother wondered how he got ahold of it, and he said, "Ah, they made a mistake!" The son-of-a-gun, he was down there in one of them holes makin' whiskey nights. He was sellin' it wholesale to some bootleggin' outfit. He'd sell it five, six gallons at a time. That was in '24, '25, '26. … Colorado was dry. … It went dry in 1916. [Elwood Barber]

I was going to school at University Hill and the neighbor came in the house and said, "Lets go to school," and I said, "I can't do it. I've got a little job." He says, "What are you doing?" I said, "I'm capping some home brew for my mother." He says, "Oh, I'll wait; I'll wait." [Bauldie Moschetti]

Just put water, and we got a can of hops and blue-ribbon malt. … You had to wait; you couldn't drink it right away you had to … let it age, but some of the boys would go drink it out of the crock. I said, "Don't drink that, I'll give you some of the good one!" [Gentina Moschetti]

I remember the day Prohibition came off, and they opened up the saloons. Everybody had a big time. [Joseph Malcolm]

The Depression

The Depression—goodness, that's almost current history! My youngest child was born at that time, and she's about sixty now. [Frances Thompson Mabee Waldrop]

I remember there was a flurry of excitement ... among the guests [of the hotel]. Lots of phone calls and everything, and the crash came that October in 1929. [Alberta Nicholson]

'Course the crash of '29 was very difficult times and a lot of people had their money in the Niwot State Bank. It ultimately went broke, and some of the farmers and the local people in Niwot area lost, if not all of their holdings, a sizeable amount of their holdings. I had all my life savings there. I was only just a little kid, but I had twenty-six dollars there, and you'd a thought it was a million dollars! [Howard Morton]

When people learned that there were banks closing hither and yonder, they'd hear it on the radio or read it in the paper. Then there would be a rush on the banks, and everybody'd go in and want to draw their money out. Many of the banks folded. ... I've seen queues of people at banks two or three blocks long trying to get in to get their money. [C. Clarence Waneka]

I know a few banks went under. ... One bank ... see I was workin' for the mayor of Boulder at the Imperial [Tea Company]. ... He was the vice president of the National State Bank and ... when they had a run on that bank ... people would come in and want their money. Then they'd go down and put it in postal savings. Postal savings would bring it right back and put it in the bank again, because they wasn't equipped. [Hugh Smith]

We didn't have any money in the bank to worry about the closure of it. We didn't have anything to lose, because we didn't have any money. My husband was earning twelve-fifty every two weeks, that would be twenty-five dollars a month at one place and about—oh, I don't think we had an income of more than seventy-five dollars a month. Our rent was twelve-fifty, and our lights and gas were much cheaper, of course. [Della Friedman]

Well, I can recall when I first got out of college, ... [I] tried to get a job teaching, and jobs were very rare. But I did finally find a job. They paid me seventy dollars a month for nine months. In other words, I taught for six hundred and thirty dollars a year. ... Of course, that seventy dollars a month was worth seventy dollars then. [C. Clarence Waneka]

During that period of time we had what we called the dirty thirties, when we had the big Depression and all of the dust bowl here. There was farms up here on Gunbarrel Hill where the fences were completely covered up with dust. [Howard Morton]

165

It wasn't so bad in this area [during the dust bowl years]. We had droughts, there is no doubt. The crops were limited. The big problem, of course, during that Depression era was the fact that the crops weren't worth anything. They couldn't sell their livestock; they couldn't sell wheat. Milk was a glut on the market. I can recall that at that time you could buy milk for a nickel a gallon. ... Some of the people [lost their farms]. [C. Clarence Waneka]

I can remember my mother and father talking about how hard it was for them to get money to buy groceries [for their grocery store], because in those days people didn't pay cash for groceries. My dad had lots and lots of credit, and people just couldn't pay their bills on time. Lots of times Dad had to carry people for quite large sums. People would usually get paid once a month, something like that. The only thing that I really think about of the Depression was that times were difficult, because [my parents] were having a hard time collecting money in the store. That just continued almost as long as my father had a grocery store, because he always carried people on time. [Alberta Nicholson]

They used to have a little tablet like this, and everybody who bought groceries—the things they got they wrote down on there and the price. Then they gave you a slip, and the grocer kept a slip. Then when the end of the month came, payday, you came in, and you paid for your groceries according to this thing, and the grocer gave you the little booklet. Of course, in the Depression, a lot of those people didn't pay for awhile. They couldn't pay. Then later on they got cars, and they went to Longmont to buy groceries ... all those receipts and bills that were never paid to my dad. That's how come he went bust. [Cecilia "Sallee" Gorce]

Dad was still in the store, but Dad lost a lot of money, you see all his investments went. It just hit us real hard. Dad died that year, in 1932 in May, and it was the very week I was graduating from college. [Elizabeth Graham Demmon]

This particular neighborhood, I can't say that [the Depression] really affected this neighborhood a lot except a lot of the little businesses began to go in and out. I think that was the time you saw less and less stability in people. They became more mobile. We had a shifting of a kind in the neighborhood. The young people would get jobs and move away, though I don't think Boulder felt the Depression like they did in lots of other places. We felt the Depression probably more in terms of what you could do. You learned to do without. You learned to make your own fun, for instance. That type of thing. But churches went on, schools went on, businesses went on, everybody pulled up the slack a little bit. ... I did hear a lot of young people saying they couldn't find a job. [Frances Bascom]

I remember Boulder during the days of the Depression, because I have often thought since that Boulder would probably have become a ghost town if it had not been for the University. The University was about the only thing that was a going concern during the Depression, and of course, people came to the University to go to school. ... Many, many people left Boulder, and lots of businesses closed. ...

On the campus, of course, we had cuts in salaries right across the board. Many schools just dropped a lot of their faculty, but here they said, "We're going to try to keep everybody, but everybody has to take a cut." Raises were completely out of the question. ... Finally, they said it would be [a] fifteen percent [cut]. [John B. Schoolland]

[Depression] really didn't affect our family, because we were raised that if we didn't have the money to buy something, we didn't get it. My folks never had a grocery charge bill. They always had a credit coming from the butter and eggs that they took over to trade. My mother did all our sewing. We had a new dress for Christmas, and we had a new dress for Easter. Prices went down, but what we bought went down, too. We all lived well. We never went hungry. We'd butcher a calf or a pig, and we'd put the meat down for the winter. We just didn't spend money if we didn't have it. [Mabel Andre Thomas]

Of course, my family having the farm, they weren't hungry. They had milk cows, ... they had gardens and fruit trees. They really didn't suffer like people who were off the farms. They had enough to eat. Very few people had money. [C. Clarence Waneka]

We'd always take our case of eggs into town, you know, and trade them for groceries. [John Axelson]

We had fifty chickens, which we would keep and use as fryers. They had eggs [that] we took over and traded for feed or something else. You did a lot of barter trade. ... [Our neighbors] ... had a cow. We had fresh milk from that cow, and we would trade eggs for the milk. [Frances Bascom]

My folks moved in from the country, and a lot of the different working people in the family lost their work. There was eight children in the family. ... We got hungry, but Mamma made corn bread. We dug great big pans full of dandelions in the summer. We had dandelion greens and corn bread; we ate it every day, because that was what we had to eat, and it tasted very good when you're hungry. Then in the wintertime Mamma baked bread, and we had homemade bread and coffee. That was all we had. She used to joke about it. ... She'd say, "Do you want coffee and bread, or bread and coffee?" and we'd argue about which one we wanted, you know. I weighed ninety-eight pounds when I graduated from the ninth grade, because I was hungry. [Father] was making, I think, thirteen cents a week when he did work, but lots of times he wasn't able to work. [Ena Jenner Bolton]

Back during the Depression, when there wasn't any meat or anything, every once in awhile she would come up with a piece of deer meat in her cooler outside. She usually knew [by] the way it was wrapped who it was from. 'Course she never told who it was from; just cooked it and enjoyed it, but that was one way of paying for your tobacco. So, if you had butter you could trade it. … She'd sell butter to somebody that didn't have it. She'd give you salmon or whatever else you wanted or needed like sugar or whatever you happened to need. Oh, a pound of butter was a dime; sugar was ten cents a pound, too, and everybody congregated there for mail, three times a week, which was Tuesdays, Thursdays, and Saturdays. She usually sat in that east window where she could see the store and the post office. Anybody'd come, they'd just go up on the porch. If they weren't in a hurry, they'd just run in and talk to Grandma for a little while. It wasn't anything like what it is here now. Grandma never saw a stranger, and if there was anything doin' everybody was invited. Everybody, I don't know everybody liked everybody else, and there was never any of this clannish clique that they have here now—that this one won't talk to that one, and somebody else won't talk to somebody else, and— fiddlesticks! If they'd learn to live by the code of the hills, they'd be a lot better off, and that's: You treat everybody just the same as you'd like to be treated. No, that's the way it always was. … You helped everybody; everybody helped you. [Maude Washburn Wagner]

The Depression hit us rather hard, but it was an integrated community. There was not much hardship here. Some of the people in the mountains reverted to using wild game rather than be known as people on the dole or a breadline or accepting charity. They were that type of people. Very independent. Particularly the hard-rock people in the mountains. Most everybody in those days hunted and fished for recreation. [D. M. "Dock" Teegarden]

They were mostly miners up here. They were a different breed of people I would say. In those days, why it used to be if you needed help, you had help. If you had a loaf of bread you shared it with somebody that didn't. The neighbors were just—well, nobody had anything, and you didn't have anything so you shared what you had. [Delores S. "Dee" Bailey]

Well, I don't think the people up here actually had it any rougher than they did anyplace else. Maybe not quite as bad, because they did have, you know, some of their own stock and that kind of stuff. Then there was always the possibility of going out and gettin' somethin' else to eat like wild meat or somethin' like that. I do know that one of the guys on WPA that worked there—they were workin' on the road out north of town—and he didn't have anything but potato peelings in his bucket. I know [when] you say that, people say, "Ah what the hell." But that's all he had. You know, a lot of times we would have more in our bucket than the guys that were living in town. [Sanford Wagner]

COPING WITH THE TIMES

There was one woman over here. She even came and shot herself. She couldn't stand it. She killed herself, a suicide. And her husband made one hundred dollars a month, that was good wages in them days. She wasn't satisfied. I was always happy-go-lucky, never worried too much. That's what my kids always said; I never worried too much. "Well," I said, "those who worried too much, that's it." Well, I know, some people had to have everything convenient. That woman, you see, she never got used to it, you know. She told all the neighbors around here that she hated to live [here]. You know, she was used to all modern in town. All at once she had shot herself one night, when [her husband] was workin' night shift. [Elna Craig]

We always had three meals a day. We never missed a meal. It didn't cost you a fortune to eat in them days. You could live on a dollar then where you couldn't live on five dollars today. [Charles Perkins]

Prices disappeared. Things were free. A hamburger was five cents when I was a freshman in college. A cup of coffee was a penny, a candy bar was a penny, and a room to rent was five dollars a month. So we were richer as a family ... because the prices went down. ... We didn't have a problem with shelter, or clothing, or food, or [to] go to school. [Howard Higman]

I remember paying less than a dollar for shoes most of my life until I was married, which was 1916. I think I never had a pair of shoes that cost more than a dollar, and they were high shoes with buttons. Money meant something, you got something for it. When I came to the University, first you could get a good meal for fifteen cents and a quarter was just more than you were supposed to pay. [Hester Phillips]

I started out to earn a little bit of money, because money was tight, you know. You had to see it to believe what it was like. Anyway, I started out to earn a little bit of money. I used to sweep the shop out and used to deliver shoes on a bicycle. Back then I used to go all over town on a bicycle delivering shoes. A pair of lady's shoes then was twenty-five cents a pair, but still you would deliver, you know. That was your service. ...

They made shoes then [in the '30s]. They had a shoe they called "Friendly Five", and they made a shoe for five dollars. You could buy new shoes for five dollars, and it was made correctly with leather insole. It was a good shoe, and we'd charge to put on a pair of leather soles and heels a dollar and fifty cents. Today we charge to do that job, thirty-five dollars. [George Perry]

That's when the farmers was all broke, you know—in Roosevelt's time. That's when most of the businessmen was broke, too. That [was when] just about everybody was broke. In 1932, and from '28 to 1932 it was really rough. You couldn't buy a job. Nobody had much money. ... You could rent a whole three-room basement like this for ten dollars a month, see. You'd go down here with five dollars and buy enough to last you a week. Eggs was twelve cents a dozen. [Oscar Faye]

I remember talking to my dad about the Depression and he said, ... "I made more money than anybody in town bein' a druggist at that time. Thirty-five dollars a week." That was a lot of money, I guess. [Frank Streamer]

I and my sister came out here in 1929. ... The folks moved out here. That was the Great Depression you know and the folks lost their farm. They moved out here to live with my older sister. ... I'll tell you it was rough. Twenty-five cents an hour was all we got for housework and worked eight hours. No coffee breaks, no nothin'. ... There was no work for men really, so Mother and I were the only ones in that household that worked. We usually got a roast for Sunday dinner, that was all. The rest was soups, chili, and things like that. Dad was on WPA for awhile. ... They're very proud people. Nobody goes to welfare, you know. We don't go along with that. My husband and I were married in 1934, and in 1935 he had his first job. He was a coal miner before. ... He went into the coal mine when he was fourteen years old. His mother signed him so he could work. ... He was a worker, that guy. Hardly ever missed a day of work. [Alma Nielson Scohy]

The lucky ones were the ones that worked for the government, because they weren't worried about losing their jobs. [Della Friedman]

They enabled an employer to employ more men, because they only had to pay sixty dollars a month for them, and more people could have jobs. WPA—Works Progress Association [ed: Works Projects Administration]—in which they worked on roads and things like that. It was paid for by the federal government. All the local government had to do was provide the plans and maybe the overseers and stuff like that. Under NRA I worked at the service station. [Robert Gruen]

The WPA had a program that put men to work building roads with shovels. 'Course that was a very inefficient way of doing it, but it did employ people. Nelson Road was graded by men working with shovels and trucks. Shoveled the dirt onto trucks instead of using the power machinery that we have now. ... I think the WPA was the best they could do. It served the purpose. [Andrew Steele]

In the '30s poor people, the government gave them three days work on the road—WPA. Well, everybody was so poor, the work [was] all shut down, and, oh, in the cities they was on soup lines. WPA gave everybody in Sugarloaf three or four days work. [Elna Craig]

There were lots of WPAs. We lived on letters—CCC, WPAs and all of the rest of them. We used to laugh at the speed, or nonspeed, of work that was done by some of these groups. Their heart wasn't in it, but they were doing it because they had to. [Frances Bascom]

Coping with the Times

I tried to get on the WPA. Nick Coughlin was road boss there, and fixin' this road, and I didn't have ... well, I wouldn't buy any of his whiskey was the big trouble, and so I didn't get on. [Ernie Ross]

I remember CCC camps. ... The CCC camps came in because Roosevelt picked up the unemployed, and they made roads, they wrote books; they did all kinds of things. It made them feel like they weren't on the dole. The CCC camps were good in that instead of having young people roaming around in the city, it put them out in mountains, in nice healthy conditions, the government fed them, but they were working. I think it was a good idea. [Elizabeth Graham Demmon]

But then the Depression years came on in '32, '33 and I was out of a job. I went into [a] CCC camp for a month here in Boulder on Sixth Street. ... Then NRA came into being, and so I left that and got a job at sixty dollars a month, which is what NRA guaranteed their men. ...

We had a very difficult time living during the Depression. My husband worked in the CC[C] camps and all that sort of thing. To make a living. It was very meager, and then my father and my mother—my mother was getting quite poorly—and so they wanted us to move up here. The cabin up above here was our old hog house, so we fixed it until it was livable. We lived there until my mother died, and then I lived here with my dad. I've been living here ever since. [Gertrude Tower]

It was bad. I was gettin' twenty dollars a week when the Depression hit, and 'fore it was over, I was gettin' fourteen—thirteen eighty-six they took off the Social Security. [Hugh Smith]

There were a lot of people out of work. There just weren't any jobs for everyone, and you would hang onto any job you could get. [Robert E. Gruen]

They'd stop me, and they'd want a job just as soon as I had an opening. The best we paid was for shaft sinking ... five dollars a day, and then machine men got four, and muckers got three dollars and fifty cents. [Clyde Boyle]

Mining was sort of a Depression industry. ... It was a promise of high returns although that was a gamble, particularly gold mining, and that's what I went into. Finally the mine ran out of ore—that was the Grand Republic over by Salina, and it produced over a million dollars in those roughly two years that we operated. It put a lot of men to work during the Depression. ... It's a hard life. Unhealthy, underground, and the air isn't the best sometimes, rock dust in the old days before they had electric drilling. The young fellas found they could get out and make better money elsewhere so mining sort of died out here. The mines here are not for big companies [with few exceptions like Jimtown]. ... Mining, although it was a hard life, it picked up. It was a Depression industry. Just like coal. [Joe Smith]

Bill Arthur was a graduate from the University and practicing law but in those days ... the [gold] standard was raised. It was valuable to come out and work the old mine dumps. Bill Arthur leased a shaft, an old mine. He would go way down in the evenings, and he was workin' down in there. [Irvin Demmon]

A lot of people started panning in Boulder Creek, all the way down from the canyon down past the Seventeenth Street bridge. They'd get down there and pan and get a couple of dollars a day. That was quite a little pay then. ... I can still see them panning gold all the way down Boulder Creek. [John B. Schoolland]

It shut out when Roosevelt put the gold standard on in ... 1933. [Delores S. "Dee" Bailey]

I come down here, and that was right in the Depression and oh boy, oh boy, she was tough. For about two years I couldn't hardly get enough work to keep a-goin'. [Charles Perkins]

I wanted to teach kindergarten, but as I told you ... there were no jobs when I graduated. I don't think even engineers got jobs those two or three years. I got this job up at Magnolia up Boulder Canyon, because Dad had worked for the Democrats, and the superintendent of schools, Mrs. Mayhoffer, was a Democrat. She said that she'd get me a job. She was nice, and she got me this job. [Elizabeth Graham Demmon]

But it seemed as though in those days you'd work for somebody for a while, and they'd run out of money. Then pretty soon they would come into a little bit of money, and we'd go back to work for them. This seemed to be the general run for the whole country during that period. [John Jackson]

Oh, I've been laid off during the summer months and then went back again in the winter, sure, a lot of that. That was just a good rest, that's all that was. No, we never suffered during the Depression that I can recall. We didn't have T-bone steaks for supper every night but we got by, you know what I mean. We didn't get rich either. But we kept aboveboard, I'll say that much, you know. That was the trouble about working the winter months. You worked October, November, December, January, February, March. That made it six for six. Then what you made in the first six months you worked, well then you went through that the months you were idle. [Jack Davies]

I know one other thing that struck me—but this struck me more in the '30s than it did right after the crash—was the great number of itinerants that came in. People coming in off the railroad would come to your backdoor and ask for handouts. We had a housekeeper for quite a bit of the time when I was a kid growing up, because Mother was teaching and Dad was teaching. ... Mrs. Johnson had a very soft heart for anybody who came to the door and wanted a handout. She didn't invite them in but she would always see that they had something to eat. We never had any trouble about it, you know. But evidently the house was pretty well marked, because I don't think there was a day that would go by during this time that there wouldn't be somebody coming. [Frances Bascom]

If [a tramp] would come to the door, [my father] would have them go and do some work before he'd feed them. They could mow the lawn or do something, whether it needed it or not. He felt, whether he was giving them dignity or that he should get something for his money, I don't know. ... He just would not give a handout without some service. ... There's no way to know whether our house [was marked] or not. [Dorothy Woodbury]

The trains come through Boulder. ... It wasn't exceptional to see a hundred men ridin' on those trains. We thought they we're all bums, but they were men out of work. So they'd come in. Lots of times they'd camp on the creek right down there by Water Street, and they took their coffee. We'd give them dried coffee. Everyone would come in. Boulder City Bakery would give them day-old bread and rolls, and Rocky Mountain Grocery used to give them can goods that had been battered in shipment. ... They'd stay around a few days and then go on. [Hugh Smith]

Depression days were bad. I can remember goin' down to the railroad tracks ... and I counted a hundred and twenty bums ridin' on a freight train comin' through town. There was no work. That was all. ... Those were hard times. There was just no work for people. [Joseph Malcolm]

The [railroad] company had guys that carried guns. They rode on [the railroads] too, you know, and they'd kick everybody off. They called 'em railroad detectives. [Joe "Cotton" Fletcher]

You used to see the freight trains goin' through. They were just loaded with people just riding—people out of work. ... It went through Niwot, and [there was] just any number of them, maybe a hundred or so, just riding the train, the freight train, from here to there to get work. That was Depression, for sure. [Ruth Dodd McDonald]

You could just look and every car had people sitting on top and in the boxcar. They just went from one place to another, you know ... and they weren't bums. They were just out of work, and that's how they got around. [Inez Dodd Johnson]

We had this farm, and I had lots of chickens and lots of eggs. The men that got off of the train, we didn't consider [them] bums or hobos; they were men looking for work, and they would come to our farm. I made every one of them a fried-egg sandwich. I made homemade bread so I had plenty of bread, and I made everybody a sandwich, and I gave them a pint of coffee. I expect I fed them by the thousands. They would work for us if we had any work. If we didn't have any work they would go on to another place. The train went right through our place. They must have had my place marked, because they did not go to the neighbors. They came to my house. They never came inside the yard. I would take everything out to the gate. Had a police dog, and he used to sit out by the gate. They would chop wood and do anything they could see to do while waiting for their meal, and they all got that egg sandwich. That's all I ever had for them, but they seemed to appreciate it. Nobody left without eating. [Ruby Roney]

The only real hard times I saw happening before we lost the ranch, there used to be people on Highway Forty going out I guess from the east to the west. They used to stop at the ranch for food, and we had so much food at the ranch we always fed them. ... I have fed eight or ten a day lots of times. We had so much food we just fed them. We knew they had our mailbox down on the highway marked, because very seldom anyone went by without stopping. They used to tell us about the hard times. ... As far as anyone we knew personally, we didn't know anyone who had hard times unless [they] were too lazy to work or something like that. ... The men who came by would ask if they could do some work [for the meal], and one woman opened up her suitcase and offered to give us some of her silverware that she was carrying to pay on the way. Of course, we didn't take any. It seemed to me they were trying. [Wilma L. Hyatt]

The area north of the creek was still switchyards for ore cars to be loaded, and there was a hobo jungle on the north side of the creek. I recall [in the] evenings there would be a fire there, and you could see [them] cooking their food. But the hobos in those days traveled by freight car. They'd hit the bars underneath the train and just ... what they call ride the roads. There were a lot of them. Hobos on the run. ... After 1936, I remember cautioning the children never to go near that creek, especially at nighttime. [Robert Gruen]

The hobo camp that I remember was just where the gypsy camp had been. The gypsies were gone, and then the hobos were there. They used to come up; my mother would never turn anyone away. She used to get pretty mad at them. She gave them something they didn't exactly relish but ... they used to come and [my] uncle used to declare that they used to put a mark on the sidewalk, because they all came here. But Mom was very generous. And often times they would ask if they could do some work. [Elizabeth Wiest Farrow]

I can remember a few [gypsies]. They used to park up under the beet dump up there. When I was a kid when we were walking home we would go way around, because we were scared to go by there. They would stay a couple of weeks or so. [Irene Wright Lybarger]

That was another thing I remember as a child was gypsies. Everybody just didn't like to see them come. They rode in the covered wagons, and maybe there would be four or five covered wagons. They would just go to a farm and beg and steal and just do whatever they could do. I remember them coming to our house one time. They would get out into the barnyard and grab chickens. They just plundered. That's the way they made their way along. I remember going home from school one time when I was a little girl. I think there were just two wagons then, but I know I was awful glad to get by and to get home, because everybody had a horror of the gypsies. I don't know what people they were. They just called them gypsies; they just roamed around and pillaged for their living, I guess. [Ruth Dodd McDonald]

We'd go down [to Boulder Creek] to get dandelion greens. ... We were a little cautious when we were quite young, because originally there was a gypsy camp down there ... and of course, Mother always told us they would kidnap us ... so we stayed away then. After that it was a hobo jungle, and then it was the CCC campground. [Elizabeth Wiest Farrow]

We were all poor and happy. It was good times, really. Really, ... people were closer together. In my family for entertainment, we'd all get together and play cards in the evenings, because we didn't have the money to run around. [Amy Sherman Cushman]

Well, it wasn't too severe on us. Most farms could make their own living. We weren't employed. I never worked for wages in my life. It didn't affect us like it did so many people. The farms got by better—felt it less than the other people in the population. [Andrew Steele]

I don't think it affected my life very much, simply because my father worked for Pike's Chevrolet. And they worked on what they called a flat rate, which means that you didn't get paid unless you did a job, but he was such an excellent mechanic that he had all the work he could take care of. ... I didn't really feel that we suffered because of it. ... They had to have their cars fixed. But my mother did go to work in the '30s. [Dorothy Woodbury]

You lived a pretty happy life. We all were happy. We didn't have anything, you know, in fact nobody did. There were lots and lots of poor people up in that area trying to make a living and a lot of them did during the Depression years, mining and working for mines that could afford to hire people. 'Course the wages was awful low those days. Something like a dollar a day. But everybody was in the same boat. All of us poor. We shared and shared alike. [John Jackson]

And I think the best time we had in our life was during the Depression! We enjoyed the Depression. We had just married; we've been married forty-five years. We were married in '30, and we just had more fun. Everybody was in the same boat. No one had anything. If you had a job you were lucky. Everybody shared and shared alike, and we'd all pool our [resources] … never did you go hungry. … We'd have bridge parties or whatever and everybody would bring something. I remember bananas being five cents a pound, and milk was five and ten cents a quart. My mother would cook enough food for their dinner at noon, and she'd always cook enough for us for leftovers. … So we never did go hungry. Couldn't afford to drive a car, couldn't afford the license, couldn't afford the gas. I remember one time, we couldn't afford a license, so we would wait until it was dark and sneak the car out and take a little ride at night! We had a little radio and listened to *Orphan Annie*. [Della Friedman]

We run away and got married. … But you know at that time, most people couldn't afford any fancy weddin' [during the Depression]. … I had a new dress and it was blue, I remember that. [Freda Brown]

I was married and had one child. We didn't have much money that was for sure. My husband worked driving a truck to Billings, Montana, for sixteen dollars a week. Paid his own expenses, and I did sewing: dressmaking or anything I could do to stay home with my child and take care of her. I used to walk—in '32 I think it was. I walked to the old Longmont Hospital. It was quite a walk. Worked the split shift and did cooking there for eighteen years. [Irene Smith Lybarger]

It was a hard time. … But we did survive. [M. Helen Carpenter]

BRIEF INSTRUCTIONS
FOR INTERVIEWING

The first step in making an oral history is to define the *purpose* of the tape. All questions should be within the framework of this purpose, whether it be for historical research of an area, for family remembrances, or for a narrower topic such as the development of a company.

A desire to *listen* carefully to what other people have to say is the most important quality of an oral history interviewer. Although a basic knowledge of local history is advantageous, no amount of expertise will substitute for a good listener. When an interviewer is paying close attention, not only will he be able to ask appropriate questions, but also the narrator will respond with more enthusiasm.

An interviewer can be an active listener *without interrupting.* There are many non-verbal ways to show that you are listening: nod of the head, eye-to-eye contact, smiles, etc. Verbal confirmation is also important, but this should be kept to a minimum, since the narrator's voice is the one that should be heard. There is nothing wrong with moments of silence: the narrator needs time to think before speaking.

Politeness is essential during the interview. Do not contradict stories or facts. This will only inhibit and antagonize the narrator. Remember, these are not historians being interviewed; they are people who are telling their side of a story—what they remember about an incident. In oral histories, factual information, especially dates, is not vital, since these may be found in history books. A narrator will remember events in relationship to other events, such as when he was married or in high school. If, however, there is confusion about a fact, the interviewer may state what he has heard or read, giving a chance for the narrator to react.

The one date that is important, however, is the narrator's *birthdate* if your purpose is to record an individual's life story. Starting a tape with *"When and where were you born?"* is an easy, informational opening. This is not an embarrassing question at the beginning of an interview and immediately dates the tape. Subsequent dates are no longer vital, although they will enhance the tape. Obtaining this information later in the tape may be awkward. This question also leads to inquiries concerning parents and grandparents.

Encourage the narrator to discuss relevant topics even if you already have heard or read about them many times. *Plead ignorance*. A researcher may only turn to that particular tape for information or may only be hearing about the subject for the first time. Also, your narrator may explain the event in a completely different way than the next person. A good example of this is the Depression.

Every interviewer will have his own style of interviewing. Every narrator will also be unique. There is no perfect way. What is important is to *do the interview* before it is too late. You will learn from your mistakes.

Telephone first: Explain the project carefully on the phone and give any reference names that you may have. If the prospective narrator is uncertain about the idea, you could explain the value of the tape for historical research, offer to have him listen to several other tapes you have done, or simply try to talk him into it on the phone. An example of some questions you would be asking (e.g., what school did he attend, who were his favorite teachers and why) might help to convince him. Another strategy is to send a letter first; this is especially advisable if a narrator is hard of hearing.

Short conversation upon arrival: Some narrators love to tell stories and will begin before you get a chance to turn on the tape recorder. Although it is nice to have a short talk before taping, do not let this last too long, because most people do not want to tell the same story twice at the same sitting. You will get a less enthusiastic account the second time. Start right in taping with the good talkers. With the shy people, explain again what the purpose of the project is, allow them to become a little familiar with you and with the tape recorder.

Test: Always test both voices before beginning an interview. This usually relaxes people quickly as well as ensuring that your equipment is working. NEVER record secretly.

"Tail": Before you begin the tape, allow a short time after the buttons have been pushed. At the very beginning and end of each tape there is a "tail" that will not record, so your words will be lost. If the narrator is into a story when the tape-side ends, it is a good idea to play back what has been recorded before turning over the tape (remember the tail on the new side) to hear how far into the story the tape was recording.

Appendix

Begin: All tapes should begin with the name of the interviewer, the date, the name of the narrator, and any other information you feel is pertinent. If you are doing more than one tape, it is a good idea to carefully label each one as you go along. It is amazing how quickly it will become complicated if you do not.

Order of questions: The first question should be "When and where were you born," followed by questions about the narrator's parents. With many, that will be all the questions you need to prepare; the rest will follow automatically if you pay close attention. Write down facts and any questions you think of as the narrator is talking, and have some knowledge of what your project covers. It is a good idea to have found out a little about the narrator first, so that you at least know what his profession is/was or what his interests are. This is not always possible. Interview without the information rather than waiting to acquire the information. The narrator will tell you, and you will not have lost the opportunity.

Questions: There are always the questions: who, where, what, when, how, and why. Try to avoid questions that ask for "yes" and "no" answers. These do not stimulate the narrator and the interviewer begins to control the conversation instead of the narrator. In the same manner, a rigid set of questions will stifle all spontaneity. Allow the narrator to lead as long as he stays on relevant topics.

Brief questions: Questions should be one at a time and should be BRIEF. They need not be perfectly phrased: a few fumbled questions on your part will put the narrator more at ease.

Unrelated topics: If a narrator wanders off in unrelated tangents, listen politely until the first break and then bring him back with, "getting back to … " or "returning to…," etc.

Reading: If a narrator wants to read a script he has written, try to discourage it. A reading is not nearly as lively and entertaining as a person talking naturally. If there is no way to avoid the situation, allow him to read his account, take notes, and then ask many questions starting back at the beginning—if he will allow it. Once in a long while, you will come across a person who simply does not trust himself to talk freely on tape (possibly because he has "colorful" language), and there will be nothing you can do.

Props: If props, such as photos, clippings, or maps, are used during the conversation, be sure to describe them, since the person listening to the tape will probably not have these in front of him. If you can entice the narrator into giving you the "prop," wonderful! Keep in mind, though, that props are an awkward technique when recording, and if they are used, the person listening to the tape should not be forgotten. Along the same line, when a narrator says, "It was so big," using his hands to measure, quietly mention into your microphone approximately the size he is indicating.

Descriptions and anecdotes: Ask for descriptions and anecdotes as frequently as you like. You are trying to paint a picture of the times through the narrator's memory, so the more descriptions and stories the better.

Limit pause-button use: Try to avoid turning off the recorder. Although many narrators will ask you to pause, this is a dangerous game: (1) you may lose out on a story and (2) you may forget to turn the recorder back on. If the telephone or doorbell rings, however, you have no alternative. If there has been any interruption, be sure the recorder is running when you begin interviewing again.

Looking at the recorder: Do not look at the recorder any more than you absolutely have to. It is distracting to the narrator, and it implies you are not paying attention.

Spelling: It is very helpful to researchers to have the correct spelling of names and places. If possible, either ask the spelling at the time the name is mentioned or write it down and ask later, while still recording. If not mentioned on tape, the spelling may be noted in the summary.

One-on-one: Interviews are much more successful if there are only two people present: the interviewer and the narrator. When there are more present, they will often interrupt, talk simultaneously, or tell "in" jokes, which will be meaningless to those listening. There is also confusion many times as to who is talking. This type of interview is successful, however, in special cases.

Length of interview: The standard length of an interview is one hour to one and a half hours. Do not let it go on too long. You usually are more than welcome to come back if the narrator has more to say, and if you have done a good job of paying attention, you will be exhausted. But as always, there are exceptions.

Both sides of tape: Use both sides of the tape and try to end the tape with a thank you so the listener knows that it is the end.

Punch out tabs: As soon as you get home *after* the interview, punch out the two black tabs on the top rim of the cassette that you see when you first open the plastic holder containing the cassette. Since the tape cannot record with these tabs punched out, your interview will be protected even if you mistakenly push the wrong button on your recorder while listening to the tape.

Equipment: An inexpensive tape recorder with two small microphones is sufficient to make a worthwhile recording. It is a good idea to take two ninety minute tapes with you incase one is flawed. No matter how good the equipment, however, the recording will be difficult to hear if you are sitting in a room with the TV on or with the spouse vacuuming in another room. The interview should take place in a quiet setting. You can do this by telling the person when you make an appointment that you need to be in a quiet place (usually his house). When this is stressed at the beginning, it should not be too embarrassing later if you find the place noisy and have to say so.

Release Form: It is a good idea to have a release form signed for every tape made if you are planning on using the information in some type of publication. When asking for the signature, explain that this releases the use of the tape to the public. If the narrator would like to put restrictions on this use, simply write in what these restrictions are, e.g., not to be used until after death, not to be used for any publications, etc. Usually the people who volunteer to be interviewed are not at all concerned with restrictions; if they are writing a book about their lives, they will not want to be interviewed in the first place.

Ideas for questions: Ask about grandparents/parents, other family members, a special family gathering, schools attended, teachers, neighborhoods, pets, natural hazards, hospitals, churches, careers, social life, dancing, theaters, travel, the Depression, world wars, transportation, unusual holiday celebrations, modern conveniences, buildings, shops, stories, anecdotes, sports, home remedies, cooking, chores, hobbies, etc.

ORAL HISTORY INTERVIEWS

Oral history interviews used in this book by narrator, interviewer, tape number, and date of interview.

Allebaugh, Flossie, by Elizabeth Keiser, Pat Whitehead, OH 40, 1975.

Altman, Samuel J., by Ann Bramhall, OH 363, 1987.

Alvarez, Teresa, by Theresa Banfield, OH 137, 138, 1976.

Amicarella, Henry, by Anne Dyni, OH 530, 1990.

Amicarella, Lawrence, by Rachel Homer, OH 7, 1978.

Armstead, Wanda Burch, by Ruth Major, OH 646, 1993.

Arnett, Robin, by Rachel Homer, OH 8, 1978.

Axelson, John R., by Cynthia Coccia, OH 540, 1991.

Bailey, Annie A., by Lana Waldron, OH 139, 1978.

Bailey, Delores S. "Dee," by Catherine Petito, OH 457, 1989.

Barber, Elwood J., by Vennard McCann, OH 483, 1990.

Barker, Jane Valentine, by Dorothy Hale, OH 587, 1992.

Barr, Anabel T., by Mary Baker, OH 142, 1976.

Bascom, Frances R., by Robin Branstator, OH 401, 1988.

Baum, Lois Huston, by Beverly Carrigan, OH 642, 1993.

Beasley, Maude Moomaw, by Rachel Homer, Anne Dyni, OH 9, 542, 1978, 1991.

Benway, Prudence, by Cynthia Coccia, OH 539, 1991.

Betasso, Ernie, by Hess, S. K. Levin, John Graham, OH 225, 227, 1976.

Bolton, Allen, by Anne Dyni, OH 529, 1990.

Bolton, Ena Jenner, by Betty Terrell, OH 249, 1985.

Boyle, Clyde, by Jim Mahoney, Vennard McCann, OH 484, 1990, 1991.

Brillhart, Sarah, by Gayl Gray, OH 252, 1985.

Brown, Freda, by Joan Plyley, OH 601, 1992.

Brown, Richard, by Joan Plyley, OH 601, 1992.

Carpenter, M. Helen, by Jewel Wolcott, Ann Bramhall, OH 327, 1986, 1987.

Caywood, Crain, by Dorothy Hale, OH 298, 1985.

Chaussart, Albert, by Anne Dyni, OH 547, 1991.

Chaussart, Evelyn, by Anne Dyni, OH 547, 1991.

Conilogue, Clarence, by Anne Dyni, OH 370, 1987.

Cox, Gary, by Joanna Sampson, OH 462 (Columbine Memorial), 1989.

Craig, Elna, by S. K. Levin, John Graham, OH 231, 1976.

Crossen, Forest, by Gayl Gray, OH 271, 1985.

Crosslen, Jerrine Sylvia, by Maria Rogers, OH 251, 1985.

Cushman, Amy Sherman, by Anne Dyni, OH 436, 1989.

Darby, Edmond D., by Anne Dyni, OH 500, 1990.

Davies, Jack, by Rachel Homer, OH 12, 1978.

Davies, Ruth, by Rachel Homer, OH 12, 1978.

Deavenport, Mrs. J.A., by Ruth Bussey, Lenore Greene, Elizabeth Keiser, OH 42, 1975.

Demmon, Elizabeth "Dee" Graham, by Jewel Wolcott, OH 403, 1988.

Demmon, Irvin, by Jewel Wolcott, Anne Dyni, OH 404, 501, 1988, 1991.

Oral History Interviews

Dexter, Rodney, by Anne Dyni, OH 580, 1986.

Dodd, Beth, by Anne Dyni, OH 18, 1987.

Dodd, John, by Rachel Homer, OH 18, 1978.

Eddy, Harold, by Anne Dyni, OH 578, 1986.

Edmondson, Mabel M., by Sarah Jacobus, OH 124, 125, 1977.

Ensz, Marguerite Treadway, by Vennard McCann, OH 569, 1991.

Estey, Robert F., by Ann Bramhall, OH 464, 1989.

Evans, Hannah, by Ed Peck, OH 51, 1972.

Faivre, Hazel, by Frances Light, OH 151, 152, 153, 1977.

Farrow, Elizabeth Catherine Wiest, by Kay Stiewig, OH 369, 1987.

Faye, Oscar, by S. K. Levin, John Graham, OH 228, 1976.

Fernie, Robert, by Joan Plyley, OH 453, 1989.

Fitzpatrick, Jessie, by Josie Heath, OH 43, 1974.

Flarty, Mary Todd, by Glenna Carline, OH 328, 1987.

Flarty, Russell, by Glenna Carline, Anne Dyni, OH 346, 531, 1987, 1990.

Fletcher, Joe "Cotton," by Marilyn Brand OH 681, 1984.

Fling, Roy, by Catherine Petito, OH 485, 1990.

Flowers, Ruth, by Theresa Banfield, OH 154, 1976.

Folsom, Franklin, by Adrienne Harber, OH 393, 1988.

Folsom, Mary, by Adrienne Harber, OH 392, 1988.

Franklin, Walter B. "Pete," by Maria Rogers, OH 586, 1991.

Friedman, Della, by Victoria Gits, OH 157, 158, 1976.

Friese, Raymond, by Jewel Wolcott, OH 281, 1985.

Gibson, Margaret, by Anne Dyni, OH 530, 1990.

Gladden, Sanford, by Sanford Gladden, OH 72, readings, 1975.

Goldberg, Harry, by Vennard McCann, OH 546, 1990.

Gorce, Cecilia "Sallee," by Joan Plyley, OH 599, 1992.

Gould, Evan, by Anne Dyni, OH 362, 1987.

Graves, Lois Muriel Caywood, by Dorothy Hale, OH 302, 1986.

Greene, Dorothy Allen, by Liz Caile, OH 342, 1987.

Gruen, E. Robert, by Ann Bramhall, OH 321, 1986.

Hall, Hazel, by Jewel Wolcott, OH 628, 1993.

Hall, Rosena, by Stephen Beale, OH 598, 1992.

Herzer, William, by Sarah Avery, OH 621, 1981.

Higman, Howard, by Maria Rogers, OH 200, 1987.

Hodgson, Elden C., by Anne Dyni, OH 582, 1986.

Houston, Clifford G., by Sue Lacey, OH 402, 1988.

Husted, Alma Leatherman, by Betty Terrell, OH 354, 1987.

Hyatt, Wilma L., by Jewel Wolcott, OH 359, 1987.

Jackson, John, by Joan Plyley, OH 553, 1991.

Jackson, Ruby, by Lana Waldron, OH 163, 1978.

James, John, by Unknown, OH 49, 1974.

Johnson, Inez Dodd, by Rachel Homer, OH 18, 1978.

Jones, Nell N., by Stephanie Widener, OH 164, 165, 1976.

Jones, Robert, by Stephanie Widener, OH 313, 1976.

Kelsey, Rosalie, by Anne Dyni, OH 291, 1985.

Kerr, Thomas, by Rachel Homer, OH 17, 1978.

Ketterman, Grovenor, by Dorothy Hale, OH 287, 1985.

Ketterman, Lorena, by Dorothy Hale, OH 287, 1985.

Kindig, Jean, by Eldora History Celebration, OH 639, 1993.

Kingdom, J. H., by Kathy Kaiser, OH 301, 1985.

Knaus, Carl, by Rachel Homer, OH 18, 1978.

Knaus, Isabel, by Rachel Homer, OH 18, 1978.

Lee, Stella Charlotte Wilson, by Marilyn Brand, OH 680, 1984.

Lehmann, Jessie Velez, by Unknown, OH 89, 1978.

Lewis, Elmo, by Anne Dyni, OH 52, 57, 1987.

Logan, Earl B., by Anne Dyni, OH 560, 1991.

Loukonen, Leonard, by David Brodie, OH 447, 1989.

Lybarger, Irene Wright Smith, by Betty Terrell, Anne Dyni, OH 250, 495, 1985.

Malcolm, Joseph W., by June Holmes, OH 535, 1990.

March, Marian Cook, by Vennard McCann, OH 631, 1993.

Martinez, Rick, by Unknown, OH 53, 1978.

Martinez, Sally, by Anne Dyni, OH 530, 1990.

Mather, Birdie, by Pat Whittaker, Elizabeth Keiser, OH 44, 1975.

Mayhoffer, Isabel, by Josie Heath, OH 45, 1972.

McAllister, Louise, by Jewel Wolcott, OH 278, 1985.

McCrone, Emma Soward, by Sarah Jacobus, OH 96, 97, 1977.

McDonald, Ruth Dodd, by Douglas Campbell, OH 382, 1988.

Miles, Mary Lou, by Cynthia Coccia, OH 539, 1991.

Miller, Frank, by Lafayette Elementary School, OH 54 , 1976.

Miller, Ralph Clinton, by Ed Peck, Anne Dyni, OH 55, 376, 1971, 1988.

Miyasaki, Jack, by Anne Dyni, OH 319, 1986.

Moon, Blanche, by Anne Dyni, OH 530, 1990.

Morrato, Edna, by Jeanne Bensema, OH 563, 1991.

Morton, Howard, by Anne Dyni, OH 379, 1988.

Moschetti, Bauldie, by Joan Plyley, OH 537, 1990.

Moschetti, Gentina, by Joan Plyley, OH 537, 1990.

Nicholson, Alberta, by Joan Plyley, OH 418, 1988.

Nilon, Charles Hampton, by June Holmes, OH 486, 1990.

Ortega, Roseann Chavez, by Anne Dyni, OH 579, 1986.

Paddock, Laurence T., by Roz Brown, OH 509, 1990.

Parker, Edith, by Sarah Jacobus, OH 98, 125, 1976.

Parsons, King K., by Cynthia Coccia, OH 549, 1991.

Parsons, Martin, by Forest Crossen, OH 682, 1963.

Perkins, Charles, by Unknown, OH 76, 1971.

Perry, George, by Vennard McCann, OH 588, 1992.

Peterson, Delia, by Toni Boone, OH 385, 1988.

Phillips, Hester, by Forest Crossen, OH 696, 1972.

Pooschke, Marie, by Betty Terrell, OH 295, 1985.

Roney, Ruby S., by Ann Bramhall, OH 567, 1991.

Oral History Interviews

Ross, Ernie, by S. K. Levin, John Graham, OH 228, 229, 1976.

Rowley, Jack, by Ron Collins, OH 629, 1993.

Rubright, Richard Dickson, by June Holmes, OH 636, 1992.

Rugg, Charles R. "Binks," by Joan Plyley, OH 456, 1989.

Sampson, Joanna F., by Anne Dyni, OH 4, 1989.

Sawhill, George, by Anne Dyni, OH 336, 1986.

Schlagel, Jacob, by Anne Dyni, OH 503, 1990.

Schoolland, John B., by Rachel Homer, OH 31, 1977.

Schott, Bertha Hartenagle, by Anne Dyni, OH 574, 1987.

Scohy, Alma L., by Rachel Homer, OH 30, 1978.

Seymour, Charlotte Ball, by John Avery, OH 284, 1985.

Shanahan, Byron, by Joanna Sampson, OH 634, 1989.

Sherman, Marguerite, Betty Terrell, OH 29, 1985.

Smith, George, by Joan Plyley, OH 630, 1992.

Smith, Hugh, by Robin Branstator, OH 419, 1989.

Smith, Joe, by Rachel Homer, OH 32, 1977.

Snively, Charles E., by Maria Rogers, OH 399, 1988.

Specht, Elbert "Al," by Grace Patterson, OH 272, 1985.

Specht, Ruth, by Betty Terrell, OH 294, 1985.

Steele, Andrew D., by Rachel Homer, OH 35, 1978.

Stevens, Harold, by Unknown, OH 76, 1971.

Streamer, Frank, by Dorothy Hale, OH 493, 1990.

Switzer, Lyndon, by June Holmes, OH 592, 1992.

Tallman, Cleo Turner, by Anne Dyni, OH 548, 1991.

Tallman, Glenn, by Anne Dyni, OH 548, 1991.

Tanner, Mildred Harris, by Unknown, OH 75, 1971.

Teegarden, D.M. "Dock," by Joanna Sampson, OH 42, 1989.

Thomas, Mabel Andre, by Anne Dyni, OH 577, 1987.

Tower, Gertrude, by B. Betcone, OH 177, 1976.

Valentine, John B., by Francis Shoemaker, OH 232, 1984.

Van Ek, Jacob, by Jewel Wolcott, OH 279, 1985.

Varra, Louis, by Anne Dyni, OH 547, 1991.

Wagner, Maude Washburn, by S. K. Levin, John Graham, OH 230, 1976.

Wagner, Sanford, by S. K. Levin, John Graham, OH 230, 1976.

Waldrop, Frances Thompson Mabee, by Ann Bramhall, OH 458, 1989.

Walker, Dorothy Burch, by Anne Dyni, OH 575, 1991.

Walter, Albert, by Anne Dyni, OH 543, 1991.

Waneka, C. Clarence, by Rachel Homer, Anne Dyni, OH 37, 572, 1978, 1987.

Waneka, Charles, by Anne Dyni, OH 571, 1987.

Warembourg, Helen, by Anne Dyni, OH 581, 1991.

Warembourg, Klubert, by Anne Dyni, OH 581, 1991.

Warren, Paul E., by Rachel Homer, OH 38, 1977.

Washington, Helen, by Charles Nilon, *Boulder's Early Black Settlers*, Video Recording, 1990.

Wells, Mary Hummel, by Anne Dyni, OH 337, 1986.

Westermeier, Therese, by Ian Yale, OH 48, 1976.

Wild, Ina Gerry, by Anne Dyni, OH 559, 1991.

Wolcott, Roland H., by Jewel Wolcott, Joan Plyley, OH 256, 283, 609, 1985, 1992.

Woodbury, Dorothy, by Robin Branstator, OH 431, 1989.

Yager, Ara Kossler, by Maria Rogers, OH 326, 1986.

Yates, Ralph, by S. K. Levin, John Graham, OH 229, 1976.

Yocom, Pearle C., by Rachel Homer, Stephanie Widener, OH 205, 306, 1978, 1976.

Zarina, Peter, by Maria Rogers, OH 373, 1988.

Further Readings

Coel, Margaret, *Chief Left Hand, Southern Arapaho*. University of Oklahoma Press, Norman, Oklahoma, 1981.

Dyni, Anne Q., *Back to the Basics: The Frontier Schools of Boulder County, Colorado, 1860–1960*. The Book Lode, Boulder, Colorado, 1991.

Dyni, Anne Q., *Pioneer Voices of the Boulder Valley, an Oral History*. Boulder County Parks and Open Space Department, Boulder, Colorado, 1989.

Galey, Mary, *The Grand Assembly: The Story of Life at the Colorado Chautauqua*. First Flatiron Press, Boulder, Colorado, 1981.

Knox, P. L., et al., *The United States: A Contemporary Human Geography*. John Wiley and Sons Inc., New York, New York, 1988.

Kraus, Michael, *The United States to 1865*. The University of Michigan Press, Ann Arbor, Michigan, 1959.

Schoolland, John B., *Boulder in Perspective—From Search for Gold to the Gold of Research*. Johnson Publishing Company, Boulder, Colorado, 1980.

Schoolland, John B., *Boulder Then and Now*. Johnson Publishing Company, Boulder, Colorado, 1982.

Smith, Phyllis, *A Look at Boulder from Settlement to City*. Pruett Publishing Company, Boulder, Colorado, 1981.

Steiner, Stan, *The Ranchers, A Book of Generations*. Alfred A. Knopf, Inc., New York, New York, 1980.

Taylor, Bayard, *Colorado: A Summer Trip*. University Press of Colorado, Niwot, Colorado, 1989.

Young, Otis E., *Western Mining*. University of Oklahoma Press, Norman, Oklahoma, 1970.

INDEX

INDEX